# THE KING OF CASINOS
## Willie Martello & the El Rey Club

# "LONG LIVE WILLIE MARTELLO"

*Richard B. Taylor,*
Author, historian, Las Vegas casino owner

# THE KING
# OF CASINOS

*Willie Martello & the El Rey Club*

Andy Martello

FIRST EDITION: December 2013
FIRST REVISED EDITION: May 2014
ISBN-13: 978-0615894591
ISBN-10: 0615894593
LCCN: 2013920096

# DEDICATION

## To April

*I can say without hesitation that without her*
*this book would have never happened.*

## To my parents, Don & Wyn Martello

*Although they are no longer around to read this, they would be the*
*most amused, if not most surprised, to learn that their son,*
*who hates to read, has written a book.*

## To Willie

*He said, **"I never had no book-learnin',"** any time someone tried to talk*
*down to him or make him look foolish. History has painted him as quite*
*the unsavory fellow. I'm hopeful those who spoke ill of him will now get*
*a little book-learnin' of their own.*

# CHAPTERS

# FOREWORD

*By Mark Hall-Patton*

A ndy Martello has written a fascinating biography of Willie Martello, an unsung pioneer of post-war Southern Nevada. He was a gaming entrepreneur who created one business, the El Rey Club, which helped keep Searchlight, Nevada's economy alive in the first decade and a half after the end of World War II.

In 1946, Searchlight was a very small, somewhat forgotten community located along the road that led from Boulder City south to California. Though it had boomed in the early part of the century, production from its mines slowed by the 1920s, and the small community began to slowly dry up. The railroad was closed in 1924. The highway was completed in 1927 and bypassed the town slightly. The population plummeted to about 50.

The town did not die though. It spread out, building toward the highway, and served the few local mines that were running as well as ranches in the area. The huge Rock Springs Land and Cattle Company, which covered 1600 square miles of Southern Nevada, California, and a bit of Arizona, went bankrupt in 1929. It was split up and the northern portion was sold to a Hollywood couple, cowboy actor Rex Bell and actress Clara Bow, better known as the "It Girl," when it became the Walking Box Ranch. Their home on the Searchlight-Nipton Road was the regional showplace.

With the coming of World War II, George S. Patton, Jr. located the vast Desert Training Center south of the community. Between this and the glamour of being friends with Hollywood stars Rex Bell and Clara Bow on the Walking Box Ranch west of town, there was some growth during the war years, but it was short-lived. By 1946, the community had less than two hundred residents and seemed to be on its way to again being little more than a gas and food stop for the few travelers heading north or south on Highway 95.

However, one man saw potential in the small town. This was Willie Martello, one of seven brothers who had grown up in California. He bought an existing hotel/restaurant and proceeded to create a must-see casino for the small town. While it was not the only casino in town, Martello's casino quickly became the best known and brought with it a "big casino"

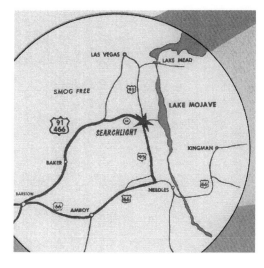

look with a friendly small-town feel. The El Rey Club quickly became the largest business in Searchlight.

Even the demise of the original El Rey in a spectacular fire in 1962 is well covered and quite interesting. Andy has done a superb job of making that evening real in the reminiscences he has collected and used in this account.

You can view the El Rey as part of the post-war entrepreneurial boom of the west when men who had been in the service or unable to build during the war decided to create their own futures. Andy Martello's book is a fun and informative look at the history of Willie Martello and his enterprise. It is a long needed addition to the history of Southern Nevada, covering one person who brought together much of the post-war spirit seen throughout the west in individual enterprises.

Andy Martello's biography of Willie Martello should be of interest not only to Southern Nevada historians but also to anyone who is interested in the expansion of the west after World War II. It is a long-awaited addition to my Nevada history shelf, and I am sure it will be to many others.

*Mark Hall-Patton is the administrator of the Clark County Museum System in Nevada and serves as a respected expert on The History Channel's popular program, Pawn Stars.*

# READER'S GUIDE

If I do my job correctly, this book will not be your typical book on Nevada history nor will it be a biography on someone you should know. It is my intention for this book to be both informative without seeming like a text book or a historical volume AND entertaining in the same way a work of historical fiction or, perhaps, a gripping documentary might be. They do exist, you know. While there is no fiction within the piece, I want it to read as if I were right there in your home telling you about the El Rey Club.

I tend to be very conversational with my writing style. Being an entertainer in my real life, I strive to make things read the same way you watch a movie. I've always been a visual person who hates to read but loves to write. Knowing the rather immediate nature of media in the Internet age, I am certain you will find a way to let me know how thoroughly I either let you down or succeeded in my goals.

Now that you have a better understanding of what I hope to achieve with how I present you this material, please allow me to explain a few things about what will and will not be discussed.

In any other book trying to detail the life of an unknown man whom the author is CERTAIN should be a household name, you would have to read the complete history—Birth...Life...Death—with anecdotes of the life he lived, the loves he lost, and a perspective of that person's place in history would all be covered. While there will be some of those traditional elements within these pages, I can say with certainty a lot of that will be absent, and I will surely face some sort of wrath and acrimony for its rather overt, almost deliberate omission. History buffs want the details, dammit! I will apologize in advance if you feel as though you are missing those aforementioned details.

I never really gave a damn about Willie Martello's upbringing: where he was born, what his childhood was like, or how he became the man he became. I was first brought into this with a rabid curiosity about the guy who ran a casino and brothel in a Nevada town near Las Vegas. This story will cover some of Willie's life before Searchlight and Las Vegas, but it is the time IN Searchlight and Las Vegas that will be covered at length. THERE is where you will find your details. THAT is the story I personally wanted to hear the most and THAT is the story that would compel one to read this book.

This should also explain a bit better why there is not a lot of mention about Willie's younger brother **Buddy**, who was also very active in the running of the El Rey Club. Buddy and **Albert Martello** started the place in 1946, but by 1947, it was essentially Willie's joint. So much of the heart and soul of the El Rey Club was Willie's heart and soul and, therefore, there is not as big a focus on Buddy's role in the place. This is not to suggest that Buddy was not integral to its success nor is it to say that his life is not as interesting as Willie's. By comparison, nobody's life is as interesting as Willie's. I'm just saying the *real story* of the El Rey Club lies within Willie's involvement.

It also bears mentioning the El Rey Club, like any other business or casino, has a birth and death date. The historical record will show there was an El Rey Club in existence between 1946 and 1973. The truth of the matter is, when you are talking about the El Rey Club, the REAL El Rey Club and its hey-day, you are referring to the place as people knew it between 1946 and 1962 when Willie owned it and his brother Buddy was by his side. THAT was when the El Rey Club was THE El Rey Club. When a fire in 1962 caused it to meet its end, it truly ceased to be the El Rey that people knew and were willing to talk about fondly.

Willie was involved with the El Rey as it floundered, trying so desperately to rise from the ashes. He hung around during the time when **Warren "Doc" Bayley** owned the place and tried unsuccessfully to make his dreams finally come true. However, in the words of **Bob Martello**, Willie's nephew, *"It just wasn't the same."*

With the deaths of Willie and Doc Bayley, the place was later run by **Judy Bayley** and eventually found itself as one of the tiny cogs in the crooked gears of **Allen Glick**, **Gene Fresch**, and the notorious **Argent Group**. By then it was little more than a place for money to be skimmed by the crime syndicate or a place where common rabble went to get into a bar fight. Though it had the name, that was NOT the El Rey Club people remembered.

Moreover, by all accounts, Willie was not a mobbed-up gangster. He certainly knew several of the syndicate figures in and around Vegas as did most any businessman in town at that time. During that period in Vegas, knowing a gangster was not unlike knowing your mailman. Reportedly, Willie would even *"occasionally entertain a few guests from Chicago"* as one of Martello's accountants would tell me, but when the offers came from the broken-nosed sorts, he NEVER took them. Everyone agrees that when it came to organized crime, Willie was as clean as his glistening white suits.

There MAY be some interesting tales from the days when the Argent Group was involved, but a dead writer writes no books, V.C. Andrews not withstanding. I will certainly not be the guy asking questions about those dark days, nor will I be the guy to tell those tales.

Throughout this volume I'll speak to the almost mythic qualities about Willie, how he seems more like a tall tale/Paul Bunyan-like subject than a regular man who tried to run a casino. The reason for this is not to create a puff piece about Willie or overstate his importance in Southern Nevada history. It is more to relay how he was perceived to others through his own outrageous antics and clever methods with which he promoted himself and his business ventures. I also intend to shed some light on the ways his influence has been overlooked or overshadowed largely due to his brief association with the world's oldest profession, something that has a history in Searchlight longer than Willie's time on Earth, much less his time offering ladies at the El Rey Club.

Continuing with the notion of Willie's larger-than-life persona and innovations, I will make no claims that Willie invented a whole lot of the promotional tactics and gimmicks used at his casino, though I'll confess his clever use of wild burros is very likely unique. Many of Willie's innovations stemmed from seeing what other casinos were doing and elaborating upon them. There was some truly visionary thinking from him, something his niece called *"Willie Wheels"* in reference to the ever-spinning wheels in his head, and I will detail that in full.

I do not intend to suggest he was the guy who brought telephones to Searchlight, airplane shuttles to casinos, and so on. Searchlight, Nevada was a genuine boom town during the gold rush days. It was on its way to becoming one of the larger and more prosperous towns in Nevada at the time. If the mines had not run out, you might not need a ridiculous Sarah Palin rally or a McDonald's stop-in by Oprah to alert you to the presence of this town.

The truth is Searchlight HAD telephones as early as 1907. Willie was just the guy who had a rather unorthodox and inspired solution when those lines were taken out of the town decades later and was instrumental in getting permanent, dedicated lines for Searchlight. The town had fire hydrants, hotels, bars, thriving businesses, a landing strip, and many other amenities that most communities take for granted today.

Much more is known about Searchlight's early days than during the time between 1940 and 1970. You could say Searchlight didn't become a part of the "wild west" until after the 1940s began, and it lost a lot of its civility and modernity. As **Jane Overy**, historian for the town of Searchlight points out, things became quite different when mining stopped being THE claim to fame for the town. *"By the 1940s, people just weren't paying as much attention to Searchlight anymore and very little was written about it. There's not as much of a public record as there was in the early 1900s. All we have are the stories, and those can often be exaggerated."* It is for that reason among others that stories about Willie Martello and the El Rey have a flair for the dramatic and lend themselves so well to bravado, either on the part of this writer or on the part of the people who relayed those stories to me.

I tried as much as possible to verify or confirm stories through newspaper accounts and other methods. However, I am still a writer and an entertainer, and it is as much my goal to be entertaining as it is to be factually informative. If you can remember that, I know you'll enjoy all I present here.

You should also know the names of a few of the people who are quoted so frequently in this book. There are many more people and family members who have also provided memorabilia as well as stories, and they'll be mentioned in the acknowledgements section for a proper thank-you. Knowing to whom I am referring will keep me from having to repeatedly say things like **"Bob Martello, Willie's nephew,"** as I did several paragraphs earlier. I'm confident I'll still make those references as I try to follow some of the literary rules of the road, but I also know, when I've had to read the same information over and over in similar books, I often wondered why the author didn't just provide me, the reader, with some sort of key. **Robert Graysmith,** who was instrumental in convincing me I could write a good book and find a publisher, does this in his true crime novels, and I think it is more than appropriate I take a hint from the pro by telling you now Bob Martello was Willie's nephew without always having to say **"Bob Martello, Willie's Nephew"** at every instance.

Here are some of the people with whom I owe a great debt of thanks for their kindness, forthright information, and generosity.

**Bob Martello**, Willie's nephew, ( DAMN, I'm funny!  NEVER forget that I am a comedian at heart and, therefore, full of snark. ) Bob was the first of Willie's family I was able to interview on the phone.  Sadly, he passed away long before this book was finished, but his contributions and friendship were both invaluable to me and this project.

**Sharon Richardson**, Willie's niece, daughter of **Harold** and **Marie "Honey" Blasiola, Willie's sister**.  Probably the person I spoke with the most, mostly because she was always the most vocal of the Martello family, wanted some recognition for her uncle, and because she was (and is) just a hoot.

**Ethel Martello**, Buddy Martello's wife of 50 years and the last of the original gang of Martellos who ran the El Rey.  Probably the person I've spoken to the least, though I know she's the one I should have been calling every damn day.  Ethel is a wonderful woman who still, to this day, hasn't the foggiest idea why anyone would even care about what the heck happened in Searchlight.  Although she has always been kind to me and offered information without hesitation, I have always felt intimidated by her and felt I was a noisy little intrusion into her life for asking such questions.  While I know this was not the case, I also felt she more than deserved her privacy and any contact I had with her would be my honor, not my right.  I'm certain I'll be taken to task by other historians for not calling Ethel a few more times, but I stand by my decision.

**Suzan Riddell** (Suzan Martello), **stepdaughter to Willie.** Finding Suzan, or rather, Suzan finding me has been nothing less than a treat. Not only has she provided me with some amazing artifacts and anecdotes, but she helped unveil a marriage that many of Willie's other family had all but forgotten about. I can't say that Suzan's mother's marriage to Willie was a secret, but it provided great fun "introducing" her to other members of Willie's family. She also paved the way for me to meet so many others in the family.

**Jerry Schafer**, **Hollywood filmmaker and good friend of Willie's.** Jerry is easily one of my favorite people in the world. He's been nothing but supportive of me in this and all of my projects. He's also had one of the most fascinating lives. I told him if I manage to get this book off the ground, a book about him would be next on my list. That is assuming he'll slow down long enough for me to interview him again. I am grateful to Willie and his El Rey Club for providing me the opportunity to make friends with Jerry Schafer.

**Dick Taylor** (Richard B. Taylor to the Nevada historian sect), a former business associate of Doc Bayley's, past owner of such legendary Las Vegas casinos as the Hacienda and Moulin Rouge, and principal developer of the Mount Charleston resort properties. Dick provided me with a previously unheard story of Willie and Doc's grandest plans for Searchlight and the El Rey as well as put me in contact with many people whom would probably never have taken my call without a referral from Dick. He was also a good friend.

**Tony Lovello, Kenny Laursen, & Joe Veronese** of the Tony **Lovello Revue.** Three musicians who provided the most vivid accounts of the night the El Rey Club burned to the ground. They were very familiar with the El Rey and Willie. Kenny still lives in Las Vegas and has on several occasions provided me with some colorful tales and more than a few laughs.

**Joyce Dickens Walker**, one of the original bartenders at the El **Rey.** Just another of the people I feel privileged to have met along the way. She always had some great stories and she provided me with some wonderful photos.

Lastly, I'd like to address something that you won't find in the book, something I know you would ask me about were I not to mention it here.

You will not find much in the way of new stories or quotes from **Senator Harry Reid**. The Senator is very likely to be the reigning "Most Famous Searchlight Resident," though he certainly would have some stiff competition if past famous residents were still alive today. For the record, numerous attempts to make contact with the Senator have been unsuccessful. Letters and emails to his offices throughout Nevada have gone unanswered. Requests from mutual friends have not resulted in a phone call or other correspondence. Blanket requests online and repeated pleas across all available channels have led nowhere. It seems it really is much harder to get the ear of an elected official than one would think, even in a state as relatively small as Nevada.

It is not my intention to make this some sort of indictment on the Senator's character, nor is it an invitation for the overly-charged political zealots from either side to spout hatred or praise based upon their hair-trigger urge to do so. I realized during the course of my research Reid had gone on to publish another book, became the Majority Leader, and found his dance card was far too full to spend any time talking with a Nevada transplant with an interest in his home town, even though I vote.

Reid has in fact written about Willie Martello in his two books, *Searchlight: The Camp That Didn't Fail* and *The Good Fight.* He has also spoken about Martello in numerous interviews. It is partially because of what he has had to say about the subject of my book that I've so badly wanted to speak with him.

While Reid has said some positive things about Martello, calling him a *"kindly bear of a man"* and referring to him as one of the few positive male role models in his life, much more has been written to cast a negative shadow across Martello's name. He would bandy about phrases like "pimp" and "whoremonger" as casually as you or I would say "mom" or "dad" to our own parents. At every opportunity he would paint a picture of Martello as little more than a common criminal who had little to do with furthering Searchlight as a town or keeping it from disappearing off the map entirely.

Reid's story is quite remarkable. To come from such a tiny town, without much support from a father figure or affluence and ultimately to end up the leader of the Senate is truly commendable. To think that a man who learned to swim in a "whorehouse pool" and whose mother would make ends meet by washing the laundry for the brothels in town (including the El Rey) would rise up to such heights is quite actually the embodiment of the American Dream. Despite anyone's politics, he has a story that most folks seeking public office would dream about having themselves.

I understand the *politics* of it all. He is a staunch Mormon and would certainly have an aversion to prostitution, even in Nevada. He is also a politician and therefore knows he can use the poverty and adversity that comes with his story to his advantage while also having to distance himself from the seedier aspects. To this day some conservative radio hosts will only refer to the man as "Whorehouse Harry," hoping to use his past against him. I get the motivations for his actions. I just wish he didn't have to let such a minor aspect of the El Rey story be the focal point of his accounts of an upbringing in a tough mining town.

I've wanted to speak with Senator Reid about his times in Searchlight. I've wanted to hear stories he hasn't yet shared in his own books. I've wanted to buy some of the El Rey memorabilia in his collection. I've wanted to ask him how he could so gladly accept a gift of Searchlight property from Buddy Martello's widow in one instance and then slur the Martello name in print so easily. I've never wanted to play "gotcha" games with him nor do anything to tarnish his distinguished career. As I have done with everyone I've spoken to during this quest, I have simply wanted to know the truth. I have LOVED hearing stories, good or bad about the El Rey Club and to have audience with any senator, much less this particular senator would have been my honor. Sadly, it was not meant to be.

So let me say to those who would think to ask me, A) I have indeed TRIED to reach Harry Reid, and B) Long after this book is published I would still welcome the chance to speak with the Senator any time. The stories and the memories are what matter most to me. I hope they will matter to you.

# PREFACE

This was just supposed to be a hobby. In fact, it started out as more of a joke among my wife, a few friends, and me. This joke turned into a hobby, one of many useless time-wasters in my life I might add. I was supposed to do a little snooping around to learn just enough facts out about a brothel owned by a guy with the same last name as mine in order to share some stories with a few friends. MAYBE, I would try to collect a few trinkets from the place.

THAT WAS IT!

I was not supposed to become an "expert" on a relatively unknown casino.

I was not supposed to care about a lesser known Nevada mining town.

I was not supposed to write a book or even pretend to be a historian.

I was supposed to be laughing with my wife over a beer about how I could inherit "the family business" and become a casino magnate and/or pimp.

I never asked for the hobby to turn into a "MISSION."

Instead, I have spent my days calling complete strangers, many of whom are in their 70s, and asking a lot of questions about their lives in the Las Vegas area and what they know about some guy by the name of **Willie Martello**. I've had to contact people, all of whom were very sensitive about the rather poor public perception of their beloved family member, and convince them I'm neither a cop nor an opportunist looking to exploit or further tarnish the reputation of an otherwise great man.

I've rooted through rattlesnake-infested junk yards, dusty antique stores, and the homes of people most would consider "a bit off" as I looked for clues, artifacts, or photos of some long forgotten casino called the El Rey Club. In my home, already filled with incredibly useless collections of things only important to someone like me (well over 500 versions of the song "Louie Louie" come to mind as an example), I was suddenly getting into bidding wars on eBay for things like ashtrays, poker chips, brochures, dice, coasters, stationery, and even some kind of gaming table—**A GAMING**

**TABLE FOR CHRIST'S SAKE!**—all so I could add more clutter to my closets, more kitsch value to my already cluttered and kitschy lifestyle, and more historic mementos from a place I would never be able to actually visit.

I became involved in the lives of people I have never met while I prodded and poked at soft spots and waited for the juicy bits of the fruit to come out. I've asked women 30 years my senior about their sex lives. I've forced myself to learn how to use the antiquated technology of the microfiche just so I could glean a few more tidbits about a place that burned to the ground eight years before I was even born. Thanks to my newfound expertise in ancient research technology, you could see me crying in a public library after reading about the death of Willie Martello despite knowing for years he'd been dead since 1968.

I needed to prove my honest intentions to the remaining members of a somewhat scorned family and convince them this was a story that deserved to be told. **Ethel Martello**, widow of Buddy Martello and a woman who was there for so much of the El Rey's history, frequently called **Sharon Richardson** and asked in a nervous tone, *"What does this guy WANT?"* Thankfully, after I had gained Sharon's trust, she explained, *"He doesn't WANT anything. He's hoping he can learn about the El Rey and share some of the great history that took place there."*

I did all this because every single fact I learned, every single friend I made, and every single bit of arcane crap I purchased during this joke-

**The El Rey Club circa 1946-48.** *Photo courtesy of Joyce Dickens Walker*

turned-hobby-turned-MISSION enhanced and brightened my life in ways I had never imagined. As the story unfolded in front of me, I became more and more fascinated. As relatives of Willie Martello came out of the woodwork and somehow got past the fact a nosy punk from Chicago wanted to ask a lot of questions about their family in Searchlight, I found I truly had something very special within my grasp. I had access to the many wonderful tales of Willie Martello and his rather innovative little casino that could, The El Rey Club.

As it happened I was not the only one who thought the world should know more about Willie Martello. Many of Willie's family members felt the same way. I eventually realized that Willie Martello SHOULD have been a household name, at least as famous as Steve Wynn is in Las Vegas today. Instead, what little was out there publicly was not all that flattering. If I believed the few written reports about the man and his club, I'd know he was something of an outlandish man who ran a casino as a front for his prostitution empire. Outside of building a swimming pool and helping with the installation of some phone lines in Searchlight, he was nothing more than a pimp in a white suit. Some of these reports came from a U.S. Senator, no less.

Thankfully, I found out there was more to the story and felt compelled to get those details out into the open. I'm grateful to the Martello family for embracing me and treating me as their own family as well as their encouragement and support in my quest to share a bit more about Willie Martello, warts and all. He was no saint, but he was far from the sinner his reputation and the words of a future Senate Majority Leader would lead you to believe.

There's a lot of responsibility that comes with trying to write a book about a man's life, especially a man as unknown or misunderstood as Willie Martello. You can't tell one story about the man without having to open a few windows into the lives of the people surrounding him, like his brother Buddy Martello among others. The more people involved in the overall story, the more difficult it becomes to get the whole story, especially when there are so many who simply aren't alive to help you get the facts straight. I'm not a journalist by trade. I'm a juggler and comedian from Chicago living in Las Vegas. When I decided there was a book worth writing, I wanted to get the truth out there. Getting the truth, as it turned out, was a much harder task than I ever imagined. Allow me to explain.

If you are trying to write a book about a casino in 1940s through 1960s Las Vegas, you are going to have your fair share of people who *"don't know nuthin' about nuthin'."* It comes with the territory. If you move the setting from Las Vegas to a much smaller town 57 miles south and add a few factors like illegal prostitution, scandalous topless movies, and adultery, you'll find that not only does nobody know nuthin' but EVERYBODY wants to stand in line to tell you exactly what you got wrong. This all comes with the understanding *"You didn't hear nuthin' from me!"* It seems a lot of the long-time Las Vegas area residents love to tell stories about the old days, but nobody wants YOU to credit them even if the tales are ultimately harmless. Nobody in Las Vegas wants to get blamed (or worse) for telling tales out of class or ruining someone's reputation. Serving as an agent for the truth, being a guy hoping to tell a few good and bad stories about a man almost universally loved but equally tainted by a nefarious reputation is not an easy task.

There is also a problem when trying to get EXACT details about so many business deals and operations from that time. Even though 1946 is not THAT long ago, 1946 in Searchlight, Nevada may as well be Pompeii. Records of all kinds were kept, but good luck to the poor juggler-turned-historian hoping to find them. Back then, especially in Southern Nevada and the casino business, a handshake meant as much, if not more, than a signature on a piece of paper. In truth, because of the nature of some of the business going on, it was best to keep the pen in the pocket anyway. I've tried my best to assemble as accurate a timeline as possible and fill the blanks.

If I were an investigative journalist, I'd have to get third party verification of all facts, stories, or allegations. However, since so few from that era want to be accused of talking out of turn and the fact there are so few left to speak to, getting confirmation on all facts is nearly impossible. What I've learned is getting third party verification is very hard to do when the first and second parties are already gone. In some cases, I've had to resort to echoing the stories most often told to me, knowing, if not hoping, someone will come forward one day and either correct me or add more to the tale.

Even though so many details fall into that same category of *"nobody knows nuthin' about that,"* I believe this to be as close to THE story as anyone has ever gotten. Of course, if the book sells well and enough people emerge to tell me just how badly I screwed it all up, the sequel should be just as much a page-turner as this one.

One thing everybody loved to talk about was the same subject everyone seemed to remember about Willie and his casino: prostitution. *"The girls,"* as so many folks called them, easily stood out as the lasting legacy of Willie Martello in the Las Vegas Valley. While very few seemed to show any negative thoughts about the presence of prostitutes, we were talking about N-E-V-A-D-A after all, and they certainly shared no need to judge or castigate Willie Martello, most everyone I interviewed for this book felt it necessary to inform me about the girls. In fact, many of the folks I spoke with, mostly people of colorful and seasoned character in their own rights, would actually get a sort of hush-hush tone when referring to the ladies' services in Searchlight, often taking care to look around the room before quietly asking me, *"You know about the girls, right?"*

As you'll soon find out, I did (and do) know about the girls in Searchlight. It may have been what started me on this ridiculous journey, but thankfully, it is not where I stopped. Long after this book is published I know I'll still be gathering more photos, writing down more stories, and avoiding more rattlesnakes in junk yards. I am hopeful that along the way people will stop asking about the girls and stop using words like "pimp" to describe Willie Martello. With some luck, this book will help clear the air a bit and even inspire others to investigate the history of the myriad of colorful places in Nevada's gaming history.

With all this being said, I am constantly reminded of something said to me by Ethel Martello in our first interview. Of all I've heard from all those I've spoken with, this may be my favorite quote:

> *"I don't care what you write about the place so long as you write the truth. The problem is, whatever you write isn't going to BE the truth because nobody really knows what went on there. Anybody who did know is probably dead and anybody alive who tells you they knew what went on there is full of it. Nobody knows what went on there because they weren't there. They don't know nuthin'! Those who say they were there, weren't there, you know what I mean? I WAS there! And I don't know nuthin'."*

And so, what follows is a collection of all the *nuthin' I don't know.*

# THE KING OF CASINOS
## Willie Martello & the El Rey Club

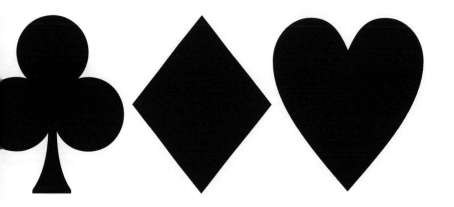

I n 1915, a woman walked in to the local Sears & Roebuck store with at least seven children in tow. All boys. All her sons. It was her intention to purchase matching outfits for the boys so they could pose for a family photograph.

Having come from a large and loving family, she now had a large and loving family herself that included two girls. The original plan was to have eight sons in the photo, but sadly, one had passed away some years earlier. This photo would serve as a wonderful keepsake within the family for generations.

She walked through the aisles at Sears and searched for the perfect outfits. As she looked at the fake calf skins, the beads, and feathered headbands the mother decided she found it! **"The Seven Little Indians"** would soon be a fixture in the Martello family albums. She purchased the matching outfits and tucked the receipt away in her bag. It was time to take the photo.

As the children all changed into their costumes, one boy, the seventh of her sons, began to make a terrible fuss over his costume. Just barely a toddler, young William adamantly refused to take off his shoes. It seemed this youngster was rather fond of his fancy shoes and didn't want to be seen as a barefoot Indian. Even at a young age **William Joseph Martello** was rather particular about his clothing. Equally telling, he would do whatever it took to stand out from the crowd and get what he wanted. The shoes stayed ON.

The photographer snapped an adorable photo and the mother was so very pleased to have such a memory of her 7 boys. After the boys changed back into their own clothes, the mom went right back to the counter at Sears.

She set the Indian costumes on the counter, presented her receipt, and asked for a refund.

# INTRODUCTION

Two dollars and fifty cents spent in Las Vegas changed my life. Okay, it was actually five dollars that changed my life, but I'll get to that later.

While it is not uncommon to hear Las Vegas stories with a similar beginning, this tale is not at all what you'd expect. This is not a story about a big win at the tables, nor is it one of a man hitting bottom by gambling away his last $2.50. I did not wager a cent in this Las Vegas story.

A quick rereading of the opening sentence reveals that I spent my $2.50 in Las Vegas. I actually bought something that altered the course of my life, although I don't really have any tangible object to show you. I didn't buy a souvenir or some useless trinket to commemorate my time in the desert.

Instead, I spent my $2.50 on admittance to an exhibit of Vegas area history.

The **Lost Vegas Museum & Store**, then located in the Neonopolis Shopping Complex of downtown Las Vegas, was a typical souvenir shop filled with all sorts of the aforementioned trinkets. Thanks to the now booming Fremont Street Experience, millions of tourists from all over the world head downtown and look for that perfect piece of crap to bring home to their friends. There are many such shops throughout Las Vegas, and if most people are anything like my wife and me, they stop inside many of these shops hoping to find the lowest prices on the cheapest of items.

It was just that sort of scenario that found April, my wife (at the time) and I wandering into the Lost Vegas Museum & Store. Prior to living in Las Vegas, we'd travel there a couple of times a year if possible, and we always checked this kind of store.

By the time we wandered into the Lost Vegas shop, our day had already been filled with items from Las Vegas' history. We also ventured to destinations most would consider to be off the beaten path.

As it turned out, friends of mine, **Ed & Lynne Clemmens,** happened to be on a Vegas vacation at the same time. April and I, being somewhat Vegas-savvy when it came to places most people missed in their pursuit of free beer and single deck Blackjack, met up with them to show them a little of downtown Vegas. The highlight of the day's trip was a visit to the **Neon Museum**, a most fascinating collection of discarded neon signs from throughout Las Vegas' history.

The Neon Museum is truly an unknown gem of the Las Vegas landscape. With all the drinking, the naked pleasures, and gambling offered in Las Vegas, places like "The Boneyard" at the Neon Museum are often missed by the tourists. For those who are interested in seeing the delightfully tacky and surprisingly beautiful sides of Las Vegas, past and present, the Neon Museum is simply the place to go. The gaudy elegance of the forgotten neon signs seems to transform you from a simple tourist into a Vegas insider. While you are walking among this graveyard of glam, you are overcome by a certain feeling of Las Vegas chic.

Perhaps, it was being at "The Boneyard" that made it such an easy decision to spend an extra few dollars at the Lost Vegas Museum & Store. I'm not altogether certain the gift shop had as much appeal to us as the museum inside. After a long day of keen observation and wide-eyed admiration, it seemed more than appropriate for the four of us to walk into an otherwise unobtrusive gift shop and indulge our need for more Vegas history. We wanted more pieces of the past to complete our day. The only real deciding factor would be the price of admission.

That's where the simple figure of $2.50 comes into play. Admission to see all of the artifacts & photos inside the museum was a meager $2.50 per person. Knowing that was all we needed when making our decisions. In reality, it was $5.00 that changed my life as I also paid my wife's admission. The storyteller in me just couldn't start off a book with the sentence, *"Five dollars spent in Las Vegas changed my life,"* even though it is actually a tad more accurate. I am hopeful other writers out there understand.

Artistic license aside, it bears mentioning that paying for April's admission into the place was really what spurred the life-altering moment. She was the one who actually found the single photo on the wall that would one day bring me to the writing of this book.

The museum was actually a very pleasant surprise for all of us. We expected to find something of an afterthought of a museum, a reasonably simple way to get an extra $2.50 out of each customer without providing much in the way of substance. Thankfully, we were quite wrong.

Every inch of wall and cabinet space was filled with some sort of arcane relic from the storied past of Las Vegas and the surrounding areas. Old posters promoting legendary acts, photos, programs, dice, and gambling paraphernalia of all kinds festooned the place. Everywhere you looked you found something designed to make the nostalgic heart swoon.

This was an actual museum, filled with items from well beyond the 100 years of Las Vegas existence. Anyone walking into the place found themselves thinking that the $2.50 to get in was a STEAL compared to other high-priced tourist attractions found within the tourist trap that makes Nevada famous. Highlights from the old west up through modern day Vegas lined the walls and provided the exact extra bit of historic content we craved. There was almost too much to see.

In fact, I walked right by the photo that would come to mean so much to me without so much as a single glance. I don't know how I missed it, really. It was actually in one of the most prominent and visible locations of the museum. Thank God for my wife, who not only found the photo, but stood in amazement laughing at me for missing it altogether.

On the wall was an old black and white photograph of a long gone and certainly not all too spectacular building boasting to be a casino called the **El Rey Club**. April grabbed me and insisted I look at the photo and hoped I would become astounded at what I saw. I glanced at it and made a remark to placate my wife as if to say, **"That's nice,"** and feigned some sort of interest. She tugged at my arm before I could move on and once again told me to *L-O-O-K* at the photo. I was a little curious, but I was really more interested in humoring her and moving on. After all, there were antique Roulette wheels and Elvis photos to look at.

I took a better look at the photo. The building was small, with a few cars in front of the place. The town where it stood was obviously some sort of western ghost town with more dust and vultures than residents. Other than the fact my wife was mysteriously taken with the photo there was no reason for me to even notice it at all.

*"Don't you see?"* my wife asked.

I thought for a minute that perhaps the neon sign was where I needed to focus my attention. We did just come from the Neon Museum and there was a sign suspiciously similar to the one we saw at the Boneyard represented in the picture. Like a moron I commented on the sign and how I thought we saw it in person earlier that day.

I imagine April wanted to smash my head into the photo at this point.

**THE photo that started it all.**
*Photo from the Author's personal collection.*

Her eyes popped out of her head as if I'd completely missed the sight of a tutu-wearing elephant dancing through the room. She pointed at the top of the photo and the caption that had been placed there in vinyl letters.

*"Willie Martello's El Rey Club & Brothel On Way to Laughlin"*

Now I understood what April was so excited about. Two words in that caption were most fascinating to me; *"Martello"* and *"brothel."*

I found the word, "brothel" amusing for the silliest of reasons. A little back story is in order here.

Some years back, while at a Thanksgiving dinner with April and her family, I went on a bit of an improvisational comedic rant about prostitutes. Being a professional comedian, it is not uncommon for me to riff on a theme during a conversation.

Before I get into the details of this discussion, I must preface this by letting you know that the members of this family tend to enjoy alcoholic beverages during holiday gatherings. Football, turkey dinner, my wife's family—all of these things make the presence of alcohol not only enjoyable but quite necessary.

At one point I found myself in front of the TV set watching football with the women in my wife's family. For whatever reason, whenever the conversation came my way, I would say something about the women on the broadcast being whores. It didn't matter who was on the screen, I would boldly proclaim that woman was a whore.

*"Hannah Storm? Whore!*

*LeAnn Rimes? Whore!*

*Mother Theresa? BIG Ole Whore!"*

Yes, I know, I'm going to Hell. No need to remind me.

I wasn't just bandying about the term "whore" because the women may or may not have been dressed like some gal on the street or it seemed a good insult. I was stating that these women were all genuine whores, with pimps and everything. If she was a woman and on TV, I had a singular and completely inaccurate conclusion about her. I would make these claims because, *"I could tell just by looking at them."* I even cited numerous explanations as to how I knew these ladies were whores.

Before too long, people were asking me how I knew all of this factual information. I told them it was because I was once known as a *"smooth pimp."*

Did I mention that alcohol gets consumed at these family functions?

I went on and on about my secret life as a smooth pimp and how I had to get out of the business because I'd run out of crack. In my diatribe, I'd determined that crack was all one would need to become a pimp. *"All you need is some crack and a woman and BOOM! You've got yourself a whore."* Soon, I was pining away for some *"starter crack"* so I could reassemble my fictional stable of whores. This insane rant inspired my mother-in-law to actually give me a bag of rock candy with a label which read, *"Starter crack...for your stable of whores,"* as a Christmas present.

You'll just have to believe me when I tell you that it was all much funnier at the time than it is in print. A classic example of a *"You had to be there"* story. It became something of a famous impromptu routine of mine among the family. Thank God we all have somewhat twisted senses of humor.

Seeing the Martello name associated with a brothel anywhere near Las Vegas just brought back all sorts of ridiculous memories from that past holiday. April and I both laughed as we relived the moment. Near as we figured I now had historical documentation of my "family history" in the prostitution business and, should the discussion ever enjoy a holiday revival, I'd be prepared with all new material.

Tasteless holiday humor aside, the more fascinating part of that photo was seeing the name "Willie Martello."

In my life, I've only encountered three random Martellos, meaning people with the same last name who were more than likely not related to me in the slightest.

The first came into my life via the television. My younger brother and I were watching "The Price is Right" one summer morning. That show has always made the perfect background noise as well as a worthy pastime, and on this day, it was just surface sounds to occupy our time while we did something else. The speaker on the TV set brought us all away from whatever else we were doing when Johnny Olson burst out with the phrase, *"Thomas Martello...COME ON DOWN!"* It provided a good laugh and much speculation as to whether there was a Thomas in our family. There is not, as far as we know.

Next was a young girl named Sarah. She was a student at a south suburban Chicago area school where I was performing. I'm a comedian and juggler and I travel to schools throughout the nation. I often get to shake hands and meet the students after the show. She walked up to me and asked, *"Are you related to me?"* If you've spent your life traveling across the country as a performer and you're a single man in his 20s, hearing a second-grader ask, *"Are you related to me?"* is quite actually the stuff of nightmares. As it happened she was just as amazed to meet someone with the same last name as herself and was curious to know if we were family. In case you are curious, we were (and are) not related.

The third of the mystery Martellos in my life was found printed in vinyl letters, hanging on a wall in a downtown Las Vegas museum.

As you can imagine my last name is not all that common. I'm not 100% certain on the numbers, but it has been estimated there are 600 – 1,200 Martello families in the world. Seeing a Willie Martello listed as the owner of a casino and brothel in old Las Vegas was absolutely the most startling and intriguing thing to cross into my brain in some time.

Who was this guy? Where was this club? Was the casino merely a front for a house of ill repute? Was it at all possible I can be somehow related to this man? I was filled with questions.

I stayed in the museum for a good amount of time after I saw this photo, but I couldn't get my thoughts off Willie Martello and this place called the El Rey. Every time I wandered over to another piece of memorabilia on the wall, I found myself wanting to walk back to that old photo of the El Rey Club and look for clues that would lead me to the Martello family in the west.

One thing I did notice was the phrase, *"Searchlight, Nev.,"* written in white letters on the photograph. At least now, I had a town to work with if I chose to do a little research on this place. However, in reality, I didn't have much to go on at all.

I was in a constant state of wonder about Willie Martello and his club during the remainder of the trip. I actually found myself eager to end my vacation so I could begin searching for information on this casino. I'd made a decision I would try to find any memorabilia from the casino that may have survived the years. With the power of the Internet and the vast wasteland of miscellanea that is eBay, I figured I'd have at least a small shot at learning a little about the club and owning a piece of history. A new hobby was born.

Being a writer as well as an entertainer, I knew I'd have at least one day's worth of interesting content to write about in my weblog regardless of what I found. I had no idea what I was about to uncover.

After I saw that one single photograph on the wall, I unearthed stories about a man who many saw as the most generous and outgoing man they'd ever met. This man had no regard for money or personal wealth and was known to provide employment and shelter to more than one out-of-work family who passed through town.

While conducting my all-too-unorganized research, I found the man who owned a brothel in a mining town was the same man who drove a car boasting the area's first car phone and that car featured the state's second license plate, **"Nevada 2."** **"Nevada 1"** belonged to the Governor.

I heard stories about one man's unparalleled vision and desire to create modern-day Las Vegas in tiny little Searchlight, Nevada long before there were pyramids and exploding volcanoes on the Strip. This same man would offer gourmet meals, champagne flights, comps, and top-notch entertainment in a place where most folks would simply drive by altogether if someone had not thought to put a resort and casino there.

In a town with plenty of desert sand and little else between Needles, California, and Las Vegas, Nevada, one man made it possible for the likes of *Frank Sinatra, Betty Grable, Martin & Lewis, Errol Flynn,* and *Louis Prima* to hide out and enjoy "civilian life." That same man provided a place where a future senator would learn to swim in the same pool where prostitutes would relax and escape the desert heat.

I came to know someone who was not only a casino and motel owner, but someone brash enough to be the self-proclaimed owner and mayor of the town. This self-made man would marry a Countess and would rarely be seen without his brilliant white suit and wide-brimmed hat, and even the wild Nevada burros would wander into the resort for a carrot or two handed out by the man in white.

I learned about a war veteran, a gambler, a husband, and a man who, as a child, refused to be pictured as a barefoot Indian alongside his six brothers.

Stories about this man's entrepreneurial endeavors and fantastically outlandish escapades sounded more like the stuff of a folk hero than that of a man who profited from gambling and lonely servicemen.

Could one man REALLY have installed the town's first telephone, swimming pool, and school baseball field?

Did one man build an airport large enough to land today's Space Shuttle so visitors could leave California and travel to Searchlight, Nevada, instead of Las Vegas?

Did noted film director, **Francis Ford Coppola**, REALLY make his directorial debut while working on a "nudie cutie" filmed in Searchlight at the El Rey?

Clearly, I had more than a new hobby. I had a lot of unanswered questions.

In the time since my wife's fateful discovery of that old black-and-white photograph, I came to know a man who, in all likelihood, is not related to me in the slightest and yet, I have his family photos among my own. I "met" a man who died a couple of years before I was born. I get sad when "family outsiders" know this man only as a brothel owner and not as a great, bigger-than-life character. Thanks to the keen eyes of my wife and the photo that once hung in a now defunct Las Vegas museum, I KNOW Willie Martello.

**A young & ever-stylish Willie Martello.** *Photo courtesy Sharon Richardson.*

Photo courtesy Sharon Richardson

# THE KING

**Two El Rey Beer bottle labels.** *From the author's personal collection*

The Martellos had long-standing ties to Southern California and Southern Nevada. In the late 1920s, **Angelo Martello** ran a very successful fruit distribution business in Los Angeles, the L. Martello Fruit Company. Throughout the years, many of the Martello children found themselves working for Angelo. By 1951, **Louis** and **Achilles "Kelly" Martello**, along with partners **Mike Maini** and **Angelo Marsala,** would travel to Las Vegas to branch out and open an equally successful produce warehouse and distribution firm, M & M Produce, at 1524 Fremont Street. By then, there were already a few other Martellos located an hour's drive away in a town called Searchlight.

Over the years, the Martellos became rather entrenched in the night club business. One such place was Marsal's bar and restaurant in South Gate, California. The night club game seemed a good match for the Martello family. **Tony Martello**, Willie's brother, was a bootlegger in the 1920s. By 1930, he had decided to get out of bootlegging and would soon apply for a legitimate liquor license. After prohibition ended in 1933, Tony secured one of the very first liquor licenses in Los Angeles, California. In 1939, he opened a bar in South Gate, California called The El Rey Club and employed plenty of the Martello brothers along the way.

"El Rey" means "The King" in Spanish, but to Tony and his brothers "El Rey" meant something else: BEER! Their favorite beer at the time was El Rey Beer, brewed by El Rey Brewing Company and later by Grace Bros.

Brewing Company of Santa Rosa, California. They liked the beer and they liked the name. With that, they arrived at an appropriate name for their new bar. The King was born. Long live The King!

Prior to arriving in Searchlight, Willie Martello, a man known for his confidence and charm, was something of a lost soul. A Navy veteran, he was in Hawaii on shore leave from the U.S.S. Arizona during the Pearl Harbor attack and felt distraught, even guilty after losing so many friends on board. Willie took odd jobs after his own military service ended, many of them through his family connections. One such job was that of a truck driver. Presumably, he delivered

**Brothers Willie Martello (in Navy uniform) and Vincent "Buddy" Martello alongside their mother, circa 1940s.**
*Photo courtesy Sharon Richardson.*

goods for his family's fruit company as well as other family ventures in California.

Willie, like all of the Martellos, showed a knack for business and certainly enjoyed the action he found within a night club more than behind the wheel of a delivery truck. Eventually, with concerns for Willie's well-being, he was simply told by Tony Martello in 1946, *"Why don't you go out to Searchlight and see what you can do."* Willie's brothers, **Vincent "Buddy" Martello,** the youngest brother, and Albert Martello, a bit older than Willie and the man who would one day own the original El Rey Club in South Gate, were already in Searchlight.

During its heyday, Searchlight, once a thriving boom town during the gold rush days, claimed a larger population than that of nearby Las Vegas. It was a dusty town that drifted along the Mohave Desert and was located halfway between Las Vegas, Nevada and Needles, California.

Contrary to its name, there was no actual searchlight in the town. Some history books state the town was named after a man named Lloyd Searchlight; however, those accounts have proved to be inaccurate. In

Original tourism brochure for Searchlight, NV, circa 1950s-1960s.

reality, the town's name came from one of the least glamorous of places: a box of Searchlight matches. Of course, you can find the best and most often told explanation for the name, if not the most quaintly entertaining, proudly printed on a 1958 travel brochure for the desert town.

*"Early 1898 found prospectors Gus Moore and Fred Colton discussing the potential values of an outcropping they had found north of the rich and productive Quartette mine. The opinion of one was explosive and negative. His remark that 'a searchlight would have to be used if there were values there' was instrumental in naming the claim 'Searchlight'."*

Over the years, Searchlight had its fair share of noteworthy residents. Hollywood celebrities **Rex Bell** and the glamorous **Clara Bow** (Hollywood's "It Girl"), as well as legendary Hollywood costume designer, **Edith Head**, made Searchlight their home. Military and aviation heroes **John Macready** and **William Harrel Nellis** once hung their hats in Searchlight. Ragtime composer Scott Joplin reportedly named the Searchlight Rag after the Nevada mining town. By 1946, Searchlight was best known for...well, for being located halfway between Las Vegas, Nevada and Needles, California.

The origin of the El Rey Club has always been uncertain at best. The Martellos had purchased some land in Searchlight several years back, possibly from the power company although some reports suggested the spot where the El Rey once stood belonged to the Marshall family. It was believed the El Rey Club was previously an old barn which was retrofitted by the Martello family to serve the needs of a bar and casino.

Bob Martello, son of Tony Martello, recalls that Buddy and Albert were living there to raise livestock, but accounts from other members of Willie's family do not believe this to be so. In fact, the El Rey Club was once known as Searchlight's **Wheatley Hotel** and was eventually purchased by the Martello family.

What else is certain is Buddy and Albert were embarking on a plan to open a bar and casino in town. The Martellos entered into a partnership to run the El Rey which brought their family history in the night club business to the table. Taking it as a sign of good things to come and wanting to continue a family tradition of fun places to drink and have a good time, they named their new venture the El Rey Club. They opened their doors on March 9, 1946.

The original El Rey was run by the Martello brothers, Albert and Buddy. However, it was a third partner, **Lloyd B. Allen**, who was often referred to as the owner of the El Rey Club. Though nobody in the Martello family today can confirm or remember a Lloyd Allen or his involvement with the El Rey Club, Mr. Allen is listed as the owner of the El Rey Club in the debut issue of the *Searchlight Journal* newspaper on August 29, 1946, the same week a devastating fire claimed three buildings in Searchlight and

Four Martello brothers inside the original El Rey Club in Southgate, CA, circa 1940s-1950s. Left to Right: Willie, Buddy, Joe, & Tony Martello. *Photo courtesy Sharon Richardson.*

scorched the side of an outside wall of the El Rey Club.

It is my belief Lloyd Allen chose to leave the bar and casino business soon after the 1946 fire in Searchlight. By December 3, 1946, the *Las Vegas Review-Journal* listed Allen, along with Buddy and Albert Martello, in a notice of dissolution regarding the El Rey Club partnership. While it is unknown exactly when in 1946 Willie came to Searchlight, it was around the time of the dissolution that Willie Martello became the owner of the El Rey. The new King assumed his rightful place on the throne.

*"Willie arrived in Searchlight, Nevada with thirteen bucks in his pocket and a couple bottles of booze,"* according to Sharon Richardson. When Willie met up with his brothers and saw the El Rey in the desert, he found more than just some familiar faces. Above the bar, along with an impressive collection of handguns owned by brother Buddy, was a framed photo of seven young boys dressed as Indians.

The Seven Little Indians, circa 1915. This photo hung above the bar at the El Rey Club. Notice Willie (2nd from left) is standing in his familiar casual slouch and is the only Indian wearing shoes. Left to Right: Buddy, Willie, Louis, Mickey, Albert, Joe, & Tony Martello. *Photo courtesy Sharon Richardson.*

Photo Courtesy of Nevada State Museum, Las Vegas [J. Florian Mitchell Collection]

# GAMES PEOPLE PLAY

A mountaintop view of the bustling town of Searchlight, circa April 1946. This image features the main drag along Hwy 95. On the far left you can see the building that would become The Crystal Club (under construction). In the center lies the Searchlight Casino, and just a bit farther north sits the El Rey Club. *Photo by Ullom. From the author's personal collection.*

It is certain that prior to the legalization of gambling in Nevada in 1931 countless establishments across the state offered some form of gambling. However, being able to track and report such places becomes something of a daunting task, especially in a town as small as Searchlight. Tough as it may be, **Harvey Fuller** seems to be the reigning expert on the subject. Though certainly not complete or definitive as new information about gaming in Nevada is being discovered every day, *Harvey J. Fuller's Index of Nevada Gambling Establishments,* is an excellent resource.

According to Fuller, in 1946, there were at least six places offering gaming in Searchlight, three of which were reportedly in operation for a maximum of one or two years. *"The competition was horrible,"* recalled Sharon Richardson. *"With a 'nothing town' as small as Searchlight having to compete with the bright lights of Las Vegas nearby, it was a miracle any club could survive past a couple of years."*

The **Desert Club** *("Where Old Friends Meet")* and **The Golden Eagle** opened in March and July of 1946 respectively. Newspaper advertisements for the Desert Club boasted affordable alcohol as well as *"Honesty, Courtesy, and Hospitality."* At the Golden Eagle you could enjoy nightly dancing and live entertainment and *"a cool drink expertly mixed."* However, all of the honesty, courtesy, hospitality, and alcohol in the world could save neither operation from fading away. Both clubs closed in 1947.

**Junior Girard Cree** opened the *Union Bar - Casino* in 1946 and transferred ownership to **Ernest "Sandy" Sandquist** in January of 1947. Despite offering *"A Square Deal to All,"* it would close some time in 1948.

One of Searchlight's most historic buildings, the **Hotel Nevada,** also known as the **Kennedy House** (named after **Bill Kennedy** who built the hotel and would later take his own life by throwing himself down a mineshaft), was built in 1900. This Searchlight landmark from the gold rush days offered slot machines, blackjack, craps, and poker to the gambling customer in 1944 and also served as a bus stop.  The Hotel Nevada, supposedly condemned for several years prior to February 9, 1949 (the day of its demise), actually continued to offer gaming up until the day it perished in a terrific blaze.  I suppose, in the strictest sense of the term, a

A rare image of the Hotel Nevada, circa April 1946. *Photo by Ullom. From the author's personal collection*

condemned building makes the perfect place to gamble.

Contrary to Fuller's book, advertising found in original issues of the *Searchlight Journal* newspaper from the time prove there were at least three more casinos in or near Searchlight.

In addition to a bar and casino, The **Hotel Rondo** offered a modern trailer park and laundry, fully air-conditioned rooms, and *"Hot & cold water in every room."* With amenities like that, you wonder why this book isn't about The Hotel Rondo.

The *Oasis Club*, listed in the Fuller book as offering gaming in January of 1947, was known to offer a hotel, bar, and games of 21 or craps at the casino under the new management of **"Dutch" J. Del Porto** as early as October of 1946. If gaming and beer weren't enough to entice you to pay a visit, surely the lure of a *"FREE pair of nylons with every hit of the jackpot"* would be too much for ladies or gentlemen gaming at the Oasis Club to resist.

The **Silver Dollar**, a bar and casino managed by **Tex Cantrell**, proudly announced nightly entertainment by the **Sage Brush Ranch Boys**. Dollar signs were prominently featured in their newspaper ads beginning in 1946. If the live music wasn't enticing, then perhaps, the hint of cash was.

The **Crystal Club**, a club eventually owned by Willie Martello, was clearly open in 1946 in contrast to Fuller's account. An early advertisement shows that a **Ray Swisher** was the owner-operator at the time, but none of the newspaper advertisements or other research I found suggested any gaming was available. What you could find at the Crystal in 1946 was *"a drink in a friendly atmosphere"* and *"booths for the ladies."* By December of 1953, slot machines and blackjack were available at the Crystal, and it would one day serve as the temporary home for the gaming interests of the El Rey Club.

There were certainly some casinos that succeeded. Two of the more successful casinos found in Searchlight at that time would have to be the **Searchlight Casino**, and arguably the most successful in Searchlight history (depending upon your measure), the El Rey Club. The Searchlight Casino sat very close to the El Rey, just a short walk farther south, and was in operation from January of 1944 to February of 1956. It offered roulette, craps, 21, and slots.

Fuller lists the El Rey Club opening, or at least, first offering gaming, on March 9, 1946. According to advertisements in the *Searchlight Journal* from October of 1946, it offered at least three casino games in the early days – blackjack, craps, and poker – though very few people I've spoken with recall the game [poker] being offered at all. Additionally, I've found no photographic evidence to prove a poker table was ever found within the confines of the El Rey Club. The only Martello mentioned in any early ads was Buddy Martello who was listed as the manager. It is certain Willie Martello was in Searchlight in 1946, and by the end of 1946, he was just starting to get a feel for the business Buddy and Albert were running.

**Joyce Dickens Walker** (then **Joyce Dickens**) was hired as a bartender at the El Rey by Willie. *"My mother lived in Searchlight. I went to school in California and worked in Searchlight,"* she recalls. *"Willie hired me because I knew everybody in town and thought that would be helpful."* Photos she provided me from around 1947 showed a roulette table, but she admits, *"The only game I remember there was 21."*

Perhaps, one reason Joyce doesn't remember seeing craps at the El Rey was due to the extremely small size of the first craps tables. An eBay purchase I made during my research revealed a very rare gaming item: a portable craps table.

This was a small shaped table almost like a casino showroom dining table, one that would fit within the "U" shape of a booth, though it was obvious this was not large enough for such a purpose. The piece sat about twenty-two inches across and about eighteen inches deep with a distinct rubber and leather bank board following the curved edge of the back, which suggested it was most certainly used for rolling dice. It was clearly a professionally constructed piece and was designed to rest on top of any flat surface. In plain stenciled lettering along the front were the words **"EL**

---

**A rare photo of the Searchlight Casino, circa April 1946. The shacks to the right were motel rooms known as "cribs" and were used for prostitution.**
*Photo by Ullom. From the author's personal collection.*

REY," and on the underside of the table were the words **"Tom Jackson"** and **"Searchlight."** Further research proved this to be a layout for craps and other casino dice games. Generally, tables this small were used in only the smallest casinos, those that didn't have the space or the money to afford a larger, more traditional craps table. Thankfully, the El Rey would soon expand its business to include full-sized craps tables.

Having the tables in place wasn't enough to get gamblers inside to spend time and money. Occasionally, Willie needed to resort to some old school tactics to ease the cash out of the patrons' pockets.

*Willie would give me money to start a game and act as a shill,"* said Joyce Dickens. *"I HATED it and would lose the money as fast as I could."* Having a reluctant employee-shill, i.e. decoy, losing money was the least of Willie's problems.

I believe I first heard this next phrase being uttered by Chicago radio personality Buzz Kilman during a conversation about radio broadcasting rights, the F.C.C., and how quickly a radio station would fire an on-air personality before it tried to fight any sort of charges brought against it (a Howard Stern tirade upsetting someone, as an example). As it happened, this phrase can be applied to just about any business and, most definitely,

**A roulette table inside the El Rey Club, circa 1946. The poodles, Peppi and Pierre, belonged to Willie.** *Photo courtesy Joyce Dickens Walker*

to a bar or a casino.

*"Once you have a license, you have something to lose."*

This cannot be truer than when it concerns casino owners and their gaming licenses. It is my belief that everyone who has ever held a gaming license in Nevada has had it removed for a variety of reasons whether justified or manufactured. No casino owner wanted to lose his gaming license in Nevada, and Willie was no exception. That doesn't mean it didn't happen.

On February 27, 1950, he had his gaming license revoked for *"irregular gambling operations,"* a charge resulting from an investigation revealing a marked deck of cards in a 21 game, according to the *Reno Evening Gazette* and the *Nevada State Journal*. Willie would lose his license for six months and would testify in person that he was unaware that the deck of cards in question was marked. In May of 1951, attorney **Harry Claiborne** would apply for a reinstatement of Willie's license on the same day he would apply for licenses for a NEW club in Las Vegas owned by **Benny Binion**, called The **Horseshoe**.

This was not the first time a marked deck of cards got Willie in the newspapers. Interestingly and rather amusingly, a marked deck of cards would play a part of another bit of news which was worthy of print in July of 1960. According to an article by the *Review-Journal's* **Forrest Duke**, Willie used a marked deck of cards to help determine who would be the next "Honorary Mayor" of Searchlight, a story I'll tell in more detail later in this book. Needless to say, the tax commission was not needed and no formal hearings were necessary, though I have always wondered if it was the same deck of cards that cost Willie his license ten years prior.

Martello found himself and his gaming license in jeopardy again in September of 1953. **District Attorney George Dickerson** charged Willie with *"operating a cheating game or device."* The device was found to be a plugged slot machine. Newspaper accounts would report an investigation by Nevada Tax Commission Agents **Keith Campbell** and **Dudley Kline,** who found a **"jumper,"** or percentage changer *"attached to the center wheel of the device, making it impossible to hit two cherries."* **O.E. Glenn** of the Glenn Sales company of Las Vegas certified the agents' findings. This time Martello faced gross misdemeanor charges. The punishment for such an offense was up to a one-thousand dollar fine, six months of jail time, or both. Ultimately, Willie lost his gaming license

once again. By December of
that year, Junior Cree, former
owner of the Union Club,
acting as operator of the El
Rey on Willie's behalf, applied
for a new license for the El Rey
and was subsequently denied.
Eventually, Willie's license woes
became a thing of the past.

While the El Rey Club
was always known to be
a very above-the-board
establishment, Bob Martello
commented in an interview,
*"These things happened to a
lot of places. It wasn't like it is
today. Willie never knowingly
cheated anyone, and he ran a clean business."*

**Buddy Martello handling the chips at an
El Rey Club Craps table on February 18, 1961.**
*Nevada State Museum, Las Vegas
[J. Florian Mitchell Collection]*

Throughout the history of the El Rey, securing the services of qualified
dealers to man the tables was frequently an issue. *"He had to pay dealers
almost double in salary to get them to come out there, and they were
not always the cream of the crop,"* according to Sharon Richardson, *"and
when they did, many stole from him."* She remembered one occasion
when she caught one dealer rather blatantly stealing from Willie. *"I saw a
dealer cuff some chips. Willie was sitting in the middle of the pit. I knew he
saw him,"* said Sharon, *"I asked Uncle Willie why he didn't say anything to
that dealer. He said, 'Because I need him.'"* When the dealer was about to
leave the pit, Willie said to him very quietly, *"Be sure to leave something
for me."*

Though it would take some time to build, eventually, the El Rey would
house two craps tables, one roulette table, four blackjack tables, and thirty
slot machines. In spite of occasional money issues, thieving employees,
and licensing woes, the El Rey gaming operation found its groove as Willie
made efforts to grow both his name and his reputation in the Las Vegas
area.

# THE KINGDOM

Willie Martello always set his sights on being a big player in the Nevada gaming industry. Though the El Rey Club would prove to be where he would make his largest contributions and spend most of his time and efforts, he did try to expand his kingdom beyond the borders of Searchlight.

Although he had only been in Searchlight a few years and only recently began operating the El Rey, Willie was always reinvesting any money he had in land acquisitions and other properties. By September 1, 1949, Willie Martello's name was clearly visible in bright lights along the signage for one of the Las Vegas Strip's more storied and notorious properties, The **Red Rooster**.

The Red Rooster first opened its doors to the public in 1931 and was owned by **Alice Wilson Morris**. There, you could find a dance floor, a stage for a singer and orchestra, and a restaurant. At that time the majority of bars, nightclubs, and speakeasies were primarily found on Fremont Street. Gambling was still illegal in Nevada until March of that same year.

Since it was located on Highway 91 (The Strip), this would be one of the first places to set up shop away from downtown in an attempt to grab motorists as they left Las Vegas and traveled to California. A novel placement along the road surface was the public claim to fame for the Rooster. In reality, this became better known as an illegal speakeasy that sold alcohol during Prohibition. Federal Marshals forced The Red Rooster to cease the sale of alcohol or risk being shut down permanently. It complied with the order for a short while, at least.

Legal gambling in Nevada had only been recently approved, and the Red Rooster was one of the first twenty-five places to be issued a gaming license. On April 1st, you would find a single blackjack table and three slot machines inside The Red Rooster. The sale of illegal alcohol continued.

In July of 1931, The Red Rooster earned a unique distinction in Las Vegas history when it became the first establishment to lose its gaming license. Federal agents finally raided the club, and Morris was officially brought up on charges for the illegal sale of alcohol.

Over the next couple years, things continued fluctuating up and down for Morris' Red Rooster. By 1933, it was granted a dance hall license, and after Prohibition ended, it was allowed to sell only beer. Before the club could gain any momentum, it burned to the ground in July of 1933 and re-opened once again on December 30, 1933. It remained a popular night spot for several years before it was sold to Hollywood actress **Grace Hayes** in 1947.

With the addition of the **Sans Souci** auto court motel to the property, Hayes renamed the property the **Grace Hayes Lodge** and reportedly would entertain **Benjamin Siegel** frequently in the lounge. She later renamed the club The Red Rooster only to mysteriously sell the club to one Willie Martello in 1949.

Willie promptly changed the name to **Martello's Red Rooster** and opened his new club on September 1, 1949. He promised customers who wanted to stop by the well-known night spot *"Something New! Something Different!"*, though it is unclear just what was so new or different about the place apart from the change in name.

Willie did make attempts to promote The Red Rooster and encourage more visitors. Advertisements for the grand opening claimed *"Every Night is Prize Night"* and promised a door prize to every customer. As with all of Willie's night clubs and casinos, nightly entertainment and dancing was imperative. Folks who wanted to strut their stuff and enjoy *"DANCING at its BEST"* could tread the boards until 6 AM to the sounds of Al Crinett and his band all weekend during the debut of Martello's Red Rooster.

Not much else is known about the time when Willie owned the Red Rooster. The club continued to be successful after its rocky start back in the early 1930s, including during the time when Willie had his name emblazoned across the sign. However, it was sold back to Grace Hayes not quite one full year later. It is my belief that Martello's gaming license woes in February of 1950 led to the sale back to Grace Hayes. She would eventually sell the club again in 1953, and before long, it would make way for the **Castaways**. Today, if you want to stand on the ground where Willie briefly had his name on a marquee on the Las Vegas Strip, just stop by the **Mirage** and have a drink.

It seemed Willie's other businesses outside of Searchlight were equally brief and mysterious. Bob Martello spoke of a time when he was ordered by Willie to make purchases of property lots on Flamingo at a cost of $1,500 each, but little more is known about what happened to those lots or if they were merely investment properties for Willie.

Bill Moore, former employee of Doc Bayley's **Hacienda**, recalled Martello had ownership in a burlesque house near the **Sands Hotel** in the late 1950s. Again, that's about all that is known about this establishment

and even Martello's family cannot remember a name or a location of such an entertainment venue for Willie.

Somehow, details of an entire $250,000 resort hotel and casino owned by Willie have all but vanished.

The most puzzling of Willie's other casino ventures the **Trade Winds**, could be found near Railroad Pass on the way to Boulder City in December of 1954. The Trade Winds was located on Highway 95 and was a joint venture between **A.G. Klinger**, a businessman and land owner at Railroad Pass, and Willie Martello. It looked as though Klinger and Martello were cut from the same cloth since they were both big fish in little ponds. Klinger had owned property and maintained residence in Railroad Pass since 1933. He had a service station and machine shop there and was known by all from that area to be "The Mayor of Railroad Pass."

Construction was already well underway for the new resort. Plans included fine Italian dining, banquet facilities, and, of course, a casino and bar.

Things were moving forward at a steady clip when Klinger and Martello received an early Christmas present from the State Highway Department.

On December 24, 1954, the *Boulder City Journal* reported that construction was to be halted while the Highway Deptartment and the Trade Winds partners worked to settle a dispute of the rightful ownership of the land where the construction was taking place.

The state asserted they had the proper authority over the land, and Klinger was vehemently opposed to their claims. When a second lane was added to the road in 1950, Klinger believed he maintained ownership of the land, and he willingly ceded the land to the Highway Department for their expansion.

Martello tried desperately to get the order halted or, at least, relaxed somewhat. He testified that $100,000 in custom made furnishings had already been ordered and delivered to the nearly-completed resort. Sadly, the order stood.

From this point forward, the story of The Trade Winds simply vanishes from the public record. It is very possible the building was completed and operational for a time based on evidence such as gaming chips and other memorabilia that were available, though scarcely, in the collectors' markets. However, no information from the Martello family or elsewhere is available, and there is no evidence of such construction ever existing on Highway 95 at Railroad Pass. Perhaps, the gaming chips from the mysterious Trade Winds were actually being used in Willie's established endeavor, the El Rey Club.

If Willie was ever to expand his kingdom, he was going to have to limit himself to the confines of Searchlight. If he couldn't grow beyond the town, he would simply have to grow the town bigger. He set out to do just that.

*Photo courtesy Ethel Martello*

# CONTINUOUS ENTERTAINMENT.
# SUPERLATIVE CUISINE.

When I have taken the time to think about trying to run a casino, bar, and resort in a town as small as Searchlight, whether it is today or back in Willie's time, I found myself thinking, *"Whose brilliant idea was this, anyway?"* During the time Willie took over the place, it seemed unlikely any such business would survive. Presently there are only about 1000 residents in Searchlight. Back then there could have been as few as 50 or as many as 800, but that is pushing it a bit.

Bars, no matter how small the town, have traditionally survived on some level across the country, especially in Searchlight. Harry Reid claimed at one point there were 28 saloons in town. According to Jane Overy of the Searchlight Museum there were never more than eight or nine bars open at any one time in the town. Apparently, the town gave the outward impression it was overrun with bars. *"What would happen, as the town fluctuated, new people would come in and become an owner of the bars or saloons, change the name, and have a big celebration. There was a grand opening all the time,"* said Jane. With so many miners, even though the numbers had dwindled, by the 1940s, a bar in Searchlight was certain to stay open for a spell.

Being Southern Nevada, most any establishment that offered gambling had some hope of staying in business. In Searchlight, there were many more casinos open for less than three years than there were open three years or longer. Many believed Willie's casino wouldn't even last a full 30 days when it first opened its doors.

To be one of those businesses fortunate enough to stay open for an extended period of time required a lot of effort, a certain amount of higher quality, and more than a clever idea or two to lure people into your building.

Two staples at the El Rey Club were freshly made meals and live entertainment such as music and dancing. From day one, Willie was already interested in the promotions angle of enticing patrons to the club and offering guests a little value along with their experience. According to Jeff Reid Jr., *"I was there for the grand opening. When the first customer came into the café, Willie gave him a free chicken dinner, and then the customers came rolling in."*

It was always Willie's intention to have world class dining at the El Rey. When Willie came to town, he convinced long-time family friend and four-star chef **Luigi Scirocco,** from California, to come out to Searchlight.

*"We're going to serve nothing but the finest food and bring people here from everywhere,"* Willie said. However, in 1947, Willie and Luigi realized these were truly humble beginnings.

In the early days the café was not particularly fancy. The building was small and had little more than an old pot-bellied stove for Luigi to cook upon. Joyce Dickens Walker recalled some basic grub, but nothing to write home about. *"I do remember eating there at least once. I don't remember if there was anything colorful on the plate. Mashed potatoes, creamed cauliflower, and white bread."*

Chef Luigi, believing in his friend's dream to make something special out of the dirty little building known as the El Rey, stuck with it as everybody on hand did their share of duties not necessarily associated with their jobs. It was not uncommon to find Willie or Luigi tending bar, dealing cards at the single 21 table, or raking in dice at their one craps table. Because there was not a large staff of people in the early days, you could find the casino

**Chef Luigi Scirocco in the El Rey Club on November 12, 1961.**
*Nevada State Museum, Las Vegas [J. Florian Mitchell Collection]*

A sampling of delicacies offered at the El Rey Club's Continental Cafe. Note the menu is signed by Willie himself. *From the author's personal collection, with thanks to Sharon Richardson for the generous gift.*

*Willie Martello*

**CHEF'S SPECIAL**

Tournedos Tyrolienne served with French Fried Onion Rings and Grilled Tomatos
Bearnaise Sauce (2 Filet Steaks) ............................................. 3.75

**SEAFOOD**

| | |
|---|---|
| Australian Lobster Tail | 2.95 |
| Catalina Sword Fish — Lemon Butter | 2.25 |
| Pan Fried Frog Legs in Butter | 3.75 |
| French Fried Jumbo Shrimps — Hot Sauce | 2.25 |
| Pan Fried Rainbow Trout — Tartare | 2.50 |
| Grilled Chinook Salmon Steak — Lemon Butter | 2.50 |

Baked Idaho Potato — Home Made Bread
Coffee — Ice Cream or Sherbet

owner himself taking a mop to his dirt-covered floors.

As a little cash began to roll in and its reputation for having better entertainment grew, Willie offered a much higher quality dining experience than anyone else in town and even rivaled some of the big-time hotels and casinos in Las Vegas. Willie's **Continental Café** also featured the cooking of chefs **John Bender** and **Ed Thompson**. The El Rey Resort's cuisine was truly making headlines with their food, and the menu options were clearly a hit with the patrons' palates as well as their pocketbooks. Any one of the items listed on their menu would make you wonder if you had magically stepped out of Searchlight and into a wonderful bistro in a more exotic location.

Of course, you could find your basics such as hamburgers, salads, and grilled cheese sandwiches. However, long before you even reached that section of the menu you were dazzled by the Chef's Special, Tournedos Tyrolienne with French Fried Onion Rings, Grilled Tomatoes and Béarnaise Sauce for $3.75.

If the price for this delicacy featuring the two filet steaks and trimmings was a bit more than you'd bargained for, why not enjoy the Australian Lobster Tail for only $2.95 or the Catalina Swordfish with Lemon Butter for only $2.25? With prices that ranged from seventy-five cents to $1.25, the Continental Café offered four different "Supreme" Ala Carte cocktails that included fruit, fresh crab meat, jumbo shrimp, and fresh lobster. If you felt like splurging, a hearty New York steak could be served right off the broiler for a whopping $4.00 and would be worth every penny. But why spend $4.00 on ONE meal when for only TEN CENTS MORE you and your date could have Two Center Cut Pork Chops with Apple Sauce and a Chicken Fried Steak with Ready Potatoes? From the 16oz. Top Sirloin steak to the Double Cut Spring Lamb Chops (both at $3.50), it was clear you had some culinary options well beyond what anyone would expect to find in a town like Searchlight. The place even reportedly offered meals featuring their own home-grown pheasants. This wasn't bad for a place often described by Harry Reid and so many others as a common whorehouse.

Truly, fine dining was always something worthy of attracting a crowd. However, for the El Rey Club to be known as THE place to find all the action, there would also need to me some hoppin' tunes and lively dancing to go along with those meals.

*"Always a Lively Time at the El Rey Club - Dancing As Usual Friday, Saturday and Sunday"* was how readers of the *Searchlight Journal* newspaper read the advertisements in 1947. In the earliest days of the club, there was some sort of musical act on the weekends. Later, as the business picked up and Willie expanded the casino, he featured live music most every night of the week. By the mid-1950s there were at least two bands on the weekends, a dance band and a lounge style act.

One of the earliest bands to appear regularly was *"The Biggest Little Band in Searchlight"*, **Pappy and Prospector Jack.** "Prospector Jack" was guitar player **Jack Perkins**, the future husband to hostess and El Rey bartender Joyce Dickens. Pappy and Prospector Jack made regular appearances at the El Rey Club as well as the Golden Eagle until Jack was appointed a Deputy Sheriff of Clark County. As they say, that's showbiz.

Willie was more upset about Joyce taking up with a musician than losing a band. *"Willie was none too happy with me for dating Jack,"* Joyce would say. When she told him that she and Jack were getting married, Willie replied, *"Joyce, if you want to get married that badly, I'll marry you!"* She refused Willie's generous offer, and Willie set off finding more musical acts.

The El Rey took great pride in being able to bring in some of the best bands in the area and from around the country. One of the acts that performed at the El Rey Club was the **Walter Craig Trio**, featuring the vocal styling of **Addie Ross.**

Music and dancing were always popular draws for the El Rey Club. Since he had many friends in Hollywood and Las Vegas, Willie was able to lure some much bigger names to his little club. Some would look at it as a stopover, a "gas gig" between California and Vegas. Others looked at it as a big time event.

In April of 1959, young country singer **Polly Possum** made her way to the El Rey stage and performed three shows nightly at 10 PM, midnight, and 2 AM. Miss Possum, aka **Polly O'Neal**, was best known for her work with guitarist **Joe Wolverton** and **The Dog Patch Boys** on hit records like "Sin in Satin."

Jazz music fans could soothe their needs by stopping by the El Rey to see trumpet player and bandleader **Wingy Manone** play his biggest hit, "Tar Paper Stomp". Although his ironically titled songs like "Nickel in the Slot," "There'll Come a Time (Just You Wait and See)", and "Downright Disgusted Blues" made for a more enjoyable evening in a casino setting.

In 1961, guests of the El Rey were treated to an exciting two-week run by the very popular jazz singing star **Helen Forrest**. Forrest had performed with acts like **Benny Goodman**, **Lionel Hampton**, and **Nat King Cole** and also toured the country with one-time boyfriend **Harry James**. She was backed by the musical group **Dixieland Dynamiters**. Miss Forrest delighted El Rey crowds with her renditions of "Sunny Side of the Street," "Ten Cents a Dance," and "You Made Me Love You" as well as a medley of hits she'd recorded with the Harry James Orchestra. Noted *Review-Journal* columnist, Forrest Duke wrote about this auspicious entertainment booking on June 29, 1961. *"In both appearance and sound, the star is top drawer, proving she would be a solid nitery attraction in any situation."*

There were also occasional reports that Rat Packers Frank Sinatra and Dean Martin made unpaid appearances at the El Rey. According to Bob Martello, they were there mostly to visit Willie and be close to Vegas and California without being bothered by the fans or the frenzies of either location. *"It was a great place for Hollywood to hide out and relax. Nobody would bother them and they liked that,"* Bob said. Betty Grable reportedly made a stop or two at the El Rey en route to or from Vegas as did Louis Prima. However, even with the names of such major entertainment superstars that were known to stop into the tiny desert resort, I found while I researched and interviewed people for this project the name of one headlining act stood out among the memories of those who'd either been to or heard of the El Rey. That act was **The DeCastro Sisters**.

Whether it was the full trio or **Peggy DeCastro** as a solo act, any time the DeCastro Sisters graced the stage at the El Rey Club, it created a sense

A junket from Hollywood to Searchlight on March 12, 1961. This junket featured many Hollywood performers, stars, and starlets, including Mousey Garner (center, front row), Diane McBain (right of Garner), Sherry Jackson (next to bus driver), and Sean Flynn (left of Jackson). Willie Martello is posing with McBain on the right.

*Nevada State Museum, Las Vegas  [J. Florian Mitchell Collection]*

Chef Luigi with legendary vaudevillian, Mousey Garner on March 12, 1961.

*Nevada State Museum, Las Vegas [J. Florian Mitchell Collection]*

Gary LeMel and Peggy DeCastro at the El Rey Club on May 20, 1961.

*Nevada State Museum, Las Vegas [J. Florian Mitchell Collection]*

of electricity.  Bringing along accompanying acts like **Paul "Mousey" Garner,** their own glamorous beauty, and songs like "Teach Me Tonight" and "Boom Boom Boomerang," the Cuban answer to the Andrews Sisters always made quite a splash when they were in town.  They brought class, comedy, and a full Las Vegas lounge show to Searchlight.  Mostly, they brought in large crowds of people.

Garner, "The Grand Old Man of Vaudeville," was known by many as the last performing headliner from the days of Vaudeville and appeared in such noteworthy television programs as *The Jack Benny Program* and *The Spike Jones Show.*  He was a working act his entire life and performed on stages up until his death in 2004 at the age of 95.

On one occasion, Peggy DeCastro appeared at the El Rey Club along with a young up-and-coming star, **Gary LeMel.**

LeMel was once believed to be "the next big thing" in modern pop music.  He was signed to Vee-Jay Records within a couple of years after his appearance at the El Rey, and they released the critically acclaimed "The Gary LeMel Album" in 1964.  Sadly, LeMel's career as a pop superstar was short-lived when another act stole the spotlight.  Just a few months later, Vee-Jay also signed a promising new act, **The Beatles,** to their label.  Don't feel too badly for LeMel.  He went on to become the Executive Vice President of Columbia Pictures and the President of Warner Brothers Music before he returned to the stage in 1997.

If you were lucky enough, you would catch a glimpse of the biggest star in Searchlight, Willie Martello, taking the stage.  *"Willie loved to sing,"* remembered **Jerry Schafer.** *"I would see him get up on stage all the time and entertain the crowd, just for laughs and to have a little fun."*  Always the lover of the desert and the west, Willie's favorite song to sing when he regaled the guests with his dulcet tones was the 1959 **Lee Penny** and **Louise Massey** song, "My Adobe Hacienda".

Entertainment at the El Rey Club wasn't limited to just music and dancing.  No Las Vegas area casino would be considered a real draw without the presence of beautiful women.  If you were looking for more exotic entertainment, the El Rey was more than willing to provide you with the best!

Most notably, *"Her Sexcellency"* herself, the one and only legendary **Sally Rand,** helped bring in 1961 with style.  For three big days, Miss Rand delighted the New Year's revelers at the El Rey Club four times nightly.

Show times were at 9 PM, 11 PM, 1 AM, and 3 AM Friday through Sunday.

Sometimes, the exotic entertainment offered at the El Rey was as much about publicity as it was about sexual curiosity.

On one occasion, the confused and the curious alike were invited to enjoy entertainment at the El Rey provided by none other than **Christine Jorgensen**.

Christine, the former **George William Jorgensen, Jr.,** had gained notoriety in 1952 when she made front page news as the first man, a World War II G.I., to undergo a sexual reassignment surgery. Though not technically the first person to have a sex change operation (the procedure had been around as early as the 1920s and 1930s), she was the first to have the surgery accompanied by hormone therapy prescriptions.

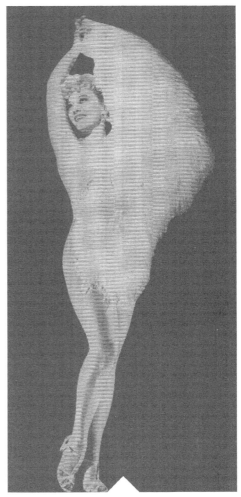

**Promotional photo from Sally Rand's performances at the El Rey.** *From the author's personal collection, a gift from Mike Madden.*

After she achieved an entirely new body, she obtained an entirely new career when she became a media sensation. Jorgensen later embarked on a career as an actress, recording artist, and night club performer where she made a quick costume change into a Wonder Woman costume and later a character of her own creation (much like Christine herself), Superwoman. Among the songs she performed in her night club revue was "I Enjoy Being a Girl."

Willie enjoyed having such a newsworthy attraction at the El Rey to bring in the crowds, but he wasn't all that certain what he enjoyed was actually a girl. *"Willie was different. He danced to the beat of a different drummer and did as he pleased,"* remembered Jerry Schafer. *"When Christine Jorgensen became such a big hit, and Willie booked her into the El Rey Club, he drilled a hole in the women's restroom so he could watch her take a leak,"* Schafer said while laughing, *"He had to find out if he'd really switched himself into a woman!"* Willie confirmed with a wild grin that, indeed, he was now a she.

Much like today's casinos, the appeal and lure of something for nothing always got more than a few people to stop in and see what the casino had to offer. The casino "comp" had been around for almost as long as Las Vegas in one form or another. The El Rey Club was no exception and offered its own unique comps.

Willie would not only offer affordable gourmet meals and frequently give meals away, he created comps worth $4 in food or gaming at the club and offered them to his guests. While $4 may not seem like much today, $4 could feed two people a heck of a good meal at the El Rey. Single, double, and family rooms were available for rent at the motel in prices ranging from $6 to $20. That four bucks could indeed go a long way at the El Rey Club.

The comps were designed to look official; they were the size and shape of bank-written checks and were even printed on actual check stationary that showed a "Pacific Safety Paper" logo on them. These checks were to be signed by Willie himself and only one check per couple per day was allowed to be redeemed. Printing the comps on check paper was a clever idea as it gave the guest a real feeling that the owner of the club was giving you money to gamble.

Other types of freebies came in the form of orange poker chips which could be redeemed for up to $1 of free play. These were chips made from the same materials as actual poker chips which gave the bearer the feeling he had real money to gamble with in town.

Some of Willie's freebies were more for show than anything else. One of the more sought after casino collectibles, at least among poker chip collectors, are El Rey Club advertising chips – black plastic chips with printed paper inside. These very clever $1,000 non-negotiable chips were mainly used as business cards for employees of the El Rey Club. These chips had a giant crown above a shield with the words "El Rey" on one side

**The El Rey Resort Hotel**
**Searchlight, Nevada**

N⁰ 1702

19____

$4.00

PAY TO THE
ORDER OF BEARER____

*Four and no/100ths* _____ DOLLARS

Negotiable only at the El Rey Resort Hotel — One Check per Couple per Day.

A $4.00 comp signed by Willie Martello
(or perhaps his secretary).
*From the author's personal collection.*

and a searchlight tower shining a light over Willie's name and the club's phone number on the other. I have seen examples of these with Willie's name, Chef Luigi, and **Marshall Sawyer**. Reportedly, Willie gave these away and encouraged people to come into the club on the premise they could redeem them for something good, usually a drink at the bar or something off the menu. On occasion, some folks thought "something good" meant an actual $1,000 and tried to gamble with them.

If you were a customer in good standing with Willie and the El Rey Club you could be issued a City Ledger Card. This card, about the size of a business card, was glossy and featured a sketch of a western wagon and Joshua trees. If you were given this card by

The clever casino chip business card. These were non-negotiable, but were frequently thought to be worth value at the casino. Today they're valuable only to casino chip collectors. *From the author's personal collection.*

Willie or anyone in management at the El Rey Club, you would be granted full credit privileges. That was, of course, if your signature matched the one on the card. I cannot imagine that many of these cards were issued over the years as it was not the most secure way to prevent someone from trying to claim a line of credit at the casino. However, the fact that these cards were also easy to lose or throw away may have made it appealing to Martello because he may have figured more cards would be lost than used.

Willie Martello, among other things, was a grand promoter. He promoted his clubs, his town, and most certainly himself. When it came to finding new ways to bring in locals or tourists, he was willing to try anything.

On September 22, 1951, Searchlight, Nevada became the location for a genuine thrill show. World champion stunt motorcyclist **Capt. Oren "Putt" Mossman** arrived in Searchlight with a two-hour show that promised a thousand thrills. Late-night television fans probably remember Putt as the man who accurately tossed horseshoes between the legs of a comically terrified **Johnny Carson** in 1973.

At speeds exceeding 40 miles per hour, Mossman hung from the edge of his motorcycle, dangled above the ground, and dared death to claim him. With his team of motorcycle acrobats and comedy performers, Mossman stood on the bike's seat and scaled a ladder all without using his hands for steering. He created a circus-like pyramid of riders and induced heart-stopping moments as the team landed on the ground moments

January 15, 1959, advertisement in the *Henderson Home News*.

before Putt jumped a ramp and missed their backs by mere inches.

While circus antics and thrill shows were nothing new to small town America, Willie found at least one way to again set himself apart as being just a bit ahead of the curve with regard to Las Vegas promotions.

All things Hawaiian were becoming quite popular in the U.S. by the late 1950s, and Hawaii was granted statehood in August of 1959. New Year's Eve of 1958 featured not only a free smorgasbord for the entire family, but music and

**Cecil Lynch and Jennie Drew at an El Rey Luau March 18, 1961.** *Nevada State Museum, Las Vegas [J. Florian Mitchell Collection]*

dancing from **Mona and The Hawaiian Glamorettes**, who made frequent appearances at the El Rey and became one of the El Rey's most popular attractions. Willie took notice of this crowd-pleasing act, and on the weekend of January 16th through the 18th of 1959, the El Rey Club proudly presented a genuine authentic Hawaiian Luau. A reader of The *Henderson Home News* wrote in its January 15, 1959 Letters to the Editor section, *"Leave it to Willie Martello of Searchlight's famed El Rey Lodge Resort to come up with a dandy idea!"*

The Luau featured authentic Hawaiian food prepared by native Hawaiians, music and dancing by the Glamorettes, and it was billed as a family event in Searchlight. *"Everybody Invited Spend the weekend! Come and bring your family and friends,"* read the half-page advertisement in the *Henderson Home News*. For three days, young and old alike came to the desert mining community. Guests felt they were in an island paradise as opposed to the actual town of Paradise, Nevada (better known as Las Vegas to those who were not from those parts).

It wasn't long before people in Las Vegas took notice and joined in on the fun. In March of 1961, **Cecil Lynch,** friend of Willie and owner of the

**The Cinco de Mayo Celebration at the El Rey Club on May 6, 1961.**
*Nevada State Museum, Las Vegas [J. Florian Mitchell Collection]*

**Fortune Club** on Fremont Street, was seen at an El Rey Luau with **Jennie Drew**, the wife of notorious mobster **Johnny Drew**. The Luaus were a tremendous success and became a regular part of the entertainment offered at the El Rey.

Theme nights were always popular at the El Rey Club. If there happened to be an accompanying holiday, it was even easier to plan an event. On May 4, 1961, the *Henderson Home News* featured a large ad promising *"Another Big Party"* during the weekend's Cinco De Mayo celebration. Willie invited everyone to be his guest and dress in Mexican costumes while they enjoyed the authentic musical sounds of **The Lisa Alonso Quartet**. If the music and fancy dress wasn't enough to bring you in, perhaps, bringing in a copy of the ad for a free drink surely would.

Other ways Willie created a stir among the Searchlighters was to have celebrity dealers at the tables. Good friend and Hollywood star **Rory Calhoun** was often seen at the El Rey Club, both as a patron and as a celebrity dealer. Jerry Schafer remembered, *"Willie would bring in people from all over simply so they could have a chance to be dealt cards from this great Western star."* Calhoun also lent his name to some of the brochure advertisements for the El Rey Club as time went on. Other celebrity guest dealers included **Sean Flynn,** son of icon Errol Flynn, and beautiful Hollywood starlets **Sherry Jackson** and **Diane McBain**.

*"I hadn't spent a lot of time in casinos before that, so the El Rey seemed impressive to me,"* said McBain of her one and only time in Searchlight. McBain, who was Sherry Jackson's roommate at the time, recalled, *"My dad*

An El Rey Resort brochure advertising celebrity dealer, Rory Calhoun, circa late 1950s - 1960s. *From the author's personal collection.*

*and his best friend set up a junket to Searchlight, Nevada to visit the El Rey Casino and meet the person in charge, Willie Martello. It was good for the casino to get the attention with young starlets and other actors. We were the attraction. I remember having a very good time."*

Many of Willie's ideas were very successful because they drew attention to the club, created a fun and memorable experience, and brought in some money. Of course, some ideas, while memorable, were not necessarily a success. One such example of an idea that should have gone better for poor Willie was the Searchlight Rodeo.

Willie absolutely loved the natural western appeal and scenery that Searchlight offered. As tourism grew in the state, more and more people were interested in coming across the Rocky Mountains and finding some authentic western landscape to hideout and enjoy for a while.

Among the popular destinations in Las Vegas in the late 1950s was the new **Stardust Hotel and Casino**. The Stardust boasted it was the biggest and the best of its day. It featured the largest swimming pool, the highest number of hotel rooms, and massive numbers of casinos. While that may not seem like something you saw in the old west, the Stardust also featured Horseman's Park, a rodeo grounds that had enough corrals to accommodate 300 horses. Even the horses had plenty of room at the Stardust.

Willie knew he could not compete with a Las Vegas resort like the

Stardust. However, he could take one of their ideas and adapt it to the pastoral grandeur of Searchlight. With nothing but wide open spaces, mountains, and Joshua trees surrounding the area, Willie decided to host a rodeo.

Willie, although he looked like a Western cowboy hero, was no cowboy himself. He hired folks to construct a makeshift rodeo arena and corral for the event and even built a special pit for a massive barbecue and planned to cook up an entire steer for all the hungry people. He made sure to get a young calf for the roping exhibition, which was the first event.

Martello spent months promoting and organizing the event. Posters were hung, bleachers were set, and there was more than enough food for everyone from miles around. He was going to feature all the rodeo exhibitions and skills, with the highlight being calf-roping. There was quite a turnout by the time rodeo day finally arrived in Searchlight. *"There were cows and cowboys everywhere, ready to party,"* said Sharon Richardson.

Willie, festooned in his white suit and hat, welcomed the crowd over the P.A. system with all the style and flair that any great promoter of his day would have. He announced the calf-roping event, and the

**Hollywood starlet, Diane McBain deals a hand of Blackjack to fellow starlet, Sherry Jackson on March 12, 1961. Willie Martello is "supervising" in the center.**
*Nevada State Museum, Las Vegas*
*[J. Florian Mitchell Collection]*

**Sherry Jackson, Sean Flynn, and friend on March 11, 1961.**
*Nevada State Museum, Las Vegas*
*[J. Florian Mitchell Collection]*

spectators gathered around the arena on the simple bleachers and eagerly awaited the chance to see a cowboy mounted atop his mighty steed as he chased after a young calf. A cheer began to wash over the crowd as the first rustler strode into view and a young, aggressive calf was led to the arena.

A gunshot sounded, and the calf was let loose. The frightened animal tore out of the chute and into the dusty circle of fencing. The cowboy, lariat in hand, rapidly gave chase. All of the folks watching, including Willie Martello, eager to see his event get off to a rousing start, watched with breathless anticipation and hoped to see that cowboy rope his calf.

The calf ran with furious speed right toward the arena fencing. Since the fence was not of professional grade construction and was somewhat hastily built, it did little to corral the animal. The calf knocked down the fence with no effort whatsoever and made a break for the mountains not too far in the distance.

A gasp of excitement from the crowd was immediately followed by laughter as the scurrying calf ran further and further away. The rodeo's only calf created a cloud of dust which formed a line all the way up the hillside and was never to be seen again. The young cowboy stared at the trampled fence and looked back at Willie for some sort of guidance or instruction. Richardson recalled, *"That was the end of Willie's rodeo. But it sure didn't stop anyone from having a great time!"*

Willie, shocked at what he saw, realized his grand event was about to end much sooner than he expected. He glanced over to his niece, Sharon, who was unable to contain her laughter. He shot her a knowing smirk that she and all of Willie's family knew all too well, and she tried to stop laughing. Willie wandered over to Sharon, looked at the calf running up the hill, the size of it getting smaller and smaller as it went, and said to her, while he tried himself not to begin laughing, *"Would you look at that son of a bitch run!"*

Photo courtesy Ethel Martello

# MEET WILLIE, YOUR GENIAL HOST!

very good book has a good story. Every good book has at least one good character. While I am far too insecure and modest to make the assumption what you are holding in your hands constitutes a good book, I can say with certainty that this book has a truly outstanding character.

I cannot lay claim to intimate knowledge of the content of other volumes revolving around Las Vegas history. However, based on the intrigue that surrounds aspects such as the mob, gambling, prostitutes, and the celebrity attached to the Las Vegas casino lifestyle in the 1950s and 1960s, I must assume books such as this one frequently offer some good stories that have a way of making you laugh and cringe at the same time. These are the kinds of stories that make you want to hang around and be within the inner circle of the main character while you're also a little glad you are not.

Among the things that compelled me to write a book about Willie Martello were the stories I uncovered with every little bit of research. While so many in this world only incorrectly know Willie Martello as a pimp if they knew of him at all, I came to find that the man I was researching was more of a folk-hero, a tall tale kind of guy, larger than life, full of flaws and obstacles, and ultimately one with good intentions. The STORIES about Willie Martello were what moved me from a guy who wanted to *"get my own stable of whores"* to a guy who thought people like YOU should really know about this guy.

I've been very fortunate that so many of the Martello family have been willing to share tales from the past regarding Willie, Buddy, et al. Most everyone I've spoken with, whether they were related to Martello or not, have had at least one good memory that got my fingers writing. Even though there are not many people left who were there to give me some first-hand accounts, I've found a wealth of documentation to back up many of the things I've learned about Willie and his club via the archives of newspapers such as the *Las Vegas Review-Journal*, the *Las Vegas Sun*, the *Reno Evening Gazette*, and others.

Of course, as the old adage goes, you can't believe everything you read in the paper.

While most of what I've found within the newspaper archives was true, there were times when embellishments were made, as evidenced by the tales told by **Ray Chesson**. Ray, a former resident of Searchlight, was a respected writer for the *Review-Journal* and was well known for eloquently painting romantic and exciting images of small towns in the west. I like to think of him as the last of the great western writers. Tales from the old west abound in magazines and libraries and many of them are accurate up to a point. It is fair to say, whether you were writing about Billy the Kid or Willie the casino owner, you took a few liberties with the truth to ensure the story you told was entertaining. Ray Chesson was, if nothing else, a great storyteller.

On February 16, 1964, Chesson published an article titled "Big Hearted Town on a Bald Headed Mountain" in the *NEVADAN*, a weekly supplement to the *Review-Journal*. It was a story about Searchlight and the colorful man who ran the town, Willie Martello. It was also, in his own words, an *"attempt to dispel the rancid fog of untruths fanned through the lowlands by unscrupulous individuals who, perhaps, are congenital haters of all towns that sit atop baldheaded mountains."* I told you this guy could turn a phrase.

He frequently described the *"peaceful and reverential hamlet"* called Searchlight as a town that offered, among other things, the one thing that folks in nearby California simply could not find: fresh air. It was the lure of the fresh air offered at no charge to the consumer, combined with the friendliest of people, that made Searchlight special, at least, in the eyes of Ray Chesson.

As lovely as this piece is to read, and it is truly a great example of a lost writing style, it is almost completely inaccurate. Take, for example, Chesson's wholly false description of Searchlight and its history associated with the world's oldest profession: *"For too many years, the voice of the disparager has been heard in the land - foul whispers that smelled of evil, that it was once even a place of bordellos. However, the bright and shining truth, as any member of the Clark County Sheriff's office will no doubt attest, is this: from the very dawn of its history, Searchlight natives would have rather perished than harbor one house of ill repute."* Powerful stuff. However, since there are more newspaper and eyewitness accounts of houses of prostitution in Searchlight than there are stories of Searchlight residents perishing, we must take this particular work of the great Ray Chesson as more of a romantic puff piece about a western town he loved.

Though not everything in this piece by Chesson is embellished so heavily, there were plenty of near truths within. Quite a few featured tales of our very own Willie Martello and included one that featured a man with a classic western character's name: **Bignose Pete**.

Per Chesson, *"Witness the behavior of the town's former kingpin, Willie Martello toward Bignose Pete. When, upon one occasion, Bignose was discovered perched upon a bar stool in the late and lamented El Rey wearing a beaver coat of noble vintage, Martello immediately stopped counting his money (Martello's own money, we're speaking of), came forward with a can of bug spray, and doused Bignose at no charge whatever."*

While I tried to wrap my head around how anyone could equate the spraying of bug spray on a man without warning or request to do so as a gesture of kindness (unless it were bug repellant, perhaps), I found references to a **"Big-Nosed Pete"** in Senator Harry Reid's book, *Searchlight: The Camp that Didn't Fail*. Reid described Big-Nosed Pete, whose real name was **Pete Domitrovich**, as a man of unparalleled strength, capable of hoisting a full 50-gallon drum onto a truck with no help at all and carrying a heavy railroad tie under each arm without breaking a sweat.

Conversations with Ethel Martello and Joyce Walker showed a decidedly less than wistful description of the colorfully named Bignose Pete. *"All I know about Bignose Pete was that he was a miner and he was always sitting at the bar drinking. I never saw him hold a conversation with anyone. Bud and Willie always spoke to him. He was always muttering but I could never understand him,"* Ethel said, *"Someone told me how he got the big red nose. He was in Alaska and it got frozen. Your guess is as good as mine as to how true this is."* At least, Chesson got the name and the nasal attribute, which are really one and the same, correct? As to Mr. Nose's coat, *"Bignose Pete came in once a week in an old truck. He'd always head right to the bar and sit there quietly, drinking to get drunk.*

*I am quite certain the man didn't even own a coat!"* according to Walker, former El Rey bartender. It seemed that one man's drunk was another man's story.

Among the most grossly inaccurate things mentioned in this piece by Chesson was the assertion Willie Martello was not present the night of the El Rey fire. Of course, if one were to believe Chesson's account, it was all for the noble cause of bringing fresh air to the suffering masses that traveled from California, *"When the thing happened, Willie Martello was on a goodwill trip to California, offering more free air to the residents of that backward state. But his brother, Bud Martello, was present and, according to witnesses, made a heroic stand against the fast spreading fire right up to the point where he fell off the roof."*

In point of fact, Ray did get one thing correct here. Buddy Martello did fall off a roof in a vain attempt to extinguish the blaze that destroyed the El Rey Club. He suffered a leg injury as a result. However, Willie Martello was most certainly there the night of the fire as many first-hand accounts and photographs will attest later in this book. The notion that Willie was on any sort of goodwill trip that promised fresh air to choking Californians while his beloved casino perished was nothing more than a great story told by a great storyteller.

Chesson related one rather peculiar and otherwise disturbing tale that Willie Martello possibly killed a man with an ice pick.

Again at the El Rey, a prospector supposedly came into the bar with a newly found nugget of pure gold for which Willie, reportedly, gave the man a fifth of whiskey in exchange as recognition of the find. However the gold nugget turned out to be nothing more than Fool's Gold, and the prospector had made out with the bottle before anyone discovered the true identity of the worthless hunk of rock, which angered Willie. Chesson waxed on, *"There were some present who feared that Martello, although never known to show anger under any manner of provocation, might, in the face of such obvious chicanery, became incensed."*

A story about that same prospector being *"tracked to earth and found flat on his belly in a slushy gutter with Martello standing over him, ice pick in hand"* had found the ears of local **Sheriff Big John Silveira.** According to Chesson this entire tale was nothing more than a misunderstanding which may have led to some of Searchlight's unfavorable reputation. Chesson wrote, *"Martello, it developed, was* *merely chopping the man out of the ice,"* which suggested that the prospector had succumbed to a harsh winter in the mountains and Martello later found him.

To the best of my knowledge, no part of this wonderfully woven yarn is true. You can imagine how hard I tried to learn more of this story as I wanted so desperately to have some vengeful murder committed by Martello himself to help sell this book to a publisher. Really, I smelled a movie deal as soon as I read this incredible tale of western revenge. Of course, even while presenting the questions to Willie's family and other folks who were around at the time, I knew this had to be hogwash. The Martello family laughed at my inquiries and showed a bit of disbelief at the notion a story of such scope existed. However, I did learn a little bit about the prospector in question—a nugget of truth to the nugget story, if you will. I think Chesson's writing style is rubbing off on me. Glad this part of the book is nearly at an end.

Joyce Walker remembered a prospector who frequently came into the El Rey with nothing more than the dust on his clothing and pyrite in his pocket. According to Walker, **"Cripple Jack"** was a prospector who used to hunt for gold at a mine in nearby Mountain Pass and regularly came into the El Rey and wanted nothing more than to get drunk. He always had little or no money on hand and would always pull out a few hunks of Fool's Gold. He would lay them on the bar and ask for a drink, sometimes the whole bottle. *"Gimme a drink,"* Cripple Jack would call out as he slammed his rocks on the bar, *"AND the change!"* Walker would say, *"He always asked for the change as if ANYONE in the place was dumb enough to give him any cash for those rocks."* Joyce told me that sometimes Willie humored him and gave him a few bucks to help the guy out and not embarrass him, but once Cripple Jack thought he had found a fool for his gold and tried the stunt again, Willie would ask him to get out of the bar.

Ray Chesson got a lot of facts right in this piece, and after Willie died in 1968, he wrote a wonderful, heartfelt, two-page piece about Willie Martello, full of more facts than fluff along with stories provided by long-time friend Chef Luigi Scirocco. I am not pointing out these "exaggerations" of the truth by Chesson to denigrate his writing abilities or show him to be anything less than a respected author. His prolific work is loved by many and reprints of his stories are still requested at the *Las Vegas Review-Journal* long after his death. The man was a fantastic storyteller.

I point these out to illustrate just what sort of a man Willie Martello was and the impact he had on Searchlight and a lot of Las Vegas. When I say that he was something of a folk hero, a Paul Bunyan-like character found in tall tales that people remember for generations, stories like these help echo that sentiment. In many respects, the antics and actions of Willie Martello were the stuff of western legend, though until now, some of the best things about him were either unearthed or clouded by the stigma of Searchlight's darkest times. Ray Chesson took those stories and turned them into larger-than-life tales in an attempt to bring more favor to a town he loved and more respect to the man who helped make that town thrive.

What follows are true accounts of the many adventures of Willie Martello and includes both the good and bad, but mostly good. Some are brief. Some are not so brief. They will add a little more detail about the man behind the El Rey before going further into the history of the casino. All of these are accurate to the best of my knowledge as many of them were relayed to me from folks who witnessed them first-hand. All help paint a better picture of the man who tried to build an empire in, with respect to the great Ray Chesson, "a big hearted town on a bald headed mountain."

Photo courtesy Suzan Riddell

# THE MAN IN THE WHITE HAT

Willie Martello, by all accounts was a man with a sense of style. Though he could look foolish at times producing a moment of hilarity, he always looked every part the dandy. Ray Chesson once described Willie as, *"a man with the dash of a George Raft - though, as numerous females have commented, a shade handsomer than Raft."*

**Bill Moore**, former entertainment director for Doc Bayley's Hacienda, noted, *"Willie was meticulous with his clothes, always dressing in the finest white suit and matching cowboy hat at night."* It shouldn't be a surprise that the man who, as a toddler, refused to take off his shoes and pose as a barefoot Indian in a family photo would grow up to care so much about his appearance. **Maxine "Mickey" Cooper**, wife of Martello's accountant **Lou Cooper**, joked with Willie when she asked, *"Willie, do you have just the ONE white suit or several identical white suits?"* It is possible to see evidence of Willie's western flair in clips from Jerry Schafer's film, **Tonight for Sure**, though Jerry jokingly described Willie as, *"the Pillsbury Dough Boy dressed white from head to toe. Yet in the middle of that dusty desert, was always immaculate."*

It wasn't enough for him to look the part of a successful casino magnate. Willie wanted everyone around him, especially family, to look exquisite whenever possible. *"I was just a young man and Willie was making sure I had very expensive mohair suits to wear everywhere,"* recalled Bob Martello. *"Willie cared a lot about people's appearance. He was all about appearance,"* said Sharon Richardson, *"He wanted my mom and everybody to always look neat and clean and look nice. He was adamant about that with his family."*

Outward appearances were important to Willie whether it was a family member or an employee. Occasionally, people with whom he did business just didn't stack up to Willie's expectations. Take the case of one **Wally Brewer**.

Willie needed a good accountant to do his books and mentioned this to his good friend, Ted Enoch. Ted owned one of the largest Chevrolet dealerships in California and frequently hung out in Searchlight. When Willie told him he needed a good bookkeeper, Ted was certain he had the right man for the job and suggested Wally Brewer. *"It seemed like a perfect match,"* remembered Sharon Richardson. Not only was he recommended by a trusted friend and businessman, but he owned his own plane and could easily make trips from California and land on Willie's runway.

**Suzan Martello posing with Willie's Woody Wagon, circa 1949.** *Photo courtesy Suzan Riddell.*

The day Brewer arrived for a meeting with Willie, Sharon got the call to go to the airport with Willie and pick him up. He flew a little Cessna aircraft that seemed a bit ill-fitted for Brewer. *"Wally was the tallest, skinniest person I'd ever seen in my life,"* said Sharon. *"He had to take out the main seat of the plane and create a makeshift seat just so he could fit inside."*

When he *"unfolded himself"* from the plane as Sharon described it, Willie and Sharon (but mostly Willie) noticed just how awkward looking the man was. He had slicked back hair, a gaunt complexion on a skinny face, and wore round, thick glasses. Sharon noticed he was tall while he was standing far away by the plane, *"The closer he got the taller he looked."* This must have put Willie off even more since he himself was not a particularly tall man.

Sharon could tell as she looked at the tight-lipped smirk that crept across Willie's lips that he was not impressed with Ted Enoch's choice for a quality bookkeeper. When Brewer finally reached the pair, the scene began to look like a Laurel and Hardy film. *"Wally is towering over us and we're both looking straight up into his nostrils,"* she said.

Sharon tried not to laugh as she watched her rather fastidious uncle suffer this fool gladly. The look on his face said it all to her. All that composure on her part was gone when Brewer introduced himself and revealed an embarrassing speech impediment.

*"Hehwoh Wiwee. My name is Wahwee Bwoower."*

With that, Sharon lost control and began to laugh. *"I wasn't laughing at Brewer. I was laughing at Willie! I knew he wasn't going to give the guy a chance because of that,"* said Sharon. Even though how one looked very likely had no bearing on his ability to crunch the numbers, Willie humored poor Wally Brewer, but was not at all pleased. He could not live up to Willie's impossible standards.

Since Willie himself lived up to his own standards, he had to broadcast the persona of success to all of Nevada. Many have described seeing Willie in either a large Lincoln Town Car or another nice car such as a Buick or Cadillac. It was always a white convertible. Photos from **Suzan Martello**, Willie's stepdaughter, also showed Willie owned a beautiful white Buick convertible and a classic "Woody" Wagon, one of the few cars he drove that wasn't a glistening white.

Presumably, the shining white convertibles were to match his suit and fit the persona of a powerful western man. His car could be seen from far away, and when he'd pass by, he had the top down so people could see him as the picture of success.

Another common thing among the Martello-mobiles was his need to advertise. On the back bumper of his Buick, people saw a metal sign under the license plate that urged people to check out the El Rey Club, located half-way between Needles and Las Vegas. His 1940s era Woody Wagon had beautiful ads for the El Rey painted on the driver and passenger doors that proudly announced the casino, bar, café, and cabins located in Searchlight.

Quite possibly, the most memorable of ways Willie convinced the world of his great wealth and success from behind the wheel of his car showed him to be well ahead of his time, yet again.

**Kenny Laursen**, a musician who played with the **Tony Lovello Revue** the night of the El Rey fire, recalled, *"Willie Martello was often seen driving down the Strip in a Lincoln convertible talking on a telephone handset that, if connected, was one of the first mobile phones in Las Vegas."*

A car phone? In the '50s and '60s? Indeed, it is true. According to Bob Martello, Willie called upon a friend of his in the army to create this modern miracle years before people were slamming into telephone poles looking for their Bluetooth devices. *"Willie asked this communications guy in the army to make what he called his radio phone and put it in his car."* This was essentially a military radio, *"a big box with all sorts of tubes and wires,"* according to Bob. This box had a telephone headset and curly wire, looked like a phone you'd find in a person's home and was hooked up to a car battery. Kenny Laursen said of the phone which sat on the car's dashboard, *"Nobody knew if the darned thing actually worked, but everyone stopped to stare at him chatting away as he drove by."*

Bob Martello insisted this was a working phone, and Willie was very proud of his **"radio telephone"** as he called it. Bob remembered one time when he (Bob) was on a date, he wore his expensive mohair

**Willie with world champion speed boat racer, Donald Campbell in November 1955.**
*Photo courtesy Ethel Martello.*

suit and drove a '57 T-Bird. *"I got caught in a flash flood and got stuck in the mud."* While in his fine suit and with his girl all dressed up in crinoline, Bob had to get out of the car to extricate himself from the muddy earth, ruined his suit, and generally made a mess of himself. When he returned to Searchlight, Willie smiled smugly and told Bob, *"You need a radio telephone!"*

If the car phone or the perception of a car phone wasn't enough to impress you, perhaps a look at the car would. Many remember Willie driving a Cadillac convertible or a white Lincoln Town Car, but several recall the license plate. While the Nevada DMV records, sadly, cannot confirm this, many eyewitness accounts relay that, when license plates were issued in the state, the first plate, **"NEVADA 1"**, went to the Governor. **"NEVADA 2"** went to none other than Willie Martello.

In the 1960s, when a cowboy dressed in white, drove his white convertible down the Las Vegas Strip, and chatted on something as incredible as a car phone, was it really a wonder he had a vanity plate?

I can't tell you how many different people told me the story of the

"NEVADA 2" license plate during the course of this research. I heard it so frequently, not only have I passed it along to new people, but I began to view this as the stuff of legend, if not one of the defining ways people recognized and remembered Willie. As it turned out, the story was more fable than fact. Another tall tale that existed within the taller tale of Willie Martello. Like all tall tales, this one was rooted in truth.

Willie Martello DID have a license plate worth cherishing, although nothing quite as memorable as "NEVADA 2." It seems that many long-time Las Vegans from the old days had

**Suzan Martello in front of one of Willie's cars, circa 1949.** *Photo courtesy Suzan Riddell.*

something of a fondness for their license plates. It showed their long-term commitment to the town. As an example, Joyce Dickens drove her car up until her dying day, and even though the car changed over the years, she was adamant about never upgrading her plate to a newer style. She wore her blue Nevada plate from the 1960s proudly and even fought the state for her right to keep it. I always joked with her there were so many registration stickers placed on the plate that one corner of the car started to sag from the excess weight. Willie was no different.

License plates were being issued in Nevada long before Willie was driving, so it is not possible he had the second plate in the state's history. Although nobody can remember the exact plate number, it was a rather low one, quite possibly the number 2, specific to Clark County and easily recognizable to people in Las Vegas. This pleased Willie very much. In fact, it pleased him so much that, at a time when Willie failed to make a few car payments and temporarily lost possession of the vehicle, he worried more for the license plate than the car itself.

***"Willie LOVED that plate,"*** according to Lou Cooper. When Willie made his payments and had regained possession of his car, he was shocked and angered to find his beloved plate was no longer there. It is unclear if the plate was stolen or simply sold to another driver, but what was clear was that Willie was none too happy and was willing to go to the highest authority to get it back.

*"I was there the day he called the Governor demanding that he be issued a new plate,"* said Cooper, laughing. *"I couldn't believe it! He just picked up the phone and called the Governor and talked to him as long as he had to until he got what he wanted."* Ultimately, Willie did not get the exact plate back, but much to Martello's satisfaction, he was issued a suitably impressive low-numbered plate by order of the Governor of Nevada himself. Lou Cooper's wife, "Mickey," put it best when she said to me with a smile, *"Willie always got what he wanted."*

As a side note, long before I'd learned the truth about Willie's infamous license plate I contacted the Nevada DMV records department for confirmation of the story. After she heard the story and the description of Willie, the clerk chimed in as she thumbed her keyboard looking for ways she might be able to help me and said, *"Sounds like a guy who should have had 'NEVADA 1.'"*

# COME FLY WITH ME,
# PART ONE: A BIRD IN THE HAND

T hroughout this book you will see the use of descriptive terms such as "innovative" and "clever" or even "groundbreaking" when describing some of Willie Martello's ideas. This one in particular fits all of those aforementioned terms, and I'm certain a few back then would have added "cornball" and "unorthodox" to the mix.

Like most great ideas, a lot of Willie's solutions to problems were born out of necessity. In early 1950, Searchlight had a communication breakdown.

Beginning around 1907 the town had the ability to communicate with the outside world via telephone by utilizing the nearby line that ran through to Nipton, California. Once that line went out of existence in the late 1940s, Searchlight lacked phones, which, as you might imagine, caused a few problems. A story that detailed just one incident appeared in the February 1, 1950 issue of the *Las Vegas Review-Journal*. This story featured Willie Martello and helped build his folk hero reputation.

Willie described a story to the unnamed *Review-Journal* reporter that involved a high-speed race to save a young infant's life. According to the RJ, the baby *"accidentally swallowed a capsule full of heart stimulant"* and needed immediate medical attention. At the time Searchlight had no doctor in town, and Martello took it upon himself to race the child in his own car into Las Vegas, 57 miles away.

At a breakneck pace Willie rushed down the road and recalled to the reporter the child's face had turned blue during the car ride. In less than

an hour's time, Martello and
the ailing infant *"arrived at
the county hospital in the nick
of time."* The child's life was
saved, but such a trip surely
could have been avoided had
the town possessed a single
telephone with which to call an
ambulance.

ALEXANDER RANG THE BELL with his telephone but Willie
Martello, Searchlight tavern owner did him one better last
week when he started a carrier pigeon service between Las
Vegas and the historic Colorado river mining camp to make
up for the absence of Mr. Bell's invention. Sheriff Glen Jones,
left holds one of the little birds, while Martello, right attaches
a message to one of his pigeons for delivery to Searchlight.

Willie's generosity toward
others was well known by
people in Southern Nevada.

Carrier Pigeons End
Dilema of Searchlighters

This story was well within his character, but it is not
beyond the realm of possibilities that this was a story Martello told to
encourage the installation of telephone lines into Searchlight. After all, no
politician or bureaucrat wanted the death of a child on his conscience.

Martello certainly led the fight for permanent telephone line installation
for the town. At the time, Martello and Searchlight only sought a single
telephone for emergency use. Certainly, Martello also thought about the
future of his El Rey Club and his dreams for Searchlight. A modern town
would require modern technology.

Willie fought for his town for two years to no avail. The installation of
one telephone would require the stringing of nearly 40 miles of new line
from nearby Boulder City, the closest significant town to Searchlight that
already had service. Getting this new line simply wasn't going to happen.
Thankfully, both Willie and Buddy Martello were there with a solution.

Buddy was, at one time, a member of the U.S. Coast Guard. It was his
time with the service that brought about what the *Review-Journal* would
describe as *"their old, but still new idea."* The Martellos would introduce

carrier pigeons to Searchlight, Nevada as a means to communicate with Las Vegas. Willie commented on this scheme, *"It beats smoke signals or flashing semaphore."*

According to the *Review-Journal*, Willie purchased around a dozen of the birds to act as two *"squadrons"* for service. He would house six pigeons at the El Rey and six at Willie's home in Las Vegas. Buddy would act as the *"airline's chief of operations"* and train the birds. Admittedly, training was a term used loosely by the Martellos. Buddy's job was not actually to show them the route between Searchlight and Vegas so much as teaching them the location of their home and letting their inherent abilities to find their home lead them along the path. His efforts were remarkably successful.

The *Review-Journal* article reported, *"The first flight over the 48 air-line miles between points was made in 40 minutes."* This was said to be the inaugural run of the messenger service and about ten minutes faster than a drive to Las Vegas. Buddy hoped as the birds became used to their trips they would be able to fly their messages across the desert in less than 30 minutes.

Once the winged messengers reached their destinations, they entered their cages, their arrival announced ironically and loudly by an electric bell. In essence, Searchlight now had its own version of "Bell" Telephone, albeit a considerably less advanced one, if not one that would amuse and astound the folks who passed through Searchlight. What started out as a need for basic communication turned into a promotional stunt worthy of print and the topic of discussion by people in Las Vegas.

The installation of the carrier pigeons is something of legend around Searchlight and Las Vegas to this day. While I conducted research for this book, people frequently asked me if this story was true. They doubted any casino owner, no matter how ingenious or desperate for publicity, much less a means of communication, would have the patience to train a flock of birds to fly to and from Searchlight. Suzan Martello, Willie's stepdaughter, remembers them well.

*"Yes, there were carrier pigeons! Buddy built the cages in our back yard in Las Vegas and trained the birds to fly back and forth with messages,"* recalled Suzan. *"This happened a lot in the winter because the roads were icy and slick."* If there were accidents caused by cold weather that required the help of the pigeons, perhaps there was some truth to the

tale of Willie and the dying infant after all.

Willie and Buddy's squadron of carrier pigeons was in use until phone lines were finally installed in Searchlight some years later by the U.S. Long Distance telephone Company. Although party-line service was not available, and the lines were only connected to Las Vegas at first, a six-phone network was installed on Tuesday, July 15, 1952. Willie Martello made the first call.

When so many, myself included, have described Willie and the El Rey as being "ahead of its time", there is a poetic charm in knowing that utilizing a "technology" that was very much behind the times was what kept Searchlight and its residents connected to the world. In this age of cell phones, text messaging, email, and the Internet, learning that a dozen birds purchased by a flamboyant casino owner and trained by his brother could have been what kept other infants from dying in a long car ride to Las Vegas brings a bit of wonder to one's mind.

By 1955, Searchlight was appearing in local phonebooks, though there were only about ten listings at the time with the listed phone numbers starting at the number "2". Eventually, folks wanting to call the El Rey Club could do so by letting their fingers do the walking along the telephone dial and dialing the number "0603". One wonders, with Willie playing such an integral role in getting the phones installed into Searchlight and knowing of his flair for promotion, why he did not secure the number "777" for the El Rey Club.

*Photo courtesy Nevada State Museum, Las Vegas [J. Florian Mitchell Collection]*

# THE GAMBLER

The number seven has always had a mystical quality about it. It took God seven days to create the world according to the Bible. Legendary baseball hero Mickey Mantle wore the number seven on his uniform. The most famous Tennessee whiskey in the world, Jack Daniel's, also known to have mythical properties, has featured "Old No 7" on its label for generations. Snow White had her seven dwarves, and somehow, someone managed to find seven brides for those seven brothers. If I were more clever, this chapter would have been Chapter 7. Lest we forget, when put into the context of gambling, few numbers are as powerful as the number seven.

Willie Martello was the seventh son of a seventh son. Throughout the world there are legends and myths that surround such a person. In 17th century England, it was believed a seventh son was able to heal the deaf, blind, and lame. In France, a seventh son was believed to be extremely lucky and sailors would insist upon having one on board to prevent the ship from sinking. Believers in the occult and the paranormal knew that, in Romania, a seventh son was destined to become a vampire.

While I've been unable to find a soul who could assert Willie Martello was a vampire (a creature of the night, perhaps), most who knew him believed being the seventh son of a seventh son meant he would lead something of a charmed life. Given his outrageous and sometimes careless ways, it would seem Willie himself believed this to be true.

Willie loved to gamble and throw money around though sometimes the money was not necessarily his to gamble. **Stan Colton**, a long-time Searchlight resident and good friend of Willie's, laughed about some of Willie's extravagant gambling habits. *"The club might take in twenty or thirty thousand dollars in a night and Willie would take it all out of the cage and blow it at the Frontier Hotel,"* said Colton. *"The gaming control board used to have a hissy about that since you have to have a certain amount of money on-site."*

Jerry Schafer often described Willie to me as a man with an overwhelming charm and charisma with a truly magnetic personality. He also believed Willie was the luckiest man he had ever met. As a testament to this belief, Jerry offered up this story to me one day. *"An insight into the real Willie Martello,"* as he would say.

During one of Schafer's frequent trips to the El Rey Club, Willie decided he wanted to go into Las Vegas and gamble. By all accounts, Willie's trips

At the Tropicana Hotel and Casino in 1961. Left to Right: Willie Martello, Carol Anderson, Jerry Schafer, and Lou Scarcelli. *Photo courtesy Jerry Schafer.*

to Vegas were as much about being seen and rubbing elbows with his powerful friends as they were about living his life to the fullest. Willie was the kind of man who enjoyed the excesses that a place like Las Vegas offered. On this particular trip, he invited Jerry to join him.

*"This was my first experience with Willie Martello the gambler. It was nothing short of amazing. Willie put ten thousand dollars in cash into his pocket,"* according to Schafer. Martello said to Jerry, *"This will be my bank. I'll try to run it up into a big win."* The two of them drove into Las Vegas and went straight to the Hacienda where the owner, Doc Bayley, Willie's friend and eventual business partner, was there to greet them. Martello had a date with the roulette table.

*"He put ten dollars straight up on seven numbers each time he bet, seventy dollars per spin of the wheel,"* Schafer said. *"At first he didn't win at all, but then he hit five times in a row."* Since Willie's luck had started to kick in, the betting increased. Schafer recalled, *"He doubled his bets. He put 140 dollars on each spin of the wheel. Before long, he had won 22 thousand dollars."*

In our many conversations, Sharon Richardson frequently laughed and repeated a line that Willie jokingly muttered whenever he saw a customer hitting a lucky streak like that at his own club, *"Throw that bum the hell out!"* It seemed that Willie was not the only casino owner who adopted such a philosophy. Schafer continued, *"Doc Bayley came over to the table and told Willie to get the hell out of his casino!"* After both Martello and Bayley laughed at this exchange, Bayley invited them to have lunch.

Once lunch was finished, Willie cracked a smile and had a wicked thought, *"Let's go to the Desert Inn,"* he said, *"I can't go back to Searchlight with this much cash in my pocket. I HAVE to lose this money!"* Losing the money at the Desert Inn was neither in the cards nor on the table for Martello. According to Schafer, Martello won another twenty thousand dollars. If Willie was going to start a losing streak, he was going to have to find someplace else. The next stop was the Thunderbird.

With fifty thousand dollars in Willie's pocket, he and Schafer entered the Thunderbird. *"Within about thirty minutes,"* Jerry said, *"he lost every cent he had."* Having spoken with Jerry and a few of Martello's family members about this event, it was understandable why the versions of the story differed slightly. Bob Martello always remembered the story with Willie laying all fifty thousand dollars on one hand of cards. *"Fifty grand on a single hand,"* Bob said. *"Can you believe that?"* Schafer remembered the event primarily at the roulette table over that short period of time. In all likelihood, this time with Schafer was not the only time Willie would throw down an enormous wager without a care in the world. Either way, it illustrated a remarkable attribute of Willie's: he simply didn't care about money and threw caution to the wind every chance he got. That was Willie.

Jerry Schafer stood in disbelief. *"Willie laughed like it was just part of his day. As far as I was concerned, it was awful. Fifty grand was a fortune to me, especially back in the 1960s."*

Willie didn't care one iota when he lost all that cash. As Willie stood there and laughed and Schafer stood there shocked, the owner of the Thunderbird gave Willie $1000 *"to get home with,"* according to Schafer. At this point it bears mentioning again that Searchlight was not quite 60 miles away from Las Vegas and Willie had a home in Las Vegas. Even if Willie were driving a car that got 1/8th of a mile to the gallon and had to travel not just to Searchlight, but all the way to Reno, one thousand dollars was more than enough "to get home with." That one thousand bucks was not about a safe journey home to Searchlight but about respect. It was respect for another casino owner and for a man who had just made the Thunderbird fifty thousand dollars richer. That gesture also spoke about a completely different way of doing business in Las Vegas than what you see today. Of course, to Willie that was a thousand dollars he did not need to respect, whatsoever.

Willie and Jerry got into Martello's white Lincoln Town Car, but home was not their next destination. *"I thought we would head back to Searchlight, but instead, Willie drove to the Sands Hotel. He walked into the Casino and Carl Cohen, the boss, walked up to him and shook hands."*

With one thousand dollars in his hand, not even in his possession long enough to wear a crease in a single bill, Willie looked at Cohen and asked, *"How about letting me bet this grand on one spin of the wheel?"* The casino boss just smiled and said, *"It's your money Willie...Go ahead, make your bet."*

Schafer watched Martello put the entire thousand dollars, the money he had to guarantee a trip home, the last money he had in his hands, on double zero, spouting out, *"Money plays,"* as the cash hit the roulette table. *"I couldn't believe my eyes when the little white ball fell on it,"* Jerry said. *"Willie won 35 thousand dollars just like that!"*

After he tempted fate and reclaimed his magical luck, Martello handed the dealer five hundred dollars, looked at Carl Cohen and said with a smile, *"Nice to see you Carl."* The two men shook hands and Shafer and Martello exited the Sands.

*"I felt like a kid who just saw his first ball game, and his team won,"* Schafer told me *"But not Willie. That money didn't mean a thing to him."* On their drive back to Searchlight, the two men started laughing and Willie said to Jerry, *"That was a kick in the ass wasn't it?"* Schafer was speechless. *"Well, Jerry my boy, you win some, you lose some. We'll go back tomorrow and see if I can lose a few bucks."*

Photo courtesy Ethel Martello

# COME FLY WITH ME,
# PART TWO: PROJECT RUNWAY

One night in the mid-1950s, Willie Martello was enjoying a night of drinking and gambling at the **El Capitan Casino** in Hawthorne, Nevada. Willie frequently made excursions to other casinos to visit his friend **Barney O'Malia**, be visible around Nevada, and keep an eye on what other places offered their guests.

As Willie sat at a blackjack table, play was interrupted by a rather large crowd of people who were shuttled into the casino en mass. One person after another was coming inside and finding a place to enjoy his or her evening and spend some money. Willie forgot about his cards and asked the dealer where all the people came from. The dealer informed him they were flown in by the El Capitan on a junket free of charge. Willie just watched as more and more people entered the El Capitan and found their places at the tables. It was then he remembered he had a good friend with some airplanes and that Searchlight had its own runway...sort of.

The thought of bringing hordes of people into Searchlight by plane made a lot of sense to Willie. He had plenty of connections in California

**The El Capitan desk at the Burbank, CA airport on August 2, 1961.**
*Nevada State Museum, Las Vegas [J. Florian Mitchell Collection]*

through his family's liquor and night club businesses to get the word out and plenty of space to land the planes. A stopover in Searchlight would be much less of a hassle than the ever-growing airport in Las Vegas and would promote more of that western tourism surrounding Searchlight that Willie wanted to develop. People wanting a taste of the western life, the smell of the fresh air, offered by the Joshua Tree Forest, the beauty and fishing of Lake Mohave, and the thrill of a little bit of gambling could find it all in Searchlight.

Aviation and Searchlight were frequent partners. Among some of Searchlight's more famous residents in its history were William Harrel Nellis and the legendary Col. John Macready. Macready's noteworthy career includes being the only pilot to win the prestigious Mackay Trophy three times for his many flying achievements. Of course, with so many of my own family from the Ohio area, I prefer to think of him as the man responsible for executing the first successful crop dusting demonstration in Troy, Ohio back in 1921.

Over the years, there have been at least eight fatal plane crashes in or near Searchlight. The most famous one occurred on August 3, 1970. The Naval plane, Zulu Echo Six, was a Lockheed P3-A Orion. It was on a training mission, flying from Nellis Air Force base to San Diego, California when it encountered rough thunderstorm activity. A lightning strike caused the plane to descend, which killed all ten crewmen on board. Thanks to Jane and Carl Overy a memorial was erected in Searchlight in 2004.

Jane Overy, Searchlight's resident historian, was quick to inform me there was indeed a previous landing strip in Searchlight long before Willie came to town. *"It was right in the town, unlike the one Willie is credited with installing, and John Macready himself historically landed on it,"* Overy said. However, much of that landing strip was gone by the time Willie arrived and he wanted an airport of his own.

Since I was never one who would suddenly decide for myself to build a runway in a town of a few hundred people, I can only speculate about the "chicken vs. egg" battle occurring within Willie's head. Where do you start if you're a small-town casino owner wanting to offer big-time amenities like air travel? Do you build the runway and then try to find the planes, or do you secure the planes and worry about where to land them afterward? It seemed logical to Willie to start with the runway, and he began to expand on a strip just south of the El Rey Club.

The runway Willie helped the town of Searchlight fully realize was not technically his. He was merely the strongest proponent of a functioning airstrip in Searchlight. There was something of an existing landing strip a couple miles south of town, just over the hill. Willie hired fellow local casino owner Ernest "Sandy" Sandquist to take a road grader and attempt to make the stretch more level. However, since rumor has it Willie paid Sandquist mostly in beer, the road was not likely to be any safer after the treatment than it was before.

This road was really nothing more than a long and somewhat flat piece of dirt and rock road that had been established by the military years before as an emergency runway. Ray Chesson remembered it as being Nevada's portion of a seldom-used, unpaved road, *"the Nipton cutoff from Searchlight to the Los Angeles Highway, an A-1 tire buster,"* as he described it. There had always been talk about eventually paving that stretch of land, and the people of Searchlight had been paying taxes to the county on that land for years with that in mind. Willie took it upon himself to remind the Clark County Commissioner's office of their "obligation" to the people of Searchlight.

Willie lobbied the Clark County Commissioner's office on behalf of the

| | |
|---|---|
| **Willie Martello and an unnamed man discussing plans for his new runway. May 3, 1961** *Nevada State Museum, Las Vegas [J. Florian Mitchell Collection]* | **Willie standing proudly on his new runway. May 3, 1961.** *Nevada State Museum, Las Vegas [J. Florian Mitchell Collection]* |

The El Rey Club desk at the Burbank, CA
Airport on August 6, 1961. Junket Hostess,
Marjorie Brown is behind the counter.
*Nevada State Museum, Las Vegas*
*[J. Florian Mitchell Collection]*

Willie with R.A. Richardson,
celebrating the first commercial flights
to Searchlight. April 23, 1961.
*Nevada State Museum, Las Vegas*
*[J. Florian Mitchell Collection]*

town just as he did years earlier when he tried to get permanent telephone
service into town, and certainly this included his own personal gain. Willie
was going to get his runway. To quote Jerry Schafer, *"Willie Martello had
a vision for Searchlight. He would move Heaven and Earth to make this
happen."* Before too long, without the need to move Heaven even an
inch or two, Willie was granted permission to pave the runway. Martello
reportedly pumped water from the El Rey swimming pool every morning
and transported it to the construction site in order to help speed the
process.

And what a runway it was!

A beautiful 6800 foot long runway, a smooth expanse nestled within a
desert landscape with a mountain view, would soon be ready and waiting
for the throngs of people who wanted to come to Searchlight. It promised
*"complete telephone and refueling services"* and would even be lighted
at night. The *Las Vegas Sun* stated this new air field would be the fourth in
Clark County capable of handling large, multi-engine aircraft.

According to Martello's family, Willie spent close to one million

**Willie & Northern Express President R. A. Richardson, along with members of the Long
Beach Elks Club on April 23, 1961.** *Nevada State Museum, Las Vegas [J. Florian Mitchell Collection]*

dollars of his own money on this project. While the county (along with
contributions from Willie) paved the air strip, he paid for the maintenance
and fuel for the planes, as well as the crew. Now, he needed some
airplanes.

To secure the use of high-quality airplanes Willie chose to enlist the help
of two friends— one old, and one new.

Willie met with **R.A. Richardson**, the President of **Northern Express
Airways, Inc.,** to negotiate a deal that would allow commercial airliners to
fly from California to Searchlight. Since Willie always found a way to get
what he wanted, it wasn't long before the deal was sealed. Soon, Willie
Martello had his own ticket counter and office at the Burbank Airport
alongside Barney O'Malia and Warren "Doc" Bayley.

Doc Bayley, owner of the Hacienda, was already bringing in thousands
of people to Las Vegas on his own planes. Bayley and Martello had
been friends for a while and discussed ways they could work together
to develop Searchlight into a tourist and gambling destination. In an

interview with **Dick Taylor**, a former employee of Bayley's, he described Willie as *"liking the aggressiveness of Doc Bayley and his thriving Hacienda Hotel on the Las Vegas Strip."*

As it turned out, getting the planes wasn't as much of a problem as they originally thought. According to Dick Taylor, *"The Hacienda team had an airplane fleet bringing in passengers from Burbank, San Diego, and San Francisco, California."* These flights were designed not only to bring customers into the casino but also to put people in the Las Vegas mindset from the get-go, according to Taylor's description of some of the in-flight entertainment offered. *"The fleet ran a nightly schedule out of Burbank and featured a piano bar and a negligee fashion show,"* said Taylor. The two casino owners met at Bayley's personal hotel suite for a little plane talk. *"After an all-night meeting, Martello had a deal, a handshake deal, which was common in those days,"* said Taylor. *"Bayley would commit one of the Hacienda's planes* (a DC-3) *in exchange for an unpublicized part of the "action" at Martello's joint in Searchlight."* Later, Willie secured the use of Lockheed Constellations for delivery of his patrons to the El Rey Club and hired **Poddy Mercer**, among other gentlemen, as pilot for the planes.

The great **J. Florian Mitchell** took photos on May 3, 1961 that showed Willie standing, happy and triumphant, on his new runway with his arms outstretched to actually welcome guests from California with open arms. A different photo from that same shoot showed a more subdued, stoic, almost concerned look on Martello's face. It was, perhaps, with good reason. After all, when something so big gets set into motion, one almost has to ask, *"Now what?"*

Planes? Check.

Runway? Check.

Customers? Ahh yes, Willie needed the customers.

Soon, advertisements popped up in California newspapers. Across the southern part of the state people learned about the El Rey Club and a town called Searchlight. On April 23, 1961, the first commercial flight to Searchlight, Nevada carried 44 people, all members of the Long Beach Elks Club. The passengers arrived on a Northern Express Corvair and, reportedly, enjoyed a smooth landing. In the *Las Vegas Sun*, R.A. Richardson predicted *"Thousands of flying sportsmen soon would be using the facilities of the new air field, located close to the 'good fishing' at Cottonwood Cove on Lake Mohave."*

An ad placed in the September 1, 1961 edition of the Long Beach *Press Telegram* read, *"Why spend your money before you get there? FLY FREE round trip to Searchlight, Nevada as the guests of Willie Martello's El Rey Resort Club and Casino."* In what appeared to be a perfect juxtaposition of advertising and aviation lineage, on December 26 of that same year, the *Press Telegram* featured at least three ads that offered free or inexpensive flights from California to Nevada. The ads were placed by the Hacienda, the El Rey Club, and the El Capitan. The idea of affordable flights into Nevada was also being offered at the remote Mizpah Casino in Tonopah where people could enjoy their "**Silver Flite**" for only $9.99.

While it may not have been his idea, Willie Martello found himself credited as one of the pioneers in the Las Vegas area when he offered free flights to Searchlight from California. With a keen eye on the competition, Willie made certain he kept the package enticing, even if there was no cost for the plane fare. If the Hacienda offered champagne, Willie also had champagne. If the El Capitan gave each guest two silver dollars with which to gamble, Willie gave rolls of nickels to the passengers. If you wanted food, you'd get it from Willie's El Rey. Kenny Laursen of the Tony Lovello Revue recalled the complete package, *"The customer was given a free plane ride on a DC-3, a bottle of champagne, a coupon for dinner, $4 in nickels, some 2 for 1 betting coupons, and a ride back to the Long Beach, California airport."*

Sharon Richardson recalled, *"He would have a full crew, all the tables were ready, Chef Luigi would have the menus ready for these nice lunches set up for the guests. The whole nine yards."*

All of these enticing options SHOULD have been enough to encourage people to take a getaway trip to Searchlight, and indeed, planeloads of people left California and landed at Willie's new runway. Of course, not all of the junkets turned out to be profitable.

It seemed more often than not, a getaway trip was all some people had in mind when they saw the ad in their local paper. Spending money once they got there was another story. Sharon Richardson spoke of difficulties getting the cash out of the customers' pockets, *"In the summertime, it was nearly impossible to get them into the casino. Willie would find them all outside with their feet in the pool, and he'd have to chase them back inside."* Sharon laughed, *"He was mad as hell! Freeloaders showed up on those free flights all the time. They would fly in, eat their meals, and go home. Willie gave away the farm trying to get these folks to drop a dime or two in a machine and would get nothing in return,"* said Sharon.

For some, even a little starter cash, compliments of Willie, wasn't enough to encourage more gambling or commerce. *"People would pocket the rolls of nickels! It was hilarious,"* said Richardson. *"They just didn't want to spend the nickels. I can't imagine*

Not quite the high-rollers Willie was hoping for. Inside the El Rey Club, February 18, 1961. *Nevada State Museum, Las Vegas [J. Florian Mitchell Collection]*

*it being very successful, but Willie kept it going for a long time."* As the program progressed, Willie made attempts to screen potential guests a little better in an effort to find real gamblers and not just *"little old ladies with their stockings rolled down to their ankles,"* as Willie's niece described them.

A few pocket-stuffing pool-dwellers aside, people started to notice the fact that Willie's plan, at least on the surface, was working. Traffic was flowing through Searchlight, and Willie's plans to get more people into town were showing positive results. Of course, it didn't always go smoothly.

*"Willie would throw his hat on when it was time to pick people up at the airstrip,"* said Richardson, *"and he bought this old yellow bus for the guests to ride in...it didn't have any doors on it, I remember that!"* The job of shuttling the passengers to and from the airport often fell upon Willie, his nephew Bob, or others who were on-hand. That is, of course, if they were willing to drive the bus. Stan Colton, the great-grandson of George Frederick Colton, the founder of Searchlight, recalled a time when he was called to bus duty. Mr. Colton found that Searchlight did not seem all too

inviting to some. Of course, this depended on when the plane arrived.

Stan was working the mines at the time and simply hadn't had any time to freshen up or clean himself off for close to four days. The man who was supposed to drive the bus that night had taken ill and Willie asked Stan if he'd be willing to pick up the guests. *"I looked a mess,"* said Colton, *"I had an old Navy pea coat that was dirty and a blue ski cap that was just as dirty, but I said I'd be more than glad to do it for him."* The dirty and disheveled Colton got into the bus and headed a couple miles out of town and over the hill to find the plane.

Colton described the night as dark and ominous, *"It was a moonless night. There wasn't a cloud in the sky. Just stars. You really can't see any glow of Searchlight from the airport. It was DARK."* Colton found the plane and drove along the side while he waited for the guests to disembark. The folks immediately started to wonder if taking a free flight to some remote desert town was a good idea. *"As the people came off of the plane, they took one look at me and one look around and saw that they were in the middle of nowhere."* The passengers began to notice the complete lack of light and the scruffy man who told them to get on the bus. *"The women were grabbing their purses, the men were clutching at their wallets,"* Colton said. *"They were thinking we were going to load them on the bus, take them some place, mow 'em all down, bury them in the ground, and take their money!"* They feared the worst and wondered if they'd see their families again. All passengers were deadly silent as the bus made its way from the airport and back onto the highway. Soon, the lights of the El Rey Club became visible to the frightened guests. *"The sigh of relief could have blown me right out of the front of that bus,"* Colton laughed.

A rickety yellow bus with no doors and a few scared passengers fearful of a desert death isn't that bad all told. It could have been worse.

One man I interviewed, author and casino memorabilia collector **Carey Burke**, spoke of one of the earliest flights Willie brought into town. *"It was very exciting, getting on this big plane and being treated like kings just so we could gamble a little,"* he said. *"The plane was packed with people all eager to see Searchlight, meet Willie, and try out his place."*

A full planeload of people, drinks being passed round, and the promise of a good time were what entertained the guests that day. Once the plane landed, the passengers waited for the door to open and for the fun to begin. They waited...and waited...and waited some more. The pilot opened the door to see Willie and his yellow bus waiting a bit impatiently for his new customers to deplane.

*"What are you waiting for? Let's go!"* Willie said.

*"Where are the stairs, Willie?"* asked the pilot

*"The what?"* asked a confused Martello.

*"The stairs. These folks can't get off the plane without the stairs, Willie,"* replied the eager pilot.

Willie looked around and asked, *"Aren't they on the plane?"*

Willie's pilot cleared his throat and said, *"That's impossible, Willie. The stairs are too big for the plane. Don't you have stairs for the plane? A big staircase on wheels like at the airport?"*

Willie got a tight-lipped smirk on his face. He knew he was about to be truly embarrassed, *"You mean these planes don't come with their own stairs?"*

Willie, the plane's crew, and every passenger from California began to laugh hysterically. *"Everyone knew they weren't going to gamble any time soon,"* laughed Burke, *"It was too much, seeing this poor guy in his cowboy hat and white suit, scratching his head over the fact he had no stairs for the plane."*

Willie had to think of something. He wasn't about to let his potential gamblers simply go back to California without stopping at the club. He went back to the El Rey and made a few calls.

*"Before too long,"* said Burke, *"Willie had arrived with his bus and a plumber's truck following him. He called around until he could find someone in town who owned a ladder!"* Willie took the plumber's ladder from the top of his truck and set it up against the side of the plane, thankful

**HOORAY FOR STAIRS! May 29, 1961.**
*Nevada State Museum, Las Vegas [J. Florian Mitchell Collection]*

it was long enough to reach the door. In his white suit, Willie climbed up the ladder and peeked into the plane. With an exasperated laugh, he removed his hat and let out a loud, *"WELCOME TO SEARCHLIGHT, FOLKS!"* The plane roared with laughter and applause.

Though there were rarely more than two or three flights per week, Willie's flights in and out of Searchlight helped bring more cash into the town and made the El Rey a memorable stop for the vacationer. Whether it was a DC-3, the massive Constellations, or a privately owned plane, Searchlight had a runway and, with that, a new way to provide a regular flow of people into his casino.

This achievement, the building of a landing strip in the middle of Searchlight, proved to be the latest in a long line of ways Willie Martello proved himself to be an innovator and visionary figure in the casino game. Much like the use of carrier pigeons to substitute for a working telephone or wild burros as a method for stopping traffic in the desert, Willie's version of the Champagne Flight places Martello among the great promoters of his time. Even without a set of stairs, Willie was able to reach new heights.

# THE MAYOR

**B**eing the principal land owner in a town as small as Searchlight had its privileges. This included the fact you could apply a rule so many children did during playground games. That rule was, "My Ball = My Rules."

Willie did as he pleased. Willie Martello WAS the town of Searchlight during his time. As far as anyone was concerned, it *was* his town. If it happened there, it was because Willie either wanted it to happen or simply made it happen. He owned several businesses, employed many people, and brought even more people into Searchlight to visit & spend a few dollars. It should have come as no surprise to anyone that while there were certainly rules to follow from Clark County government, the Gaming and Liquor Board, and the Sheriff's Department, Willie felt he had the right to make his own rules in his own town.

**Forrest Duke**, "The Visiting Fireman," was the variety and entertainment columnist for the *Las Vegas Review-Journal*. He was also a broadcaster and host of his own radio program on AM 1340, KORK, which was broadcast seven times a week. He had the print and radio broadcast media as his platforms and had a VOICE in Las Vegas entertainment. It was an honor if you were mentioned in one of Duke's columns according to many entertainers I spoke with over the years. Forrest was also a friend of Willie Martello and frequently hung out at the club. Because of this relationship, the El Rey Club was frequently mentioned in the newspaper. Whether it was to report an appearance by blonde bombshell **Nancy Kaye** or to report Willie's first heart attack, Willie Martello and the El Rey Club came up quite often in Duke's column. Occasionally, some of the

*Forrest Duke*

*"The Visiting Fireman"*

sillier antics that had less to
do with the vibrant Las Vegas
entertainment scene found their way into Duke's
well-read paragraphs.

Willie Martello was very much the town's judge, jury, and executioner during his reign in Searchlight. To make things official, he even appointed himself mayor, though it was only honorary. Of course, with great honorary power comes great honorary responsibility and even a king needs a break once in a while.

On July 26, 1960, Forrest Duke wrote that Willie Martello stepped down as the town's honorary mayor and reported the results of Searchlight's bogus election. You knew life was simpler when the phony election of an honorary mayor in a tiny town made a noteworthy entertainment column in a town like Las Vegas.

There were three candidates interested in the fake office. It seemed when so much imaginary power was up for grabs, the candidates felt your average campaign tactics, such as shaking hands and kissing babies, just wasn't enough to gain the majority of the electorate. Clearly, one had to cheat and swindle his way into such a coveted, honorary office. Willie was beside himself when bearing witness to this chicanery. The way Duke told the tale, *"Willie tearfully announced that, since there was so much ballot-box stuffing and other underhanded activity, he was going to do the decent thing and pick the winner by letting the three candidates draw cards."*

One of the candidates, **"Black Bob" Fleener,** sneaked in a marked deck of cards and, naturally, drew the high card, a 10 according to Duke's account of the event. The other two candidates, known as **The VF** and **"Artful Dodger" Cozad,** drew the next highest cards, a 9 and a 4, respectively.

Since Willie was still the sitting honorary mayor, he also dictated the rules and results of this "election." In the end, Willie decided that Fleener,

The VF, and Cozad would all be honorary mayor of Searchlight for one month each, starting with Fleener and ending with Cozad. Cozad's campaign manager, a woman named **Barbara Ballinger**, reportedly impressed former Nevada senator **George "Molly" Malone**, who was in attendance that night. Malone, not well-regarded among the voters, was considering making another run at the Senate, and almost certainly joking, said he wanted to employ Ballinger as his campaign manager after he witnessed her efficiency running Cozad's third place campaign. One can only envision whether alcohol had something to do with this newsworthy election that evening.

I find it interesting that a marked deck of cards was used to decide the election knowing Willie's gaming license was revoked ten years earlier after a marked deck was used in a 21 game. One would hope no casino owner who lost his license once would even dare allow anyone to enter with a cheater's deck of cards. However, since this was all in good fun, Willie did as he pleased. I can't help but wonder if this might be the same deck.

Apparently, being an elected official, even an honorary one, carried some weight. Duke wrote about Willie Martello in July of 1962 when he stopped by Searchlight sometime after the fire that destroyed his original El Rey. Since it was an election year, Duke wrote, *"Willie Martello has a small army of office-seekers after him for endorsement."* Duke added, *"Seems that in the past, every candidate Willie supports, wins."* As I read this and laughed to myself, I wondered just how many Nevada elections were decided over the years by Willie and a marked deck of cards.

While this blurb in Duke's column was really more of a chance for Willie to make a minor mention of his big plans for a new El Rey Resort, which appeared later on the page, it showed that, real or imaginary, Willie liked to show the world he had some clout in Las Vegas.

My favorite tale of Mayor Willie Martello does not come from the pages of the *Review Journal* that were home to Forrest Duke's popular column. Jerry Schafer sent me an email one day that detailed how Willie ruled the town and how pressing legal issues were dealt with in Searchlight.

One day a young man rode into town and needed a tank of gas. He pulled into Willie's Texaco station and realized he had no money. **Bob Patterson**, the station manager, knew Willie would likely just give the kid a tank of gas so he could get home, went ahead and filled the tank. *"The kid left his bowling ball as a security deposit,"* according to Schafer. The young man promised to one day return, repay the money, and reclaim his bowling ball.

*"Six months passed and the kid never returned,"* said Jerry, *"so the gas station manager sold the bowling ball."* As fate would have it, within two days of selling the bowling ball, the young man returned with his father to Searchlight. Both men became very angry when they heard the bowling ball had been sold. *"The kid's father said he was going to sue Willie and the station manager,"* according to Schafer.

Martello had already decided that he was just going to give the kid the money for the bowling ball and another tank of gas, but as Shafer continued, *"Willie, being Willie, said that they had to have a trial."*

Willie asked everyone to go into the restaurant at the El Rey Club, which would serve as their courthouse. There were several patrons and hungry guests on hand to watch the trial unfold.

*"Rory Calhoun was Judge,"* said Schafer, *"and Willie appointed me District Attorney."* With Mayor Willie Martello present in the town's sacred and reverent courthouse, celebrity Judge Calhoun called the young man to the witness stand. Newly appointed District Attorney Schafer approached the youth and asked his first and only question.

*"Was this a two-fingered or a three-fingered bowling ball?"*

The witnesses in the court room, the judge, the mayor, the district attorney, and even the young man's father, broke into hysterics and the trial ended almost as quickly as it began. *"As you can imagine, everything went downhill from there,"* said Schafer. Willie issued the man his refund and justice was swiftly served in Searchlight, Nevada.

**Willie entertaining guests that included Rory Calhoun (second from right).**
*Photo courtesy Ethel Martello.*

*Photo courtesy Ethel Martello*

# A GENEROUS MAN

While Willie Martello certainly was cavalier with his gambling, his drinking, and his women, he was also reported to be a very kind man who was always willing to help others.

Stories I relayed to his family members or others that knew him, about Willie hurriedly driving a dying baby to the hospital or occasionally offering a bottle of booze in exchange for a worthless hunk of rock, have never been met with any doubt about their veracity. *"Wouldn't have surprised me,"* was the statement I heard most often. People just enjoyed the man's character and personality and knew him to be, after all was said and done, a kind and generous man.

As an example, I'll begin with a story relayed to me by Jane Overy. This story was told to her by a woman who had been to Searchlight only once before. What a trip that turned out to be!

This unnamed woman lived in California, and by her own admission, did not have much in the way of money. With her daughter about to graduate from high school, she wanted very badly to give her a special present to commemorate the occasion.

As the mother leafed through her local newspaper, she saw an ad for the El Rey Club in Searchlight that boasted free airfare to and from the casino. When she learned that Searchlight was also close to Las Vegas, it made for an even more exciting trip.

Not only was the price right, but neither had been on a real airplane before and, therefore, the choice of a gift became very easy. Soon, both mother and daughter were on their way to the Long Beach Airport eager for what promised to be an experience they'd never forget.

Unbeknownst to the mother, the prostitution sting of 1951 in Searchlight left the town with quite a reputation for salacious behavior. Even with nearly a decade of time passing between the payment of fines and the removal of the desert's sultry purveyors of pleasure, many men headed to Searchlight and thought they could find a little more than a cold drink at the El Rey Club. As it happened, many men were on board that plane the day that mother and daughter chose to have their adventure in the desert. Many men noticed the ladies were clearly not with gentlemen escorts, such as husbands or boyfriends.

As the men boarded the plane, they paid quite a lot of attention to the mother and her teenage daughter. They were like dogs at the dinner table; their eyes perked up when they saw the ladies seated there. They believed this was part of the in-flight and post-flight entertainment.

During the flight, some men worked up the nerve to start conversations with the ladies. While the two certainly understood the excitement of flying in a luxurious aircraft to an exotic destination (such that Searchlight was), neither mom nor daughter quite understood the amount of fuss the men paid them. Why would so many be so fascinated by two women on a plane? Why were there so many whispers and stares? Why would anyone be so interested, almost giddy, to hear that the two were mother and daughter and the daughter was about to graduate high school?

The plane soon landed in Searchlight.

Willie was there to greet his planeload of customers. He always wore a smile to welcome the guests. However, when the two ladies left the plane, Willie had a look of shock.

He approached the pair and tried to take them away from the male onlookers and asked them what brought them to Searchlight. The mother, now more than ready for an explanation, told Willie about her young daughter's high school graduation and the gift of a free plane ride. She told Willie they hadn't much money and couldn't resist such an enticing offer. That was all Willie had to hear.

A smile washed over Martello's face as a sigh of relief came from his mouth. He now knew the innocence of the story and saw an opportunity to make this a positive and memorable trip for them. He let them in on the little secret all the men were keeping from them. He then told them they were not allowed in his club.

Rather than embarrass them anymore or cause another unwanted leer from any man at the El Rey, he offered to take them into Las Vegas himself for a full day and night on the town, all at his own expense. The ladies, both amused and relieved, gladly took Willie up on his offer and were whisked away to Las Vegas in Willie's convertible. He treated them to fabulous meals, dazzling shows, and gave them the King's Tour of the town. Once the mother and daughter were more than satisfied with their roller coaster ride of a day, Willie, their generous host, brought them back to Searchlight and made certain they were not late for their free plane ride back to California.

All Martellos seemed to place a higher value on children and family than most other things. Since they all came from generations of large families, the thought of being there for others was always important to the

Martellos in Searchlight.

Suzan Riddell, who really was just a child during the time her mother, **Joan Gilbert**, was married to Willie, remembered feeling like a princess because of Willie's affections. *"We were friends with Rex Bell and Clara Bow, who were neighbors. We never wanted for anything."*

In addition to things any man normally provided for a family, there were extravagances that included cars and furs. While the stereotype is that all young girls wished for a pony, Joan and daughter Suzan found themselves with a most unexpected family pet: a MONKEY!

**Joan Gilbert, Suzan Martello, and Pierre (a different Pierre) at Willie's Las Vegas home, circa 1949.**
*Photo courtesy Suzan Riddell.*

*"Yes, we had a monkey named Bingo,"* said Suzan of her childhood pet. *"That monkey was very cool at first."* Bingo was on his best behavior when he first came into the Martello household, *"Until it went nuts and started tearing up the house!"* said Suzan. Bingo reportedly tore up the curtains, threw anything he could get his hands on, and made a total mess of everything that stood in his path. *"He would smash oranges on the kitchen counter and climb the dog's back,"* remembered Riddell. Eventually, Bingo simply went away and Peppi and Pierre, the poodles, were in the favor of the Martello clan.

Long after Joan and Willie had split, Suzan (age 16) and Joan went into Vegas and found Willie working at the Hacienda. As far as Willie was concerned, there was never a cause for any post-divorce animosity toward Joan and her daughter. He wanted to treat them as well then as he did when he and Joan were together. *"He was the same flamboyant, throwing money around, snapping his fingers, and saying 'get my wife and daughter anything they want' kind of guy,"* recalled Suzan. Joan carried a torch for Willie until her dying day, and Suzan always thought fondly of that crazy man from Searchlight.

To many Willie simply had a big heart. He was always willing to help someone who was down on his luck. *"No one ever left the El Rey broke or hungry,"* claimed Sharon Richardson. One story relayed to Ray Chesson by Chef Luigi in a very touching article after Willie's death suggested this was truly the case.

A man rolled into town and hoped to find work in Searchlight of all places. He strolled into the El Rey which appeared to be the town's most logical place to find activity and a promise for some gainful employment. When he found

**Peppi and Pierre at the El Rey in 1946.**
*Photo courtesy Joyce Dickens Walker.*

Luigi at the counter, the man asked, *"Any chance for a fellow to get some work so he can get something to eat?"* Willie was at the front of the El Rey and took notice of the man and the car he drove into town. He noticed a woman and children in the car outside. Martello joined in the conversation the stranger was having with Luigi.

*"You want something to eat?"* asked Willie.

The man replied with a simple *"Yeah"* and waited for a response.

*"What's the matter with your wife and all those kids out there in the car? Don't they want something to eat, too?"* was Willie's query.

The man told Martello he had intended to ask for food for his family as well and was abruptly interrupted by Willie.

*"Well, you didn't ask me! Not for them!"* Willie went outside and greeted the family still waiting in the car and insisted they follow him into the El Rey Club. *"Give them anything in the house!"* said Willie to his chef.

The family gorged themselves on food finer than they'd ever expected to find in a town like Searchlight. Reportedly, some of the kids, with bellies full and bodies exhausted from their long drive, fell asleep at the table. Willie invited them to stay at the El Rey Motel, and once they were fully rested, found some sort of work for them to do. According to Luigi's story, that family stayed in Searchlight with gainful employment from Willie for two years.

Stories of this kind of charity and generosity were not uncommon. These tales painted a much different picture than that of a lowly whoremonger. Chef Scirocco shared another tale that showed Willie was more like Santa than a sinner.

Willie frequently vacated the El Rey either on business trips or simply to get away to his beloved Palm Springs area. It was not always customary to find Martello within the confines of the El Rey Club during the holiday season.

*"Now, if I am gone, if I am over in Palm Springs or some place,"* he instructed Luigi, *"I want you to go to Vegas and buy presents for all the kids in town."* Chef Luigi was quick to point out to Chesson that money was not an issue when it meant making people feel like family at Christmastime. *"Don't get cheap stuff. Get them something that will last,"* said Scirocco. If it seemed that a present wasn't appropriate, Willie made sure Luigi knew what to do. *"Don't forget to buy food for the people that need it."*

Willie and Buddy certainly seemed to have a soft spot for the children of Searchlight. One of the highlights for the town's children was the chance to take a dip in the town's first real swimming pool located at the El Rey. Harry Reid always said the pool was open to the public once a week, but before long, it seemed as though it was really a pool for the Searchlight youth. *"The kids swam more than any visitor or guest,"* according to Sharon Richardson.

It wasn't enough to open the El Rey swimming pool to the kids in town. The Martello brothers, Bud in particular, noticed there was no real place for young Searchlighters to play America's favorite pastime and took matters into their own hands.

*"Bud started a baseball team for all the local school kids in town,"* said Jeff Reid, Jr. *"All of us, including me and Harry, were on it. He kept that going for a couple of years, and we were pretty good. We beat all the schools in the rural areas around here."*

As I have said many times, Willie was not a saint. However, he did have, with very little exception, the love of the people. He worked tirelessly in an effort to make Searchlight a real city and did what he could to find work, food, or fun for the people that needed it. Some took advantage of Willie's kindness, but from all accounts, he never ran out of that goodwill. When possible, he fed the hungry, employed the needy, and gave as much as he could.

Believe me. I looked for the dirt. As an example, when I tried to corroborate one "bad" story I was told, which I will relay in a later chapter, I was barraged with plenty of comments like *"**NONSENSE!**"* or *"**That sounds like a load of bull to me.**"* I asked everyone who would speak with me as I researched this book to give me as many bad memories as good. With very few exceptions, I received an overwhelming amount of positive memories about this common "pimp" as so many have called him. Perhaps after this book has come out, those folks who have waited to tell me how wrong I am will come forward, but until I hear from them...this is what I have been told.

For the people that knew Willie Martello, they just can't seem to remember a more kind and generous man. Perhaps Chef Luigi summed it up best in Ray Chesson's article as he remembered Willie's life, *"**Willie Martello was a gentleman. I don't care what anybody says.**"*

**Searchlight kids enjoying the El Rey pool.**
**Left to right: Ralph Stewart, Unknown, & Jeff Reid, Jr.**
*Photo courtesy Joyce Dickens Walker.*

*Photo courtesy Nevada State Museum, Las Vegas [J. Florian Mitchell Collection]*

# THE DIRT

When I started this project I didn't set out to find "the dirt" so much as I set out to find "the stories." Though I know the more sordid tales are often what get the books flying off the shelves and the pages turning faster, I wanted to know what happened in Searchlight, who Willie was, and so on. IF there was dirt to be found, other than the oft-mentioned prostitutes, I was hopeful people would come forward with the stories. If there was none to be found I was hopeful there would at least be interesting tales. I've been very thankful to find out anything at all. As it happened, there were a lot of interesting and funny details to share but only a little dirt.

While on a trip to procure some more El Rey artifacts for my collection, I came across a most unusual book of hand-written notes dated from 1957 to 1961. It was believed the spiral-bound notebook came from the home of a **Mary Patterson**, also known as **"Kissy Mary."** Kissy Mary was supposedly an El Rey Club employee and prostitute in Searchlight.

Inside was a rather odd assortment of lists, names, and dates. This woman kept track of all the legal proceedings that involved Searchlight residents and even cited case numbers and charges. There was a page listing airplanes that landed at the Searchlight runway, complete with identification numbers. I knew of the cars and trailers along with the names of owners and license plate numbers. In some cases, I knew when these cars drove through Searchlight as well as when and where they stopped. There's even a page titled "Characters" which had a list of names and odd stories about these folks. Some fascinating stuff to say the least even if decoding the book was nearly impossible.

It was too hard to tell what this book was other than a rather interesting accounting of details from somebody who had an interest in what went on in town during very specific times. **Crystal Van Dee** of the **Nevada State Museum** called this book "The Crazy Lady Notebook" as there really was no rhyme or reason to exactly what was documented in detail.

I've always thought, if this were a book written by a prostitute or an employee of the El Rey Club, it would qualify as a "cover your ass" notebook, a book filled with minor details about everything that was helpful for those who wanted to get out of a pinch. A book filled with names and dates in a town like Searchlight *could* be quite incriminating. In essence, this was a book filled with "the dirt."

Tucked away among the pages was a card that very specifically dealt

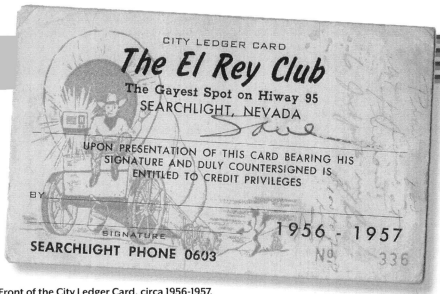

**Front of the City Ledger Card, circa 1956-1957.**
*From the author's personal collection.*

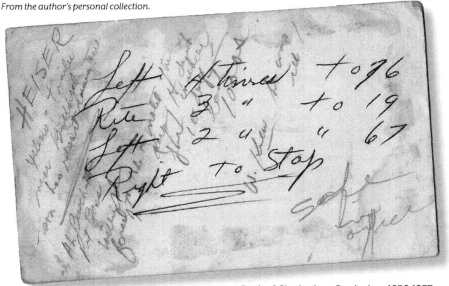

**Back of City Ledger Card, circa 1956-1957,**
**including the story of Heiser.** *From the author's personal collection.*

with the El Rey Club and made a great addition to my collection. This card was about the size of a common business card and featured a green cartoon of a western-looking covered wagon and a Joshua tree on a glossy front. It was, in fact, a "City Ledger Card" (essentially a casino credit) for the El Rey Club from the years 1956 and 1957. I've only seen two of these before, and they were very cool, to say the least.

Since it also came from the home of the same crazy lady, there were notes scrawled all over the card. The notes told a few stories. First of all, I learned someone, presumably Mary, played $1 slot machines at Fremont one day and hit six jackpots worth $100 to $200 each. Lucky girl!

The back of the card would have been blank except Patterson decided to use it as her own personal notebook. If her writing and tales were accurate, I now had the combination to the safe in the office at the El Rey Club. However, there was something a little more interesting to me than that – the story of **Heiser**.

According to the scribbled note on the card, Heiser, later referred to only as "H" on the note, was a gambler at the El Rey. He owned a yellow trailer near Bullhead City, Arizona, and his son owned a resort downtown. Where downtown, I have no idea. It seemed Mr. Heiser was drinking a lot while he gambled away at the El Rey.

A man named **Al Busch**, the apparent pit boss at the El Rey, was ordered (actually *"forced"*) by "W" (Willie) to take Heiser to the El Rey Motel and keep him drinking. The note said Al, under Willie's orders, kept him drunk at the El Rey for another ten days and Mr. H, *"lost 1000s."* Right after the tally of money lost by a drunken Mr. Heiser was one last addition to the story: *"W. knew he was ill!"*

A dark and dirty tale of how Willie Martello used his might to impart enough force on an employee so that employee maintained a high level of inebriation on a gambler who was clearly unable to make clear judgments was now in my hands. This sordid story of how Willie sold a man's health and dignity and took advantage of Heiser's weakened state all for the chance of taking a few dollars more was in my archives.

This was fantastic, whether it was true or not. I had finally found someone who said something bad about Willie. Admittedly, it was someone no longer with us to verify the story and someone who was very likely a little crazy, but I had finally found the dirt.

Of course, this story was not really much to go on if one was hoping to hear some really awful tales of illegality in the desert. Ordinarily, without having some way of backing up such a tale, a responsible researcher or historian wouldn't even print the thing. That being said, I needed SOMETHING to offset the otherwise positive stories about Willie.

As an example, when I met Joyce Dickens Walker and sat down with her for a donut one day, one of my first questions was, *"What were your impressions of Willie Martello? What kind of a guy was he?"* Her immediate response was a burst of laughter as she uttered the phrase, *"He was a crook!"* Being the comedian I am and not wanting to start off our conversation on the wrong foot, I fought the urge to ask, *"Was he a good crook or a bad crook?"*

This statement about Willie being a crook didn't really surprise me as there were very few 100% honest gamblers and casino owners in the 1940s in Las Vegas, much less Searchlight. I was hoping to hear something gritty to prevent this book from seeming like an advertisement for Willie Martello. I already knew that back in the '40s she was rather upset when she lost her bartending job at the El Rey when Willie brought in the working girls. Could this be what she meant? I simply asked if she would elaborate. The story ended up being rather harmless but was not out of the realm of crookery in 1940s Searchlight. Yes, I made up the word "crookery" for literary impact. There's not much to this chapter so let me have this!

On at least one occasion, Willie tried to collect some money from a man who had been at the El Rey the night before where he reportedly drank excessively. The story he told the now sober patron? He had borrowed money from his bartender and needed to repay it, a story which was not true in the least, according to Joyce. Not only was the man not drunk enough to forget he borrowed money, but he certainly had not spoken to her for such a purpose. *"The guy confronted me and I told him he hadn't borrowed any money from me,"* she said. *"Willie would have collected, I'm sure, if the guy had been as drunk as Willie thought he was."*

While this story does lend a little credence to the tale of a drunken Mr. Heiser, it still doesn't provide that special amount of tarnish on the teapot that some folks want from a book like this. What else have I heard?

**Bonnie Canter**, one of the last people to own the El Rey Club as one of Willie's partners, vividly recalls throwing a drink in Willie's face. *"I was so pissed at him,"* she said, *"but for the life of me, to this day I have no idea why."* Funny, but it isn't much to go on.

One person told me a tale about a night Willie and a friend went to Las Vegas for a night of fun and brought a few lovely ladies with them. On the drive into the big city, Willie, a hard-drinking man of wild reputation, found he really needed to use the bathroom. There were few if any actual pit stops along the way back then (or now, for that matter), so Willie pulled his Lincoln off to the side of the road and relieved himself. While any other man in that situation would likely have found a Joshua tree, a cactus, or a creosote bush in the desert to accept his waste, Willie decided it would be funny and certainly in character if he stood in front of his car and urinated by the light of the car's headlights. The sight inspired laughs and screams from the ladies, and Willie showed the world he didn't care who saw him living life on his terms. A little crude and certainly funny, but not really something worthy of a major exposé.

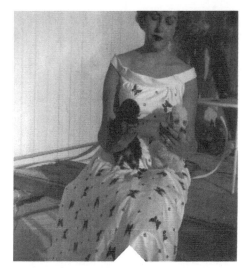

**Could this be the mysterious Margie? Taken at the El Rey Club Pool, circa 1950s.**
*Photo courtesy Sharon Richardson.*

Willie was never what you would call a faithful husband, unlike his younger brother, Buddy, who married Ethel in 1954 and remained faithful and happy during their entire 50 year marriage. Willie was married at least three times in his life and maintained relationships with several other women all the while, though it wasn't always Willie who made the first moves.

With his outgoing personality and George Raft appeal, Willie never had any trouble getting the attention of beautiful women. *"It wasn't always him chasing after the ladies,"* remarked Sharon Richardson. *"Women just wanted to be with Willie. PEOPLE wanted to be with Willie. He was so much fun to be around."*

*"He was truly larger than life—gregarious, generous, handsome, well groomed, splashy. He was very good to us. We never wanted for a thing. My mother was spoiled with furs, new cars, a nice home,"* recalled Suzan Riddell of Willie. While he was married to Joan Gilbert, many felt she and Willie were a well-suited couple. Joan Gilbert married four times in her life and, according to Suzan, was something of an outrageous, fly-by-night woman in her own right which made her a perfect match for a man of Willie's charisma. However, that compatibility only created happiness up to a point.

During this marriage, Willie regularly met up with one of the prostitutes at the El Rey, a woman named Margie. Riddell said this *"extracurricular activity"* became too much for her mother to handle. *"My mother would not tolerate it,"* said Suzan. *"According to Willie, it did not lessen his love for her.* [laughing] *Typical!"* Joan Gilbert left Willie around 1952 after she grew tired of what she described to Suzan as, *"The Italian thing."*

Of course, the rules that applied to Willie didn't apply to any of his women. While dating **Estelle Longwell**, she frequently broke up with him because of his constant cheating. This wouldn't have been a problem if Vegas was not such a small town and Willie such a large personality within the town. *"You could never hide from Willie,"* said Sharon Richardson. *"Everybody knew him and everybody loved him."*

According to Mickey Cooper, one night Estelle was having a dinner with a gentleman other than Willie. It was unknown if she and Martello were on-again as a couple at the time or even if the new gentleman was a romantic interest. What was certain was someone at the casino saw Estelle and felt it necessary to contact Willie in Searchlight and let him know Estelle was having a good time with another man. *"Before long,"* recalled Mickey, *"Willie comes storming into the casino restaurant and marches right up to Estelle's table."* An angry Martello lifted the beautiful Miss Longwell to her feet and proclaimed, *"You know, I USED to have a girlfriend that looked j-u-s-t like you! But you COULDN'T be her because no girlfriend of mine would ever be seen with a BUM LIKE THAT!"* With that, Martello made his exit and drove back to Searchlight, an hour away, but not before he was offered a drink from the bartender, presumably the man who called Martello in the first place. *"Nope,"* said Willie, *"I came here and did what I had to do!"*

Whether it was one of the girls who worked at the club or a woman he met at the tables, Willie apparently had a hunger for the ladies like none other. He even courted other men's wives or girlfriends to satisfy his needs. One family member was certain he was sneaking around with the wife of a prominent mobster from Las Vegas. At her request, I have omitted the names of the wife and the wise guy husband.

Willie was not associated with organized crime himself and tried to run a clean operation; however, he was having an awful time getting the supplies he needed to renovate and improve his club. Too many shipments were simply conveniently detoured or arrived in pieces. He went to the Stardust Hotel armed with a satchel full of money. He

**The lovely Estelle posing in front of the El Rey.** *Photo courtesy Ethel Martello*

desperately wanted to make some arrangement with the crime bosses that allowed him to get shipments of building materials delivered to Searchlight. A lunch meeting was scheduled inside the showroom of the Stardust. Willie and his niece were in attendance.

When the showroom door opened, thought to herself, *"I had never seen so many good looking Italian men in pinstripe suits in my life!"* After lunch, Sharon was not allowed to hear the business dealings between Willie and the mobsters. Willie gave her some money *"to go shopping with or something."* When the meeting was over, she came back and found Willie no longer had the satchel with him and seemed relieved with the results of the meeting.

She thought they were headed back to Searchlight and was surprised when Willie told her there was one more stop to make. This stop was the suite of the unnamed mobster whose wife was waiting there. *"I walked with him to her room right after he got done paying off her husband!"* she said. When she asked what he thought he was doing, Willie just smirked and replied, *"Never you mind!"* Sharon also remembered, *"When I came back to pick him up and she* [the mob wife] *answered the door saying, 'Hiya, hon.' I began to fear for our lives! It's funny now. At the time, it was scary as Hell."*

Willie was a charmer. That was certain. It didn't matter to him who the woman was. If he wanted her, he was going to have her. Willie's exploits were legendary. It didn't matter if the woman was the great Peggy DeCastro, with whom he reportedly had a brief affair, or a famous Hollywood actresses. His most notable exploits were with Hollywood bad girl, **Barbara Payton**.

It is quite possible Payton met Willie in Palm Springs during one of his excursions to California. The beautiful actress, who once had a promising career in

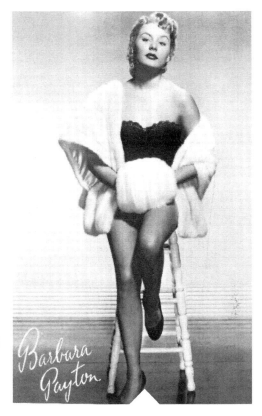

**The beautiful Barbara Payton, circa 1960s.**
*From the author's personal collection*

Hollywood and starred in films with **Lloyd Bridges**, **Gary Cooper,** and **Gregory Peck**, later became deeply involved with drugs and alcohol. She had even started selling herself to men who wanted to enjoy the comforts of a beautiful star from within the walls of the historic Palm Springs Riviera. According to the **John O'Dowd** book, "Kiss Tomorrow Goodbye: The Barbara Payton Story," she packed her belongings and headed for Searchlight after she was ousted from the Palm Springs Riviera.

Payton indirectly spoke of Willie in her autobiography, "I Am Not Ashamed." She spoke of dating a Nevada gambler with mob ties who owned a casino in Searchlight. Although Willie was not in the mob, there were almost always whispers of mafia connections when an Italian casino owner was involved.

Payton's book was quite a shocking tell-all of its day, and many details or names were altered or omitted. As an example, the Searchlight casino she referred to was a two-story place that was raided by federal agents. In fact, there were no two-story casinos in Searchlight at the time, and none were ever raided by the Feds. This could simply have been an embellishment for dramatic purposes or an effort to protect the true identity of her suitor.

It is difficult to say with 100% certainty that Willie was the man Payton dated. It is entirely possible that she was referring to California auto dealer, Ted Enoch, who reportedly visited Searchlight often and spent time with ladies that were not his wife. Jerry Schafer recalled seeing Payton and Enoch together at the El Rey, but since Barbara Payton was seen quite often with many men, this is not quite proof enough.

Where there seems to be some certainty, if not the strongest evidence within the eyes of Martello's family, is within the walls of the El Rey Club itself. Payton was clearly at the El Rey where she hung on or around Willie at almost every turn. Willie made it no secret that he and Barbara spent a lot of quality time with each other when she was in town. According to rumors, she had fallen head over heels in love with Willie. *"She thought she was going to MARRY Willie,"* exclaimed Sharon Richardson!

Much like Willie, Barbara Payton loved sex and money. Though she never referred to him by name in her scandalous book, she protected the identity of her mysterious lover with a titillating pseudonym: **Dick Fortune**.

*"We ALL laughed for a long time when we read that book,"* said Sharon Richardson. *"Who else in Searchlight could she be referring to? "There was no doubt among any of us that she was talking about Willie! She was crazy about him, but he had no plans on being that serious with her."*

All told, stories of adultery with or without celebrities are not all too surprising nor are they all that disparaging. Powerful and charming men, especially casino owners in the golden age of the Las Vegas area, were not all known to be celibate choir boys. Nobody in Willie's family and none of his friends tried to paint Willie as a Goody Two-Shoes.

There must have been more dirt.

I received a comment at my web log one day that quite intrigued me. A man who called himself **Frank Way** (you really never know WHO is posting online) left a brief but fascinating paragraph full of firearms and death threats.

*"I lived in Searchlight from 1948 - 1951. In 1951, Willie threatened to kill me. In response, my father bought a big shotgun for me and told me*

*that if Willie was to show up, I was to use the shotgun to blow a hole in him large enough through which to observe the sun rise and set. He told Willie what he had done, and Willie never showed up. I was 13-years-old at the time."*

Attempts to find Frank have been entirely unsuccessful. There is a Frank Way in the Las Vegas phone book, but a call to him revealed a man who hasn't been to Searchlight in many years, doesn't own a computer, and has grown very tired of the occasional phone calls he received that asked if he was the Frank Way from Searchlight. No luck there.

For all I know, this story never happened. Again, I include it because there is a dearth of "bad" stories about Willie to share. Maybe it did happen, but there is much to the story Mr. Way isn't telling. Was he a kid trying to steal soda bottles from behind the El Rey Club as a young Harry Reid once did? I would still love to know more. Maybe, Frank will find a copy of this book and drop me another line. Frank, if you're out there...a little contact information on where I can find you will be helpful.

**Everybody loved Willie. March 18, 1961,**
*Nevada State Museum, Las Vegas*
*[J. Florian Mitchell Collection]*

During my search, I found one last juicy story. Perhaps, some desert justice would satisfy a need for the tales of a seedier Willie Martello.

One man, who asked for anonymity, relayed a story to me about a rare instance of Willie Martello with a temper, almost a mean streak, toward a customer. Of course, this customer had tried to cheat the casino and I have never heard a "good" story about how a casino owner dealt with criminals in their place. It's not as though you'd ever hear an anecdote about a casino cheat being given lemonade and cookies for his efforts. I leaned forward and grabbed my pen waiting for this one.

According to the story, *"Willie pulled me aside and told me some guy was trying to pull a switch at the craps table,"* which meant the man was attempting to switch the real dice for loaded dice. The cheater was caught as he tried to swindle some of the house's cash and Willie reportedly instructed some rather large men, which included the fellow who told me this story, to grab the deadbeat gambler and take him out back *"to teach him a lesson."*

*"I don't want John* [Sheriff John Silveira] *to see this,"* said Willie. Far away from the eyesight of the law or any customers, Willie and his burly friends dragged the cheat outside of the casino. That man soon learned just what a mistake he made by trying to cheat Willie Martello in his town.

The man was forced to his knees, never a good thing to have happen if you've been caught trying to steal from a casino in the wild west days of Nevada, and awaited his fate. *"We held the guy down and Willie put a bucket over the guy's head,"* said my storyteller. He feared the worst, and the man trembled there on his knees, and his head sweated inside that pail as the nervous panting of his breath bounced back onto his face. *"Willie grabbed a 2 x 4 and began to whack the side of the bucket until the man's arms flew up and he fell to the ground."*

The man got up off the ground with a ringing in his ears and the start of a rather bad headache. Willie instructed the man to leave the casino and never return for fear of something worse happening to the swindler. *"We didn't have to do any more than that,"* laughed my informant, who admitted to me that none of them were even capable of doing more.

With that, the tale comes to an end. No bodies buried in the desert. No cruel vengeance from a cheated casino owner. This, perhaps the dirtiest of "the dirt," proves to be once again rather tame.

The fact was Willie was never once known for having a terrible temper or a mean disposition. Joyce Dickens always remembered Willie "the crook" as a fun-loving man who, while not perfect by any stretch, was friendly and good-natured. She recalled he frequently ambled along his day spouting quaint colloquialisms like, *"Keep laughin' and scratchin'"* to the customers and employees alike. She was quick to point out to me, *"I am quite sure Willie was never mean nor cross to anyone."* He was no hardened criminal, nor was he a choir boy. He simply was Willie. From what I have been able to gather from those willing to share, Willie had more dust than dirt.

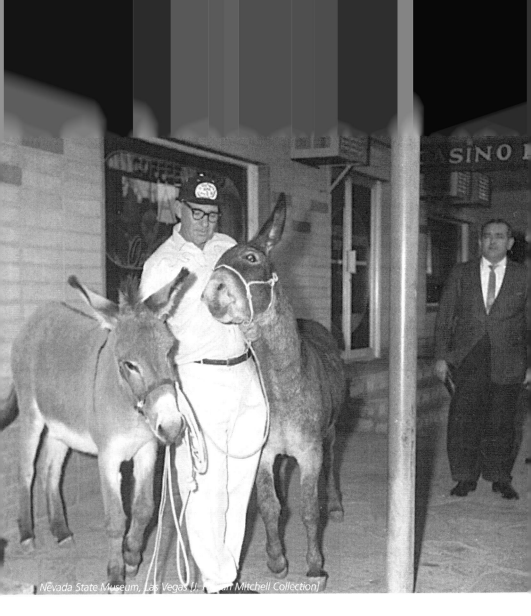

*Nevada State Museum, Las Vegas [J. Florian Mitchell Collection]*

# JACK AND JENNY

**" Willie was a wild man. There were no restrictions as far as he was concerned. Because of his dynamic personality, he was like a living magnet that could draw in people almost at will."**

That is how Jerry Schafer described Willie to me in one of our earliest conversations. It seemed the more I spoke to people who knew Martello, the more I realized this was one charismatic man. Willie indeed had a lasting affect and a magnetic personality from all accounts. However, his charms went well beyond beautiful ladies or people with whom he wanted to be friends.

Jerry Shafer called me one day a short time after our initial meeting on the phone with an odd, but charming little story. *"I don't know why I remember this, probably because it always seemed so crazy, but every day at about 11:00 a.m., a wild jackass, an actual burro, not a customer,"* Jerry laughed, *"would wander into Searchlight, down the street, and walk right in to the El Rey. People would be gambling or eating or whatever and there'd be this wild animal standing there!"*

According to Schafer, this animal wasn't lost, and the regular customers of the El Rey didn't consider it the least bit odd. You could say this wild burro actually WAS a regular customer of the El Rey. *"The donkey would walk right up to Willie and he would feed it. He always had something in his pocket to feed this thing,"* Schafer said, *"and he never got a speck of dust on his white suit!"* Nobody could recall the first time such a thing occurred, but it was a regular part of life at the El Rey. *"This burro belonged to Willie,"* according to Schafer. *"It was his burro."* After his daily feeding, the burro would wander out of the casino and back into the desert. It was just one more customer that was happy to accept a little hospitality from Willie Martello.

What seemed to be an almost mythical way Willie had with the creatures (Willie Martello: The Burro Whisperer) turned out to be a wild burro Willie had trained somewhat and made into his own personal pet. For whatever reason Willie took a liking to the ambling, dusty animal and made its presence a regular part of everyday life at the El Rey Club. Back then wild burros were common sights in Searchlight, and Willie not only took one on as his own pet but encouraged others to do the same.

Jeff Reid, Jr., cousin to Senator Harry Reid, met Willie in 1946 at the ripe old age of seven and was present at the grand opening of the El Rey Club. You could say that he was one of the first employees there as well.

Two gold prospectors from Chicago visit the El Rey and meet a local burro.
**November 12, 1961.** *Nevada State Museum, Las Vegas [J. Florian Mitchell Collection]*

*"Willie had bought a donkey named Sally,"* remembered Reid, *"He built a pen for her and named me as her caretaker."* The young Reid was charged with the task of coming out to the El Rey twice daily, once in the morning and once after school to care for Sally. *"I would feed her. I'd ride her, exercise her, he left me totally in charge of her,"* said Jeff. *"I'd be the only one she'd let ride her. Everyone else—she'd buck 'em off. I would ride Sally right into Willie's casino."*

The sight of a young boy riding a wild burro into a casino was a delight to all the customers according to Reid. *"People would want to get on her and take pictures and I'd have to hold her or she'd buck 'em off. Then they'd give me money for it,"* Reid laughed. *"I had quite a deal going there!"* Watching the people react to Jeff's way with the burro was also a joy for Willie. *"He loved it and the people loved it,"* Reid would say. He cared for Sally up until he was in the fifth grade, but he recalled it wasn't necessarily a full-time job. *"I took care of Sally for years and years, rode her all over the country,"* he said. *"But, sometimes, she'd want to escape and get real mean with me. She'd take off and be gone for a month or two. But she'd come back and I'd take care of her again."*

Tragically, Willie's wild beast met its end at the hands of a hit-and-run driver. Jerry Shafer recalled the day Willie learned of the news. *"He was furious! He grabbed his gun and set out to find the man who killed his burro."* Martello reportedly offered a $10,000 reward to anyone who could find the man who ran down his beloved burro. Sheriff Silveira had to calm Willie down and promised to find the culprit for him, though the man was long gone.

Now if this were a book about any other casino owner in any other town, the tale of a wild desert creature being drawn to the charismatic Willie Martello would end there. However, this is not a book about any other casino owner nor is this about a different Nevada town. Therefore, the burro stories continue.

Searchlight and the El Rey actually had an unusually long history with the wild burro. Jane Overy, of the Searchlight Museum, remembered some stories told to her by long-time residents and described a time when the school children of Searchlight could lay claim to their own personal equine friend. *"Every child had its own burro,"* said Overy. *"They would name them and play with them after school, but they would quit playing with them once the burros would walk into the cemetery."*

There is at least one tale of a burro ruining the grand opening of a saloon in town. The new owners had laid out a wonderful spread of food for their big day when a burro wandered into town, walked right into the bar and ate all the food. Jane told me, *"One writer said it was the worst grand opening he'd ever attended."*

Wild burros strolling into local saloons was not uncommon in those days. Some actually looked upon the bars in town as their own personal watering hole, though water was not on tap at the time. Take into account the tale of Jimmy the Burro.

Jimmy belonged to one of the families in town and this burro loved to drink. *"Every day he would go into town and hit all of the saloons,"* said Overy. *"If the miners had any money in their pockets, they would always make sure that Jimmy got some beer to drink."*

Actually, the El Rey had a burro that was more than just a regular customer. He was like family. Ethel Martello recalled one particular Christmas when the El Rey was all decked out for the holidays, including a tall, fully decorated Christmas tree. Many friends and family members were invited for a special party at the casino, and there was a little Christmas stocking for each guest. The highlights of the evening included a massive craps game as well as plenty of drinking and gambling. Among those in attendance at this gala affair was a little wild burro named Oscar. For the record, the burro had his own stocking, and he did enjoy bottles of beer along with all the guests. He abstained from the gambling.

Wild burros and the El Rey Club had something of a financial partnership according to Ethel Martello and Sharon Richardson. In an email from Sharon, *"She* [Ethel] *and Uncle Buddy used to pay the Indians to tame the burros so they could sell them,"* Richardson said. *"The townspeople complained to Sheriff John about all the noise the burros*

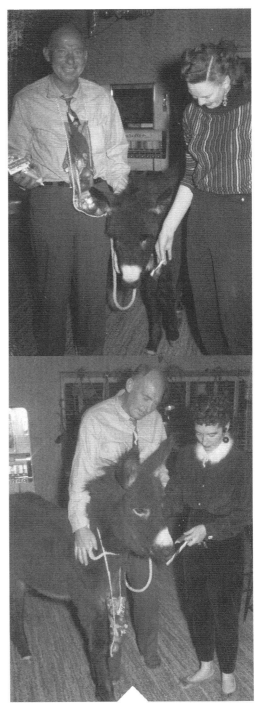

**Oscar the Burro being given his Christmas Present.** *Photos courtesy Ethel Martello*

*made all night long, so they sold the tamed burros to a guy on his way to Idaho."*

While no one recalled the name of the man who was headed to Idaho, new burros in tow, the encounters with the burro at the El Rey Club continued.

Sharon Richardson also recollected a night that involved her own mother, **Marie Blasiola** (Willie's sister), a motel room, and a wild burro. Don't get your hopes up; it is not THAT kind of story.

Marshall Sawyer, a former employee at the El Rey, was something of a cad according to the Martello family. *"My mom just didn't like him,"* according to Richardson, *"the way he would run around on his wife, bringing girls up to the club, acting like a big shot, never paid for anything – she just couldn't stand it."*

According to Richardson, one night Sawyer brought a woman from Las Vegas, who was not his wife, out to the El Rey, and Blasiola, who was there that night with a friend, had devised a little scheme to ruin Marshall's evening. *"She always denied doing this, but I was there and I SAW HER,"* recalled Richardson. *"While he was drinking with the girl, Mom grabbed a friend of hers and snuck around the club most of the night, watching Sawyer wine and dine his bimbo. After a few drinks, he took off to the motel room. She somehow got a hold of a pass key for the motel rooms and found out which room Sawyer was planning on using that night. She gave Sawyer just enough time and then she and her friend left a little present inside his room."* While Sawyer and girl were in the room Blasiola unlocked the door and placed a wild donkey inside. *"This was NO small donkey like the little beer-drinking one. It took a while before all hell broke loose. Sawyer, not a small man, chased the burro out of the room and he* [the burro] *was more than willing to leave after someone opened the door. He'd made rather a mess of the whole place. Must have scared the crap out of him! Sawyer was none too happy!"*

Wild burros are still roaming around the desert to this day. The town of Oatman, Arizona has a herd of burros that are as much an attraction to the tourists as the gift shops and the dusty trails along old Route 66. You can also frequently see herds of wild burros and our state animal, the Big Horn Sheep, roaming around beautiful Red Rock Canyon. Near Pahrump, Nevada aside from legal brothels, you can see burros roaming in much the same way you find them in Oatman. I'll refrain from making "ass" jokes when referring to the town of Pahrump.

Sadly, the days of the wild burro and the El Rey had to come to an end. Oscar, the burro that attended the Christmas party, died. No, it was not the drink or the abundance of food offered that did him in but another sinful vice that ended its life. Tobacco ultimately killed the creature. As people stopped in Searchlight to fill up their cars with gas, they emptied their ashtrays onto the ground, and the burro ate the cigarette butts.

Rather than end this chapter on a down note, I'll share with you what is perhaps the best of the wild burro stories involving the El Rey.

Finding a wild burro in the desert is truly an amazing and beautiful thing. Some desert towns, like those mentioned previously, have found ways of making their presence a benefit to the community, even a tourist attraction. However, nobody has ever found a better way to utilize the endearing nature and appeal of this gentle beast more than a certain casino owner in Searchlight, Nevada.

**Stubborn as a...burro! At the El Rey, November 12, 1961.**
*Nevada State Museum, Las Vegas [J. Florian Mitchell Collection]*

One day Sharon Richardson was driving along Highway 95 on her way to the El Rey Club. As she drew closer to the casino, she was forced to screech to a halt. *"There were these two wild donkeys standing in the middle of the road eating hay somebody left for them,"* she said. *"I didn't want to hit the darned things and kill them."* Richardson pulled off the road and into the El Rey parking lot. *"I went to grab a broom or something to try and scare them off before somebody hit them."* Willie saw her and asked what she was doing. *"I told him about these two burros in the road and asked if he'd help me move them,"* Sharon said. Willie just called out a dismissive reply to her, *"Them? Aww, that's just Jack and Jenny."* Confused, Richardson asked, *"Jack and Jenny? They have names?"* *"Sure they do,"* Willie said. *"Who do you think put that feed out there for them?"* Sharon wondered why on Earth her uncle would purposely toss feed out onto the middle of the highway, and he replied, *"They're STOPPING TRAFFIC! Nobody wants to hurt those things so they stop, pull around, and head right into my parking lot!"*

Ironically, in the days after a passerby killed one of Willie's beloved wild burros, it was the placement of two burros directly into traffic that proved to be a clever marketing tool. Perhaps, there was safety in numbers. There are many instances within the pages of this book that illustrate the innovation and ingenuity of Willie Martello. For me, that one beats them all.

The history and reputation of finding "ass" at the El Rey Club is well documented, but few have ever known about the VARIETY offered there. I said I'd refrain from making "ass" jokes when referring to *Pahrump*. Not Searchlight. No, you can't have a refund on this book.

What an ass.

Willie had a way of announcing his presence, even on the telephone. His niece described it as that of a man you should already know and should be honored by his phone call. No matter who he was calling, as soon as the called picked up the phone, he would loudly proclaim, **"This is Willie Martello!"**

She thought this was simply too arrogant for a man stuck in a nowhere town like Searchlight to think anyone would be impressed with receiving a call from Willie Martello. **"Uncle Willie,"** she asked, **"why do you announce yourself like that on the phone? Do you think anyone even cares that Willie Martello is calling? Who the heck has even heard of Willie Martello, anyway?"**

Her uncle just shot her a little smirk as if to say, **"Oh yeah?"**

He picked up the phone and began to dial, as he stared right into his niece's eyes the whole time. When the person on the other end answered, he loudly announced, **"Dorothy, this is Willie Martello! I'd like you to say hi to my niece for me."** He handed over the phone, and she took it, with a bit of nervous anticipation, only to find that the woman Willie randomly called and interrupted her day without any worry was legendary Hollywood actress **Dorothy Lamour.**

Miss Lamour was only too happy to take time from her busy day to speak with a member of Willie's family.

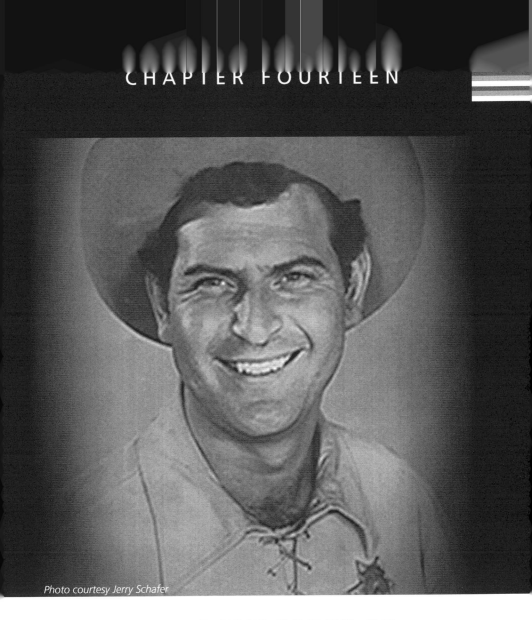

*Photo courtesy Jerry Schafer*

# PAY TO THE ORDER OF:
## JERRY SCHAFER

**Email from Bob Martello:**

| From: | "BOB MARTELLO" |
|---|---|
| To: | andy@andymartello.com |
| Subject: | willy & the el rey |
| Date: | Mon, 4 Sep 2006 10:39:40 -0500 |

Andy.... Give notice to jerry schafer and friends, if they are still out there, sign in and tell us about the movie they did at the club.

It was a fun time. And one of the first of its kind, the ladies turned up topless, wow, what a deal!!!! Shocking......There was even a story to the picture!!!

Jerry was a quick draw cowboy, stunt guy, you have seen this guy get shot and fall off buildings, he had a whole show.

erry Schafer has been a Hollywood stuntman, a quick-draw cowboy, a Las Vegas police officer, and one of the most prolific producers and directors of television shows and movies the entertainment business has ever seen.

His name has appeared in the *Guinness Book of World Records* for his fast hands with a revolver, and he has produced more live variety shows in Las Vegas than almost anyone alive. At one point, his name appeared on five separate marquees as the producer of Vegas variety shows including the Sahara, The Mint, the Thunderbird, the Lucky Casino, and the Sahara Tahoe. He even produced all the high-roller shows at the Sands. He is credited with producing the first afternoon variety show on the Las Vegas Strip (*Speaking of Girls*) and being the man to introduce Las Vegas to comedian **Frank Gorshin**. As entertainment director for the Thunderbird

Hotel, Jerry wrote and staged productions for such legends as **Judy Garland, Jack Benny, Steve Allen and Jayne Meadows, Robert Goulet, Debbie Reynolds, and Sammy Davis** among many others.

Prior to his many successes in Las Vegas, Jerry worked for Republic Studios in California, where he was one of the youngest producers and directors in Hollywood. Jerry first made a big name for himself in 1957 when he wrote and directed *The Legend of Billy the Kid*, a western television pilot which would be picked up and renamed, *The Tall Man*. The show starred **Barry Sullivan** and **Clu Gulagar** and the show's 75 episodes ran for two full seasons on NBC. While Schafer did not produce or direct any of the series for NBC, the quality of his pilot, one of the first forays into writing, directing, or producing for the young man, established him as a man who could get projects done.

While filming *The Legend of Billy the Kid,* Jerry found himself in Southern Nevada's picturesque Valley of Fire. He also did some shooting in the outskirts of a desolate town called Searchlight. At the time, he was completely unaware there was anything to Searchlight other than dust and Joshua trees. He had not yet heard of the El Rey Club or its outlandish owner. He did not meet and become a good friend of Willie Martello until late 1960.

Jerry had begun working on a script called **Wide Open Spaces.** Set in the west, this motion picture was rather daring in scope and plot by 1960 standards. He had an idea for a western comedy fantasy that involved a bashful and puritanical cowboy who fell off his horse and hit his head. When the cowboy regained consciousness, he tried to go about his daily life but discovered a rather odd end result of the bump on his noggin. Whenever the cowboy hero of the film felt any sort of residual pain from this injury, all the women around him, in fact all creatures (cows, horses, etc.), suddenly appeared as topless or completely naked women.

While this may not seem the greatest of ideas for a movie plot, the potential for great comedy was there and no such film of this type had ever been released before, which appealed to Jerry's maverick sensibilities. At the very least, the shock value of being the first film to so

**Searchlight on March 12, 1961, during the filming of Wide Open Spaces.** *Nevada State Museum, Las Vegas [J. Florian Mitchell Collection]*

blatantly parade naked women in everyday settings would succeed in gaining him some press, and more importantly, some money for more projects.

He spoke of this idea to his good friend, handsome western Hollywood actor, Rory Calhoun. Rory had just gone through a divorce and was living with Jerry at his California home at the time. Both agreed it was a daring, if not innovative idea for a film. They also assumed it was a project that would probably never see the light of day.

Willie simply loved the idea of living in such a rugged western town. He was enamored of the beauty, the fresh air, and the scenery. He kept the persona of a wealthy cowboy himself when possible and enjoyed his friendship with Rory Calhoun just as much.

Westerns were becoming the rage in Hollywood on the big screen and on television. Calhoun, who was in Searchlight visiting the El Rey and working as a guest celebrity dealer, began to speak to Willie about the popularity of westerns. It was Willie's belief he should be able to market Searchlight to Hollywood as a location for the shooting of westerns. He not only had plenty of authentic western landscape to go around, but Searchlight was not a far drive from California, and he also had a motel he could rent to the crew. Willie was certain lending his town to Hollywood would not only help bring in business and put Searchlight on the map, but would also appeal greatly to the studios. After all, having an actual western town in which to shoot would have to be better than recreating one on a Hollywood set. Calhoun mentioned to Willie he had a good friend in California who was working on a western script.

Jerry Schafer's life was about to become considerably more interesting when the phone rang at his office at Republic Studios in Hollywood.

*"Jerry, this is Willie Martello from Searchlight, Nevada,"* said the man on the phone. *"I want you to come to my town and make a movie. I'll be there in a couple of days to pick you up."* There was more to the conversation according to Schafer, but mostly of the *"What the heck are you talking about? Who the heck is this?"* variety. Once Willie had imparted to Jerry he was genuinely interested in the production of a movie, the phone disconnected and Schafer assumed he might never hear from this mysterious man again.

*"Two days later,"* Jerry said, *"a short man all dressed in white from head to toe comes walking into my office with Rory Calhoun."* Willie was carrying a satchel, which he held long enough to make his introductions.

*"I'm Willie Martello! Rory said you make movies so I'm bringing you to Searchlight,"* said Willie as he shook Jerry's hand. The men sat down in Schafer's office as Willie began to brag about his town. *"He told me he owned this town 56 miles from Las Vegas,"* said Jerry. *"He was a real salesman. He knew how to sell Searchlight* [as a location]."

Willie went on about the scenery, the locale, and the facilities his town had to offer, *"I've got a casino, a motel, a gas station..."* Willie also had that satchel with him. He didn't want to risk Jerry refusing this opportunity or understating his importance and his influence, so Willie opened the bag and emptied the contents onto Jerry's desk. *"He must have poured out about four thousand dollars worth of El Rey poker chips onto my desk. The guy knew how to end a conversation!"* said Schafer. Martello told Jerry this would serve as a partial payment if he came to Searchlight to make a movie and then invited him out to lunch. Jerry looked Willie, Calhoun, and the stack of chips on his desk up and down. Always the practical business man, Jerry had made up his mind about Rory's casino owner friend. *"I took the lunch,"* he laughed during an interview with me.

During their meal, when lunch soon turned into dinner, Willie brought a briefcase filled with photos of Searchlight, his casino, and his beautiful girlfriend, Estelle Longwell. *"What a really nice girl she was,"* Jerry said. *"He told me she was royalty. A countess. I didn't doubt him for a second."* Once all meals and drinks were consumed, Jerry agreed to fly out to Searchlight to see this town of which Willie spoke so highly.

Soon thereafter, Schafer, also a pilot, loaded up his own plane and set off to visit Searchlight and brought his friend **Dick Chapin** along for the ride. *"Willie was waiting for us when we landed on that all dirt runway of his and he couldn't wait to show us around,"* said Schafer. Willie took the men to Cottonwood Cove for a ride on his boat, showed them the scenery of the surrounding area, and of course the El Rey Club. *"I'd never known anything about Willie or the El Rey before then,"* said Schafer. *"Before I knew about it...Searchlight...if you took a deep breath while driving through, you'd miss the town!"*

Now more than aware that there was a lot more to Searchlight than abandoned mines and dirt, Schafer agreed the town and Willie's casino would make a perfect setting for his western script. However, he wasn't at all certain Willie would want Schafer around to make the movie once he found out the film's plot.

He knew Martello hoped for a film that would help put Searchlight on the map and draw in more business, so Shafer approached Willie with a little hesitation. *"I've gotta tell you something, Willie,"* said Jerry to his new friend. *"This film is a fantasy. I'm doing something that has never been done before and it may never even get released."* He proceeded to explain the plot to Willie—the cowboy, the bump on the head, the naked blackjack dealers.

*"Oh, that's GREAT!"* was Willie's only immediate reaction. This, no doubt, came as a surprise to Jerry. *"Willie, there's gonna be naked women running all around your casino,"* said Jerry. According to Schafer, Willie's reply was quite simply, *"You can have anything you'd like. Just do the motion picture here!"*

Jerry just laughed at Willie's enthusiasm. He now had a perfect location and a script. Of course, none of this meant he had any financing for the film.

Although Jerry Schafer has enjoyed a long and fruitful career in the entertainment business, he has told me many times since I began this project that he is not "a money man". The raising of cash, the finding of investors for projects like film and television shows, in his own words, *"is just not my thing."* The thought of trying to find cash for *Wide Open Spaces* back then seemed daunting, to say the least. Fortunately, some of the luck from being friends with a seventh son of a seventh son was about to rub off on Jerry.

While he visited his parents in their classic 1950s modern Baldwin Hills apartment, then a ritzy part of California, he spent some time at the swimming pool to speak with his friend, salesman **Ken Fisch**. A man named **Richard Candalaria** was with Ken, and he seemed very familiar to Schafer. *"We kept looking at each other as if we should already know each other,"* said Schafer.

When it was time for Jerry to make his exit, he mentioned he had to go back to the Clover Field Airport, now known as the Santa Monica Airport. *"I gotta fly,"* said Jerry. *"Are you a pilot?"* asked Richard. Schafer affirmed he did have his own plane and that he was a pilot. Then the realization washed over both men. *"That's where we'd seen each other before. Clover Field,"* said Jerry.

Indeed both men had seen each other before at the air field but never spoke to each other until that day. Candalaria asked, *"What do you do for a living, Jerry?"* The director explained he'd just finished writing *"this ridiculous satire"* and began to explain the outrageous plot.

Candalaria's expression remained the same, that of a man intently listening, and he asked, *"Will it make any money?"* Jerry, confident in his burgeoning production, *"Sure it will. I just need a backer first."*

Again, Richard continued his queries, *"What does a backer get out of it?"*

*"For this, a 50/50 split,"* said Jerry.

Without batting an eye, Candalaria, Jerry's newest friend, clearly stated, *"I'll back it. Do you have a typewriter here?"*

Schafer, a bit startled, told him there was no typewriter at his parents' apartment.

*"Well, I'll go to Clover Field with you,"* said Candalaria. *"I'll find a typewriter there and write you a check."*

The two men went to the airport in Santa Monica, found a typewriter, and true to his word, Richard Candalaria tapped on the keys of the typewriter to the tune of $20,000. He pulled the check out from the typewriter, signed it, and handed it to Jerry.

Schafer had just as good luck finding a second backer for the film, Israeli **Rayhavam Adie**, whom had an interest in the business of making movies. *"I never could pronounce his name correctly,"* laughed Jerry, *"so I ended up calling him Richard as well."*

Upon their initial meeting, Adie, just as promptly and with an equal amount of discussion (or lack thereof), wrote Schafer a check for just as much money. Of course, this check came with a catch or two. In classic Hollywood form, Rayhavam was hoping his girlfriend would have a part in the film. Nothing ever changes in Hollywood, it seems. Schafer agreed but, after he saw she was not quite glamour model caliber, gently suggested to Adie it wouldn't be appropriate for her to appear in the nude. Ultimately, she had a small, clothed part as a casino dealer. Since everyone wanted the film to be shot, edited, and released in a hurry, Schafer also had to concede any control over the film during his upcoming absence in England. After handshake agreements were made by Schafer and both check-wielding men, it became clear this film was going to be made!

This new genre of film, the "Nudie Cutie", had only a handful of predecessors to *Wide Open Spaces* and they all made money. Jerry and his financiers felt he had to strike while the iron was hot and get the shooting done as quickly as possible. To add to the mayhem, long before this film deal was in place, Schafer had been contracted to direct a musical comedy in London, England. He had to leave in four weeks. Jerry called Willie to let him know there was indeed going to be a movie produced in Searchlight and was pressed to get the film in the can. Willie was more than ready to accommodate Schafer's cast and crew. Now, Jerry needed a cast.

He needed at least five beautiful ladies for this film and at least three cowboys, so he held a very brief casting call. He cast the handsome **Larry Chance** as the cowboy hero who falls off his horse, as well as actors **Marcelino Espinoza** and **Lou Scarcelli**. A rather dashing Willie Martello scored a bit part as "The Pit Boss". In fact, Willie's photo appeared in *ADAM* magazine in their write-up of the upcoming film. He was described as *"a nonchalant cowboy extra."*

When it came to the ladies, Schafer cast lovely starlets like **Sandi Silver** and **Patti Brooks**. He found a blonde bombshell in the curvaceous form of one **Linda "Ginger" Gibson**.

The two most noteworthy of the movie's leading ladies had graced the pages of *Playboy* magazine. Virginia Gordon, a sultry brunette, was the Playmate of the Month for January of 1959 and had already appeared in a few films prior to this time. Marli Renfro, the stunning redheaded beauty, was not only on the iconic cover of *Playboy* in September of 1960, but she was also featured in what many considered the most famous scene in movie history. Renfro was the body double for Janet Leigh in the film,

HARLEQUIN GOES TO A
# NUDIE MOVIE

**Marli Renfro in Searchlight,
March 12, 1961** *Nevada State Museum,
Las Vegas [J. Florian Mitchell Collection]*

***Harlequin*** **Magazine story.**
*From the author's personal collection.*

**Marli Renfro, Willie Martello, and Larry Chance in the pages of** *Adam*.
*From the author's personal collection.*

*Psycho*. Though it was not accredited, any time you watched the shower scene and were not seeing Leigh's face, you were watching Marli Renfro.

In early 1961, *Wide Open Spaces* was being shot in the Nevada desert. The cast and crew were guests of the El Rey Motel, and Willie offered them all the compliments of the house. Folks traveling to the El Rey Club or to nearby Cottonwood Cove were treated to a taste of the Hollywood life as beautiful actors and actresses came to town where new locations in and around Searchlight were being used. They also caught quite an eyeful when the nude scenes shot.

The ladies of *Wide Open Spaces*, March 12, 1961. Back L to R: Virginia Gordon, Sandi Silver
Front L to R: Marli Renfro, Linda "Ginger" Gibson, and Pat "Patti" Brooks
*Nevada State Museum, Las Vegas [J. Florian Mitchell Collection]*

"*Willie was very curious about filmmaking,*" said Jerry. He wanted to know about the process of directing a movie. Of course, this may have had something to do with the five gorgeous women who were running around his club. All five women were young, beautiful, and frequently very naked. Willie was like a kid in a candy store.

It was written that "*Schafer's non-professional bit players* (meaning Willie) *behaved like true Western gentlemen in the midst of such unaccustomed nudity.*" However, this was not the case at first. He found he was particularly fond of redheads during that shoot. "*He was always trying to score with the actresses, especially Marli,*" laughed Schafer, "*but she wouldn't give him a tumble, at all!*" Jerry had to make an attempt to rein in Willie's desires.

"*I told him that this was a business relationship and asked him to stay away from the actors,*" said Schafer. The young director equated the working relationship between a director and his cast as that of an owner with his race horses. "*Willie, you wash them, you feed them, and you keep* them clean and healthy, and take great care of them, because you want them to win the race." This made for a good analogy, because not only was there a gambling element, but Jerry was on a very tight time schedule for completion of the film. The film was the race. Schafer went on, "I know these are lovely ladies, but this is business."

Willie understood Jerry's request and did not make any more plays for any of the lovely ladies of Wide Open Spaces. He even told Schafer he truly respected him for how he felt about the care of his actors. "It made our friendship that much better," said Jerry.

Shooting in the desert was not without its problems. According to popular men's magazine Adam, "The five girls chosen were unaccustomed to the discomforts of location shooting, especially in the raw. However, they cooperated without complaint."

The film shot in late winter, so the desert was rather cold and windy. Marli Renfro was cut by a piece of flying cactus during a particularly blustery day. Other scenes, including the one shot in the waters of Lake Mohave, took a toll on the actors. The Adam article asserted, "...the girls shiver apprehensively before re-entering the water, so cold it made them literally turn blue." On the last day of shooting, Ginger Gibson summed up the experience perfectly, "Thank God it's over!"

Seven days, several nude scenes, and a few cuts and scrapes from the Joshua trees later, Wide Open Spaces was in the can. The film had taken as long to shoot as it had taken Jerry to write the script. Jerry not only got his film completed on schedule in a hurry, but he also finished within the budget. He was a true professional, indeed. Of course, in retrospect, Jerry admitted he was a

**On the set of Wide Open Spaces. Left to Right: Lou Scarcelli, Larry Chance, & Marcello Espinoza.**
Nevada State Museum, Las Vegas [J. Florian Mitchell Collection]

*The Wild, Wild West has never been wilder... Beautiful babes... bashful cowboys!*

EASTMAN COLOR **TONIGHT FOR SURE!**

**WANTED**
**ADULTS ONLY**
Definitely & Strictly
An Adult Western!

Released thru PREMIER PICTURES COMPANY

MAT 103

Original newspaper advertisement
for *Tonight for Sure!*
*From the author's personal collection.*

bit green as a movie director.

*"I really had very little idea what the hell I was doing at the time,"* said Schafer, laughing. He frequently used the masters whenever possible and did not capture a second take for scene coverage. There were very few close-ups or second shots. Many of the "standard" shots and techniques that were seen and used by most Hollywood directors were of lesser importance than the timely completion of the picture. *"It was crazy!"*

Adam boasted "[*Wide Open Spaces*] *promises to be one of the funniest and most entertaining films ever to be shown,"* and added that the film was *"the funniest, sexiest film to ever come out of Hollywood,"* and *"the most hilarious horse opera ever filmed."*

The concept for the film was actually quite groundbreaking at the time. It was among the first to feature topless women in such a manner, and it utilized much of the Searchlight scenery including an old jail, a mine shaft, and Lake Mohave. *Adam* magazine laid it out for the reader, *"What makes Schafer's comedy different from previous nudie films is 1. Better looking women and 2. A funnier story."* However, Jerry has looked upon his film as being something not to include on a resumé. *"It was a FANTASTIC piece of shit!"*

**Ginger Gibson at the Roulette Table in the pages of *Harlequin*.**
*From the author's personal collection.*

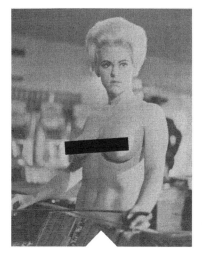

**Ginger Gibson in the pages of**
***Harlequin*.**
*From the author's personal collection.*

**Ginger Gibson horsing around in the pages of**
***Adam*.** *From the author's personal collection.*

**Renfro in the pages of**
***Harlequin*.**
*From the author's*
*personal collection.*

**Jerry Schafer directs his**
**cast, March 12, 1961**
*Nevada State Museum, Las*
*Vegas [J. Florian Mitchell*
*Collection]*

125

Jerry's original script did have its action as well as some interesting twists, not the least of which was the film's ending, filmed in beautiful Lake Mohave. To get away from all of the nudity, our hero, Larry Chance, was accused of lunacy because he saw naked women everywhere and decided he would travel to the middle of the lake for a fishing trip. This was an attempt to remove his "curse," according to the film. However, even the fish in this movie popped up as beautiful naked women as he soon found out after he reeled in a busty babe on his fishing line. When hysteria set in, his boat capsized and he found himself surrounded by beautiful, naked swimmers. After that, our cowboy hero awoke in bed in 1961 and wondered if he had dreamt the entire affair. Instead, he found all those women were with him in his room.

While the film was certainly titillating and entertaining, it was not the film for which Jerry wanted to be known. *"I was so new to the business,"* recalled Jerry, *"I was so eager, I would have done anything to make a film."*

This work, later renamed *Tonight for Sure!* by the time it was released, was not the film for which Jerry would be known. In fact, his name was misspelled as **"Jerry Shaffer"** in the credits. Plus, he was only credited as a writer. His name didn't even appear on the poster or other advertising even though he wrote and directed the film.

*Tonight for Sure!* gained a certain amount of notoriety and publicity. Released in the States on October 25, 1962, it certainly caught the attention of all the major men's publications ahead of its release, which earned the film pictorials and articles throughout 1961 in such publications as *Adam, Modern Man,* and *Hi-Life.*

Interestingly, the October 1961 issue of *Modern Man* not only listed the film as being titled *Meet Me at the Harem,* it also made the film seem so scandalous it doubted it would ever be released, a clever tactic to market the film and guarantee better attendance.

Once it was out into the world, it did get some decent write-ups from the press. *"I remember that a newspaper writer named Paul Coats wrote an article about the film after he saw it. The title of the article was: 'Billy the Kid Sings; There's Nothing Like a Dame,'"* said Schafer.

However, the appearance of the topless women during the birth of the nudie cutie, the *Playboy* Playmate, and the presence of Janet Leigh's body double were not what ultimately made this film shot at the El Rey Club one

**Promotional photo from *Tonight for Sure!* Promotional photos for magazines are believed to be shot by J. Florian Mitchell, but were largely uncredited in all publications.** *From the author's personal collection.*

that would be discussed on the internet and among film geeks for decades to come. No, there was at least one other noteworthy name associated with this film. One only needs to read the poster for the film or make one stop at the Internet Movie Database website to find this film is listed as the directorial debut for one **Francis Ford Coppola**.

Yes, you read that right. THE Francis Ford Coppola. *The Godfather, The Outsiders, Apocalypse Now*—THAT Francis Ford Coppola. I was as shocked as you when I discovered this little fact. How on Earth was it possible that this film could be the directorial debut of one of the world's most acclaimed and respected filmmakers?

Upon completion of the film, Jerry packed his things and prepared to rush off to London. His departure was so quick that only *Adam* listed Jerry Schafer as the director. By the time *Modern Man* covered the film a few months after *Adam*, their article stated, *"Producer-director Francis Coppola took over the entire town of Searchlight, Nevada for two months of shooting shapely mammaries,"* even though Coppola never set foot in Searchlight.

But how did Coppola become involved, at all?

The man Jerry had initially hired to edit the film and prepare it for distribution took ill and Jerry was essentially already gone. Producer Rayhavam Adie, whose name changed to **Ray S. Adiel** in the film's credits, had full control over the film. *"Once I was on my way to England, I had nothing more to say about it,"* said Schafer. Adie told Schafer he knew of a bright young kid from UCLA that showed real promise as an editor and suggested he take over the job of putting the footage together. *"I took a look at his reel,"* Schafer commented, *"and I was impressed."* That bright young kid was Francis Coppola.

Though Jerry never met the young man in person, *"I hired Coppola to edit the film and the rest is history,"* according to Schafer. Mr. Coppola, however, remembered it differently.

Coppola described this movie and his involvement only a few times publicly and included a brief mention on the Bravo television series, *Inside the Actors Studio.* In an email sent to the movie film buff website, ambedextrouspics.com, the Oscar-winning director had this to say:
*"Tonight For Sure was a job to combine the short film The Peeper into a film the distributors had but couldn't release (that I had nothing to do with) called The Wide Open Spaces. I used footage from both, and this became Tonight for Sure."*

*The Peeper* was a film that also featured Marli Renfro. It was about a man who snuck peeks into store windows as the ladies' mannequins were being undressed and redressed. Set in an urban city, he also fantasized that the mannequins came to life and also entertained sexy dreams about the shop girl. Since he had done some work with the great **Roger Corman**, Coppola knew if you made some films with a little naughty appeal, those projects could make enough money to pave the way toward having a chance at a much bigger project. Coppola's email to ambidextrous.com continued:
*"I made a short 12 minute film called THE PEEPER. We tried to sell it, and the only buyer had this* [black and white] *western about a cowboy who kept seeing cows as naked girls. It was un-watchable, so they bought our short, and gave me $500 to intercut it and some connecting footage to salvage their effort. When I had the titles made, I was so thrilled to see my name on a film that I myself had it say 'Directed by Francis Coppola'. In fact, I was the editor and had made the original short about the man eavesdropping on the photo session."*

A couple corrections must be made. First off, *Wide Open Spaces* was not in black and white. What survives of Schafer's film is vivid color and

starring

DON KENNEY · KARL SCHANZER

featuring VIRGINIA GORDEN · MARLI RENFRO

SANDY SILVER · LINDA GIBSON · PAT BROOKS

and LINDA LIGHTFOOT

Produced and Directed by FRANCIS COPPOLA

Released thru PREMIER PICTURES COMPANY

**Poster artwork for** *Tonight for Sure!* **The first time Coppola's name would be listed as the director for a major theatrical release.** *From the author's personal collection.*

does actually showcase a lot of 1961 Searchlight. Next, although a minor point, this film was not about a man who saw cows as naked women. In response to Coppola's comments, Jerry Schafer jokingly quipped, "*There weren't cows in the film. We were lucky to have enough money to pay for the horse!*"

I do admire a man who has achieved so much in the entertainment business admitting to almost a childhood sense of glee at the thought of seeing his name in lights and taking credit for a movie he didn't make. I'm sure far more people in show business with lesser careers than Coppola have taken credit for another person's work. Though his actual filmed contribution to *Tonight for Sure!* was about 20 to 30 minutes, young Francis saw his opportunity and made a few changes to the finished product.

He hired his father, **Carmine Coppola**, to write the musical score for the film. Among the cast of *The Peeper* was actor **Bill Freed**, a man best known in the movie business for playing Adolf Hitler twice, most notably in the B-movie cult favorite *They Saved Hitler's Brain*. Some of the other changes included changing the main setting for the film to a burlesque house and the addition of a few working burlesque stars of their day. This quite likely made this the only Coppola film to have a cast with names like **"Exotica"** and **"Electra"**.

**Larry Chance falling off his horse, as seen in the pages of *Adam*.**
*From the author's personal collection.*

Coppola also had to completely rewrite the story, finding a way to make some sort of sense out of the two films. He shot additional connecting footage and removed all of Schafer's dialogue and storylines. Ultimately, the plot for the new film was completely convoluted, oft times bordering on slapstick. The film comes complete with cartoon-like "boings", "pops", and "whistles".

Instead of a simple western tale full of bar fights and prison breaks (and a fair amount of naked women), viewers at theaters witnessed the nonsensical tale of two puritans who loathed nudity and debauchery so much they went to a burlesque house to get drunk. They watched the nudity (to reassure themselves they didn't like naked women) and then blew up the building together. All of the footage from both Schafer's and Coppola's films were seen as flashbacks. Much of Jerry's action finale in the lake was cut out. Instead of actual dialogue, much of the film, especially when set in Searchlight, was narrated with a bad voice-over.

Among the things most upsetting, at least to me, was the near complete omission of the many scenes at the El Rey Club. Fortunately, the finished film had two complete scenes inside the club that offered the tiniest glimpse of the interior of the casino and one scene that featured Willie, festooned in his cowboy attire. You can still see some footage of Lake Mohave and the former Searchlight prison. Otherwise, it simply wasn't the film Jerry intended to make.

If Jerry's film was *"unwatchable,"* this new film was unforgivable.

With all this in mind, the film did make a fair amount of money. Nudie Cuties were still new and fascinating. Theaters were eager to release mainstream movies with beautiful topless women. The film became an international success and earned more press within the pages of *Fury* and *Harlequin* magazines (*Harlequin* featured some of the only full-color images) when it was released in Japan in 1963. It was released on West Germany television under the title *Nackt im wilden Westen*.

Somewhere between Schafer's account and Coppola's account of how the Academy Award winning director became a part of this *"Rootin' Tootin' RAWHIDE REEL,"* and ultimately El Rey Club history, lies the real story. I tend to believe Schafer's memory of events is the more correct version. After all, Schafer had less to lose than Coppola in the production of a scandalous

**Virginia Gordon in the pages of Harlequin.**
*From the author's personal collection.*

**Virginia Gordon and Larry Chance in the pages of Adam.** *From the author's personal collection.*

NOW FILMING

**"Wide Open Spaces"**

a feature-length wide-screen color movie by independent producer Jerry Schafer.

Watch Scenes being
shot this week at

WILLIE MARTELLO'S
**EL REY RESORT HOTEL**

Searchlight
Nevada

picture like this one that was only shown in the pussycat theaters of their day. With Coppola's later career assuring him a place in movie history, it would be he who would have to frequently explain himself. After all, he was the producer and director of *Tonight for Sure!*

Jerry never minded being essentially cut out of his own film. He actually viewed it as an honor to have Coppola involved and something of a favor to have his name erased from the record books.

In fact, Schafer has written, produced, or directed hundreds of films and television shows. Of course, you would never know it if you did a search for his name at the IMDB. I asked him how he felt about the fact Coppola took credit for his film and why no one could locate a better listing of the work he has done over the years in Hollywood. Jerry simply smiled and replied, *"Do you have any idea how many people have taken credit for my work or simply have not given me credit, at all? The only place I really want to see my name is when it follows the words, PAY TO THE ORDER OF!"*

Jerry continues to succeed in the entertainment business. While he travels internationally, to this day, he lives in Las Vegas and is always writing, filming, or editing another project.

When he said he had nothing to say about the film after he finished shooting, he wasn't kidding. In fact, he only had reason to think of it at all a few times since he completed the project, the most recent of which was when I put Jerry in contact with Jane Overy of the Searchlight

Museum. He agreed to speak at the 110th birthday celebration for the town of Searchlight in October of 2008 and regaled the audience with many fantastic tales of Willie, the El Rey, and the odd little movie he made. After another introduction on my part, he would tell these stories again to Robert Graysmith as he researched his future best-seller, *The Girl in Alfred Hitchcock's Shower*. Should Jerry ever need an agent, I think I would make a good one for him.

Prior to that he spoke in Searchlight once to discuss the movie, only back then, it happened after he had returned from England. Willie wanted to start the promotional machine quickly so the world would know about the major motion picture that was shot at his club in his little town. While back in Hollywood, Schafer received a phone call. After hearing the typical, *"Jerry, this is Willie Martello,"* Willie invited him back to the club. *"He wanted to place ads in the newspapers announcing that Jerry Schafer, the big-time Hollywood producer, was going to be at the El Rey to gamble,"* laughed Jerry. *"He even gave me money to play with and act as a shill!"* Jerry remained good friends with Willie until Martello's death in 1968.

The only other time Schafer would be called upon to remember anything about the *Wide Open Spaces* would be when he opened a letter from me back in 2006. I took Bob Martello's email assignment urging me to track down Jerry Schafer to heart and was fortunate enough to hit pay dirt on my first attempt. Jerry was gracious enough to contact me the very same day he received my letter and we have been friends ever since.

As it turned out, he had never seen the film he made back in 1961. He had no idea how it turned out or how the great Francis Ford Coppola had approached his editing assignment. Having had such good luck in finding Jerry, I set a goal to find a copy of the film.

I found at least one place that was selling the title. **Something Weird Video** specialized in hard to find, outrageous movie titles. If it is exploitative, campy, horrific, or tasteless, the odds are you will be able to find a copy, and that's where I procured my own copy of *Tonight for Sure!* I purchased a few copies on VHS and sent them to Bob Martello and Jerry. I never heard from Bob regarding his opinion of the film, but I almost immediately heard from Jerry. Since this chapter started out with the email from Bob, I think it is only fitting to end it with the email I received from Jerry. I like to think of this as the best review any film will ever receive.

| From: | "Jerry" |
|---|---|
| To: | andy@andymartello.com |
| Subject: | Re: Check Your Mail! |
| Date: | Thu, 07 Dec 2006 09:39:33 -0800 |

ANDY.....
I received the "video" and looked at it (well some
of it) last night....

I was appalled....Holy Mother of Christ, that was
the worst piece of shit I have ever seen!

As you know I had never seen it.....God how awful.

Thankfully my name as writer is misspelled and not
on the production credits at all.  I didn't write
one word that was spoken in that ridiculous piece
of shit.

I see, or at least I think I see what Francis was
trying to do by putting the two stories together
but he elected to omit the dialog from my film
altogether.

Maybe that was a blessing too.I tell you I couldn't
watch the whole thing.

As I remember, my film was 1,000% better on its
own.....that's not to say that it wasn't a piece of
shit too, but at least it was good shit....
as you know, there's good shit and bad shit....that
thing is bad shit...REAL BAD SHIT!

It's hard to imagine that the fellow who put that
together went on to become a famous director....
it's almost inconceivable.....but, after the smoke
clears away I remain a Coppola fan and always will
be.

The one thing that touched my heart was to see Willie again in the Casino scene. God he was something wonderful, a man amongst men. Always smiling, always having something good to say, always ready for anything.

Again, I thank you for your kindness. I appreciate the trouble you went to sending me the video.

I wish you a happy holiday and continued success and, I hope that in some way I will be able to show you some reciprocity.

Jerry Schafer.

Since my luck was so good while I was conducting this research, maybe, some of that Martello luck will come my way as I attempt to find the original print of the film and restore Jerry's original film for all the world to see.

**Marli Renfro along the shores of the very cold Lake Mohave, seen in _Fury_ magazine.** *From the author's personal collection.*

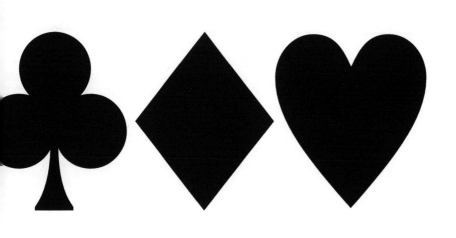

In a dusty town located 57 miles southeast of Las Vegas, an old rusty truck sat on the top of a hill near the city limits. It had been there for as long as anyone could remember, while it absorbed some of the dust from the town and made it a permanent part of its overall appearance. Finding an automobile like this was not uncommon, though generally a sight like this one would also be accompanied by a "FOR SALE" sign somewhere on the windshield, something that was clearly missing from this scene. The truck appeared to be in disrepair, possibly incapable of operating at all. People drove past the vehicle on a daily basis and wondered if the thing would even start. Those who lived within the town remembered times when they saw it running. As they motored past the four-wheeled relic, they all had the same thought that very truck itself would have had if such a thing were possible: **"God, I hope we never have to put that to use again."**

This is not a thought one should have when gazing upon a town's only fire truck.

# ACT I:
## THE TRUCK ON THE HILL

A fire in the desert is not an uncommon thing, but it still raises some concerns. The desert is arid, hot, and filled with dry tinder, making it a prime location for devastating wildfires. Placing a resort or a casino in the middle of a desert, a place that conceivably could be filled with thousands of people at any given time, many of whom are drinking or simply not paying attention to their own behavior, makes the thought of a fire breaking out that much worse. Las Vegas has had more than its fair share of fires, both inside casinos and out.

During the time I have lived in Las Vegas (since mid-2007), there have been at least three significant fires in the Las Vegas Valley. The first occurred on January 25, 2008 when the top of the **Monte Carlo Hotel and Casino** caught ablaze after molten slag from a workman's cutting torch ignited the stucco foam facade of the building. Thankfully, nobody was seriously hurt in the incident, but 17 people were taken to the hospital for smoke inhalation. In just over an hour's time, the fire was extinguished.

In 2010 and 2013, thousands of acres of the beautiful mountain resort land of **Mt. Charleston** were hit by fires. The first and smaller of the two fires was most likely started by careless campers and the second was ignited by lightning. Again, no serious injuries were reported, but the immediate and unpredictable nature of fires in the desert threatened to permanently change not just the landscape, but the lifestyles of many Las Vegans.

Of course, these are not the only fires to hit Las Vegas.

On February 17, 2003 my wife and I were resting comfortably in the **Aladdin Hotel** in Las Vegas before it became the **Planet Hollywood**. That night we watched the horrifying news reports of the **E2 Night Club** disaster in Chicago, our former home town, where 21 people were trampled to death as they tried to exit the club. I performed and worked events at that very club and recall how we always thought the layout of the club lent itself to potential dangers. My wife and I cozied up for the night in our plush accommodations only to wake up to a considerably more local news story on our television sets. While we slept, a few floors above us, a fire broke out in a laundry chute at the Aladdin, the result of a discarded lit cigarette. The 22$^{nd}$ and 23$^{rd}$ floors of the building were evacuated and several people were treated for smoke inhalation, but nobody was killed. By the time we were fully awake, the incident had been over for a few hours and it was business as usual at the Aladdin. Fortunately, this potential tragedy was averted.

Notably, the second worst hotel fire in U.S. history happened in Las Vegas on November 21, 1980 at the **MGM Grand**. There were 700 injuries and 87 deaths as a result of the inferno. Close to one billion dollars in damage was reported, and countless lives were changed forever. Less than three months later, a fire started by a lit marijuana cigarette at the **Las Vegas Hilton** took the lives of eight people.

Significant fires have been reported in Las Vegas casinos as far back as 1943 when the **Meadows Hotel and Casino** went up in smoke. One historic building, the **Moulin Rouge**, actually burned three times throughout its long history. Once in 1955 and again in 2003 when it was nearly totaled. By May of 2009, the Moulin Rouge was claimed totally by yet another conflagration. Las Vegas icons such as the **Sahara**, the **Sands**, and the **El Rancho Vegas**, as well as modern Las Vegas structures such as the **Stratosphere** and the **Palace Station** all became victims of fires at some point in Nevada history.

In a town as large and in command of as much money as Las Vegas, it makes perfect sense that a fire, even one as massive as the one that destroyed the MGM in 1980, would be unlikely to destroy the town. Fires would leave scars, but Las Vegas would ultimately survive. A town like Searchlight, however, had a much greater risk of being wiped away entirely should a fire occur. As it turned out, Searchlight saw its share of devastating fires, and as a result, the debut issue of the short-lived

From the *Las Vegas Review-Journal*, April 8, 1947

## Searchlight Asks Better Fire Wagon

Fire protection for the town of Searchlight was discussed Monday with the county commissioners.

R. E. Franklin and Jack Fisher, members of the town board, requested that the town board be allowed to purchase one of the surplus property fire trailers in California.

Said Franklin: "Anything we might get would be better than what we have now. The present equipment is falling apart. A wheel came off the fire truck the last time we went to a fire."

The board instructed Franklin to look into the possibility of purchasing one of the surplus property vehicles and report back to the board. There is enough money in the Searchlight town fund to allow such a purchase, it was reported.

Franklin said that as soon as the new water tank can be connected up so there will be water available for the fire fighting apparatus, that a volunteer fire department will be organized.

*Searchlight Journal* newspaper had plenty to write about on August 29, 1946.

When it came to Searchlight's need for fire prevention, it appeared the town had more of a flair for dramatic irony than it did for taking appropriate action. For example, I offer what retrospectively seems to be a wholly ironic news blurb: the April 8, 1947 issue of the *Las Vegas Review-Journal* wrote about Searchlight's desperate need for better fire equipment. This plea for better fire equipment came *after* one of the largest fires in Searchlight history and soon *before* another fire destroyed the town's most historic building. By the time the El Rey Club met a fiery end in 1962, it seemed little had changed in the quality of the town's ability to extinguish a blaze.

The April 1947 article reported town board members **R.E. Franklin** and **Jack Fisher** met with Clark County Commissioners with a request to allow the town board to purchase a surplus property fire trailer from the state of California. The story titled "Searchlight Asks Better Fire Wagon" reported Searchlight did indeed have the money to make such a purchase and the County Commissioners instructed Franklin to *"look into the possibility... and report back to the board."*

Franklin testified to the commissioners that a volunteer fire department would be formed as soon as the new water tank could be hooked up and ready for use with the existing firefighting equipment. What did he have to say about their existing truck? *"Anything we might get would be better than what we have now. The present equipment is falling apart,"* Franklin reported *"A wheel came off the fire truck the last time we went to a fire."*

The "last time" Franklin was referring to was not even a full eight months prior when the town of Searchlight was nearly wiped off the map by a suspected arsonist's blaze.

At approximately 4:45 a.m., Sunday morning, August 25, 1946, Searchlight awoke to a most startling sight and a horrific inferno. A man by the name of **Ralph E. Stewart**, awakened by the smell of smoke, ran out of the building completely nude in order to sound the town's fire alarm. Stewart was employed by **Fred Cobb** as the night watchman for Cobb's **G.I. Building**. It was an old military base building that was transported to Searchlight in the hope it could find a permanent home as a new two-story hotel (complete with barber, bar, and confection accommodations) in October of that year.

The first to arrive on the scene were the owners of the town's only grocery store, **Ray L. Scheffer**, along with his wife and son who all lived in a residence inside the store. The Scheffer family, who had been selling groceries to Searchlight residents for seven years, had barely enough time to gather clothes and some contents from their safe before their business and home was razed by the fire. A man by the name of **J.B. "Babe" Collins** and his wife drove up to the Union Bar to find Deputy Sheriffs **John Silveira** and **George Morgan**. Everyone who saw the blaze and sprang into action.

Deputy Morgan ran to get the town's fire truck, an *"antiquated 150 gallon Model A Ford"* according to the description reported to the *Searchlight Journal* newspaper. Deputy Silveira turned his attention to Lloyd Allen's El Rey Club which was, *"almost immediately threatened and simmering from the heat."*

It was believed the fire started in the south end of the grocery, but other reports claim it began inside one of the town's night clubs. It rapidly raged out of control and ultimately claimed three buildings. Among the businesses lost in the fire were Scheffer's grocery store, the **Miners Club** owned by **"Madman" Pizinger** and **Lee Mitchel,** and the **G.I. Building**. Fred Cobb never saw his hotel come into fruition. The Scheffers were certain insurance would not cover the total loss and felt they might not rebuild. Neither of the owners of the Miners Club, which had gone up for sale a few months prior, were available for comment in the wake of the blaze.

Things seemed suspicious from the beginning. Eyewitness accounts reported several smaller fires that broke out prior to the massive blaze that claimed the three businesses. This suspicion was later proven to be true. The historic Nevada Hotel was also affected by fire that week. In fact, in the four days BEFORE the big fire, no fewer than four small fires within the walls of Searchlight's most

Volume 1, Number 1

**nday Fire Levels Three Buildings**

Townsemen Battle Blaze With Antiquated Equipment

re of an undiscovered origin pletely demolished three dings in the main business k of Searchlight early Sunday ning.

ie grocery store owned by L. Sheffer and adjacent two- y GI building and the Miners owned by "Madman" Piz- r and Lee Mitchel were razed ie ground while tireless work partment coupled with a change

of the entire assembled popula- tion. The Union club, directly adjacent, seemed hopeless of sal- vation and the furnishings were removed into the street. A con- crete block wall between the two buildings and the efforts of towns- men and fire fighters in removing part of the burning roof of the Miners club may be given credit for the fact that it is standing. Questioned after the fire which razed the three buildings to the ground at 9:00 a.m., the Sheffers

The debut issue of the *Searchlight Journal.*
From the author's personal collection.

historic building were reported by the *Searchlight Journal.* The fifth fire at the Nevada happened on August 25. All of the fires including the big fire, started at approximately the same time of day and caused much suspicion among the townspeople. Upon the discovery of the hotel's fifth fire that week, the *Searchlight Journal* reported *"a greasy pair of trousers were reported to have been found smoldering hopefully in the oncoming dusk."*

An arsonist was soon hunted by Searchlight residents. A report in the August 25 *Las Vegas Review-Journal* stated a guest of one of the Searchlight lodgings, **Velda Simpson**, spotted *"a suspicious looking character lurking around the Oasis Club."* Velda Simpson attested she was certain some sort of highly combustible material had been spread throughout the buildings before the fire started, and cited the rather explosive manner in which the buildings erupted into flames.

Though I've found no subsequent news reports that named an arson suspect, a manhunt began in the town. The *Review-Journal* reported, *"The town became almost an armed camp as pioneer residents took up a search for the guilty party."* During the mayhem, at least two robberies were committed, the work of opportunistic looters. One man, **Wendell Fred Shore,** was captured at a camp near Davis Dam a short time after the fire and charged with stealing $350 in silver and two guns from **Bud**

Jackson's Union 76 service station.

Regardless of who started the blaze, there was certainly one unwilling accomplice that aided in destroying the buildings and businesses of Searchlight that morning: the inadequate, decrepit fire equipment. That same truck, the one with the bum wheel, was called upon to make feeble attempts to extinguish the fire. From the *Review-Journal*, ***"Fire prevention equipment appeared helpless in the face of the inferno."*** The *Searchlight Journal* also wrote that a town suffering from such a fury of flames in one week caused the citizens to sleep ***"with one eye open and a bucket of water by the bedside."*** If only that were true, perhaps, the townsfolk would have been able to provide more water than the rickety old fire truck.

While the labored and useless equipment bravely attempted to spray even the smallest amount of water, the people of Searchlight, residents and guests alike, were the real heroes of the day. Perhaps, the best description of the efforts put forth by citizens of the town were noted within a headline of the debut issue of the *Searchlight Journal*, ***"Everyone Worked."*** To quote that column, ***"In a matter of minutes, the entire town was aroused and, almost to a man, bustled about the task of removing furniture, bars, tables, and accoutrement to the streets."*** The *Las Vegas Review-Journal* wrote, ***"Hundreds arrived on the scene. The leader of which was Sheriff John Silveira."*** Protected only by a wet blanket, the Sheriff frequently entered the burning buildings and retrieved equipment, liquor, and other valuable belongings. He took a shovel and scattered desert dirt onto sections of the burning building when the thin stream of water that emanated from the outdated fire equipment was not sufficient to quell the blaze. Silveira also suffered injuries when panes of red-hot glass cracked and fell directly onto him. Other reported injuries included those to "Babe" Collins who ***"blistered the entire length of his right arm."*** Two other unnamed men reportedly briefly succumbed to ***"over-work and smoke"*** while they fought the blaze.

Countless townspeople and patrons of the businesses came out to aid the fight, including owners of competing businesses in town. According to the *Searchlight Journal*, ***"Although there is a natural competition between rival businesses, such feelings were forgotten in the stress of the emergency and it mattered not who was carrying whose luggage into safety."***

Even folks who were only in Searchlight as paid performers turned out

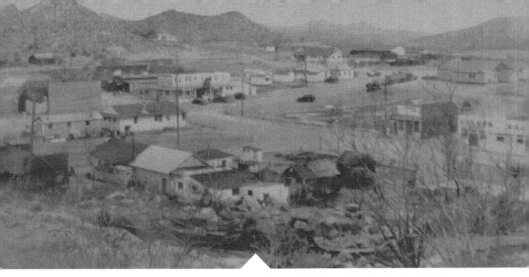

Perhaps the only known image featuring the Golden Eagle and the Union Bar & Casino (far right), circa 1946-47. Notice the charred vacant lots next to the Union Bar—the results of the first Searchlight fire.

*Photographer unknown. From the author's personal collection.*

to extinguish the inferno. According to the *Review-Journal*, **"Night club entertainers joined with the citizens generally in a feeble attempt to control the flames."** This report was confirmed by the *Searchlight Journal* when Searchlight's Justice of the Peace, **"Mac" Meginness**, also on-hand to aid in extinguishing the fire, offered commendation to one very brave guitar player, Jack Perkins, who was not playing at the El Rey, but at the Golden Eagle on that night.

The *Searchlight Journal* described the fire as having **"swept from the GI Building through the grocery store and consumed the Miners Club."** After the damage was done, the wobbly fire truck went to rest upon a hillside outside of town. Though three buildings were destroyed by the blaze, it certainly could have been much worse. The Union Bar and Casino faced potential loss. It sat adjacent to the Miners Club and only a large concrete wall that separated the two buildings protected the operation from demise that morning. The Nevada Hotel, though certainly damaged, survived the morning's conflagration and remained in business.

No matter how bad the fire prevention equipment was, at least one building claimed to be saved by the Model A with the bad wheel. That building was the El Rey Club. Saving the El Rey was about the only bit of heroism the truck saw. Two things contributed to the successful rescue of the El Rey: the valiant efforts of the people on-hand and a strong westerly

**Thursday, February 10, 1949**     Las Vegas Review-Journal **3**

# Nevada Hotel, Famed Searchlight Landmark, Razed by Night Fire

From the *Las Vegas Review-Journal*, February 10, 1949.

wind. Again, from the *Searchlight Journal*, *"The building smoldered and burst into flames several times but a vigilant fire hose was victorious and the damage was to a serious scorching of the building side and an upheaval of the Masonite flooring."*

Nine weeks later, the editor of the *Searchlight Journal* newspaper, **H. E. Mildren**, wrote about that truck *"It looks tired and defeated. Its battery is probably worse than tired."* He continued, *"It doesn't seem logical for a town to have a fire truck that has to run down a hillside to get a start for the fire."*

Mildren pointed out the truck had remained on that hill ever since the fire felled the heart of the Searchlight business district. *"Someone might at least take the truck out for a ride now and then just to limber up the grease and to remind the dilapidated old rascal that it has to be ready at all times."* The commentary by Mildren seemed to be an ominous warning to Searchlight and promoted wonder about what would happen if that rusty old truck was called into service again. Just a couple of short years later, in 1949, they would find out.

On Wednesday, February 9, 1949, the town of Searchlight again lamented the loss of its history and possibly more revenue needed to keep the town afloat. The Nevada Hotel, the town's most historic building, fell victim to a midnight fire. Built in 1900 by Bill Kennedy, the hotel was one of the few multi-story buildings in town and was one of the last remaining relics from Searchlight's historic gold rush days.

The mysterious fire started somewhere in the upper story of the building according to Searchlight Justice of the Peace **Molly Kay**. It was reportedly condemned and unoccupied during the time of the fire, but available evidence suggested that gambling was still a regular part of the Nevada in 1949.

Again, the efforts of the volunteer fire department in town were nothing less than heroic. In a *Review-Journal* story from February 10, 1949, *"the walls of the old structure crumbled in the blaze despite valiant attempts by the community's volunteer firemen to save it."* Thankfully, through their efforts, not only was nobody injured, but there was no subsequent damage to surrounding buildings. However, it was the quality of the firefighting equipment that lead to the demise of the Nevada.

The Searchlight fire truck made another trip up the hill and brought with it more hope that nobody would need call upon it for use any time soon.

With at least three significant fires in its history, it is surprising to read more accounts about the *need* for better equipment as opposed to the *purchase* of better equipment in Searchlight. Much has been written about Searchlight and its completely inadequate fire protection. The most powerful was an editorial comment by **Berta Sherman**, the local news editor for the *Searchlight Journal* in that premier issue on August 29, 1946. As ironic as the aforementioned *Review-Journal* article from April 8, 1947 was, the commentary by Sherman proved as much tragic as it was ironic. In reading the following excerpts from her column, you learned Searchlight had set a precedent of doing too little too late regarding fire prevention prior to the devastating fire of 1946.

*"The manner in which firefighters were forced to battle last Sunday exposed the negligence and lack of foresight that may be placed directly in the laps of those who are responsible for the welfare of the town – THE CITIZEN! Will citizens limit themselves to discussion or recognize the immediate need to act? There is, in view of past emergencies, some question.*

*"Some time ago, J. Bonocchi, war veteran and surplus material authority, suggested that the firefighting equipment, definitely inadequate, could be changed by the purchase of a military fire truck. The objections voiced at the time were in regards to cost. The price paid in the early Sunday morning tragedy will be a topic of discussion for some time.*

*"A community is just as strong as the citizens that live therein."*

Even though the town of Searchlight claimed it had the money in 1947 to purchase new equipment, I have been unable to find any record the town made such a purchase. That rickety old truck could not save Searchlight from harm in 1946 and could not perform adequately in 1949. After the loss of the Nevada Hotel, to the best of my knowledge, that same battered, 150 gallon Model A Ford sat on that hill for a long time and waited for its next assignment.

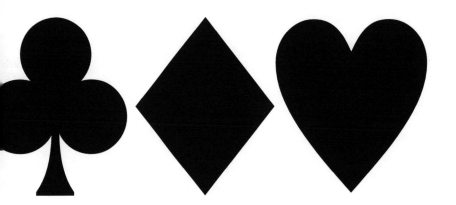

"**W**illie had a way of letting you know he just couldn't be bothered by any of your nonsense. Sometimes, it would just be a look, a telling look that was designed to say, '**Get this bum out of here.**'

Other times, he'd get caught in a bit of a mess. Almost trying to hold back laughing at himself, he held this frustrated smirk, and his face would say to you, '**I know already. But YOU'D better not know. Don't say a word!**'

If I ever had a problem, or what I thought was a problem at such a young age, Willie would ask me what was wrong. As soon as I'd start to tell him what was bothering me, he would make an instant judgment as to just how big of a problem I really had. If it wasn't worthy of his time or if it wasn't what he considered to be a problem, Willie would just stop me and dismiss me by saying, '**I don't want to hear about your ice cream cones!**'"

- Sharon Richardson

Photo courtesy Nevada State Museum, Las Vegas [J. Florian Mitchell Collection]

# ACT II:
# WILLIE'S ICE CREAM CONES

B y the 1960s, things were hopping at the new and improved El Rey. With the grand opening of the larger and friendlier El Rey Lodge (also known as the El Rey Resort & Casino) a few years behind them, the Martellos were celebrating a substantial increase in the numbers of patrons. Regular events such as Hawaiian Luaus, live entertainment from some of the biggest acts in the business, and world class dining provided by Chef Luigi Scirocco were only a few of the things that enticed people from all parts to see what the little town of Searchlight had to offer.

Hollywood movies were being filmed in the mining town and at the little casino that could. It was not uncommon to find celebrities playing or performing at the El Rey. Rory Calhoun was a frequent visitor at the club and starlets Diane McBain and Sherry Jackson, as well as the son of Hollywood icon Errol Flynn, would make appearances. Bob Martello spoke of times when even Rat Pack members Dean Martin and Frank Sinatra were seen sitting at the bar or enjoying a little time at the tables.

In the spring of 1961, Willie Martello proudly advertised his new airport runway in Searchlight. Guests from California could fly for free to Searchlight, Nevada and enjoy a "Champagne Flight," receive meal and gaming vouchers, and partake of all of the newly-provided tourist amenities such as the fishing and boating that were available at nearby Lake Mohave or the Indian petroglyphs found in the serenity of Christmas Tree Pass. When the vacationers and gamblers completed their time in town, Willie flew them back to California free of charge.

Searchlight was now a genuine tourist attraction, a viable, albeit smaller alternative option for the gambler and tourist. Whether you wanted to make the trip into Las Vegas or not, you were likely to make a stop in Searchlight. Some people simply stopped in to see the intricate mural commissioned by Willie depicting Searchlight's rich mining history. Bob Martello told me in an interview that the El Rey brought in an estimated two to five million dollars in revenue per year. Bill Moore of the Hacienda later said to me, *"If they were admitting to at least two million or more, you could bet the amount was likely much higher."* The town had the efforts of the Martello brothers, especially Willie, to thank for this new success. At one point, there was talk about rerouting historic Route 66, possibly allowing it to wind its way through Nevada, specifically through Searchlight. This thought provided Willie fuel for even larger plans within Searchlight.

Willie Martello had not only become the face of the town, he was the honorary mayor and was frequently seen as the kingpin of Searchlight. Much of the property in Searchlight was owned by a Martello. By 1962, Willie owned the Texaco service station, the Oasis Hotel, the Crystal Club, the Desert Club, the El Rey Casino, the motel, and the new airport runway, in

**Petroglyphs at Christmas Tree Pass.** *From the author's personal collection.*

addition to other properties and businesses. When the stationery for the Searchlight Business Men's Association went out, it listed Willie Martello's name as the president. When a phone call was made in the town of Searchlight, the call was made on a phone system established largely through Willie's efforts. On the surface, it seemed as though Willie Martello had it all.

The reality was Willie was deeply in debt.

**One of the only images of the mining mural at the El Rey Club. Pictured are Angelina Martello-Neese and Ben Neese (Willie's Brother-in-law).** *Photo courtesy Sharon Richardson.*

**Searchlight Business Men's Association letterhead.** *From the author's personal collection.*

Often, Willie would have to deal with thieving dealers, when he could find someone willing to come to Searchlight to work. *"They had him over a barrel and he knew it,"* according to Sharon Richardson. However, a few sticky-fingered blackjack dealers were not Martello's only money concerns.

According to Martello family member Ed Darling, the construction of the massive runway cost Willie an estimated $1,000,000 of his own money. The fuel and maintenance of the airplanes used to bring guests into town fell upon Willie's shoulders. Those flights were free to everyone but Martello.

Willie poured countless dollars of his own money in the town of Searchlight over the many years it took fully remodeling the El Rey Club. Sometimes, he paid two or three times for the exact same deliveries and supplies. As his club and his efforts to create a tourist destination to rival neighboring Las Vegas grew, certain people in Vegas began to take notice. *"When Willie wanted new glass windows for the club,"* recalled Sharon Richardson, *"most of the time they never even made it to Searchlight. Guys from Vegas would put out an order to get shipments stopped or to have the glass delivered to Willie in shards."* The story was the same when Willie attempted to bring in new flooring, paint, furniture; anything that would make a noticeable improvement to the club would end up as a financial burden for Martello.

In addition to occasional court appearances to fight for his gaming license, Willie was often involved in

**Marie Blasiola, Willie, Lucy Morano and "Aunt Sis" behind the El Rey Club.** *Photo courtesy Sharon Richardson.*

a variety of law suits. Among them was a personal injury suit filed against Willie in May of 1960. The suit alleged that a **Jesse Schultz** and her husband **Edward** of Phoenix, Arizona stopped in at the El Rey when their bus passed through town. Mrs. Schultz fell and injured her arm, hand, ankle, and foot, claiming the El Rey Club was *"negligent in maintaining carpeting at the entrance of the women's restroom."* Suits like this one in addition to court appearances for grievances from vendors, writs of attachment, and other legal woes peppered Willie's life and placed a toll on his bank account. Not including issues involving his gaming license, my research showed at least eight times where Willie or the El Rey Club was named in a law suit between 1957 and 1961.

Willie frequently owed money to many different people. When he wasn't gambling or wooing his many lady interests, he was trying to improve the El Rey. Sometimes, owing money and attempting to improve the El Rey Club were one and the same.

*"We rented a house to Willie in the early days,"* said **Donna Andress** in an interview with me where she related her and her husband **Gail's** time with Willie. *"Every month we had to track down Willie for the rent money. Every month."* Donna further described a typical encounter with their gregarious tenant. *"We had just installed a new oil heater into the property we rented to Willie,"* Andress said *"On one of our regular trips to find Willie and collect rent, Gail went to the house and found the heater was gone. Gail went to the El Rey to try and find Willie, and when he did, he not only found Willie but found the brand new oil heater had been installed into the El Rey Club!"* When he was caught with the goods, Willie offered to let the heater cool down and bring it back to the home himself. According to Andress, her husband Gail wisely said, *"I'll just sit here while it cools off and I'll help you."* It bears mentioning that, when I heard of this exchange, Donna was laughing and said in a good-hearted tone, *"That was Willie! What could we do?"*

Throughout the history of the club, Willie often had to rely on friends to act as business partners just to keep the club open, his creditors at bay, and money flowing in. At one point, **Junior Girard Cree** applied for a gaming license on behalf of the El Rey. In 1960, the *Review-Journal* reported the death of a California man, **Ted Bernhardt**, in a car crash. This same article also listed Bernhardt as a co-owner of the El Rey Club. In 1962, a lawsuit was brought against Willie by a **W. Roger Barnard** who claimed

**The VIBRANT El Rey Resort prior to the sale.**
*From the author's personal collection.*

he owned three trust deeds on the El Rey properties. That same suit listed Marshall Sawyer as an investor in the club. Sawyer himself held two trust deeds on the property in a deal signed by Martello in 1961. It was clear Willie had plenty of money problems.

*"He was willing to do whatever it took until the dream was realized,"* according to Sharon Richardson. *"Every dime he made went right back into the club."* Harry Reid would describe Willie as *"always in debt,"* while Bob Martello would have a different take. *"Unlike Harry Reid's account, Willie was NOT always in debt. Willie simply never really made a penny from his efforts there. It all went back into that town."*

In an attempt to keep all he had created up and running long enough for him to help realize his even larger dreams for Searchlight, on January 14, 1962, Willie announced the sale of the El Rey Club and all his financial holdings in Searchlight to the First Capital Development Corp. of Reno, Nevada. The sale price was a reported 1.5 million dollars, with approximately $800,000 of that value in the El Rey Club and the remainder in his nearly 400 other

# Martello Reveals Resort Sale

Willie Martello announced yesterday that he is selling his El Rey Club and all other holdings in Searchlight for $1,500,000.

From the *Las Vegas Review-Journal*, January 15, 1962.

lots and properties. **Lyman Oliver** and **Anthony Frisone** of First Capital signed the agreement on behalf of the Reno firm and First Capital would, in turn, agree to assume all of Willie's debts other than personal taxes.

While it seemed Willie Martello would soon be gone from his beloved city and casino, he remained the operator of the El Rey Club. Willie continued to run the casino while he waited for the sale to go through. Martello's gaming license continued to be used while First Capital Development Corp. awaited approval for new gaming licenses. As it happened, he ran the El Rey Club only one week longer.

On the evening of January 21, 1962, as a lone prostitute made her way into Searchlight, the sound of men trying to start a rickety old fire truck could be heard in the distance.

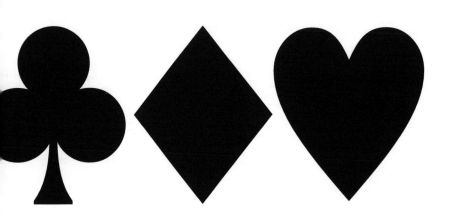

On January 22, 1962, a prostitute, new to the town of Searchlight, emerged from one of the rooms at the El Rey Motel. She had heard good things about the cash available to a girl who was willing to spend a little quality time with strangers in Searchlight and came to town where she hoped to find some action.

She was absolutely glowing with the excitement and satisfaction of knowing she made the right decision. After all, the night before she met a man of obvious charm, but what was more obvious to her was that this guy had MONEY. Her new client had spent most of the entire evening with her and was more than happy to pay her well for her services and showered her with many black $100 poker chips from the El Rey Resort & Casino. She must have earned thousands of dollars that night from this one man alone.

Soon after she exited from the man's El Rey Motel room, she went up to the cashier and wanted to know where she could cash in her fortune.

**"Lady, you aren't cashing those things in for shit. The El Rey burned to the ground last night."**

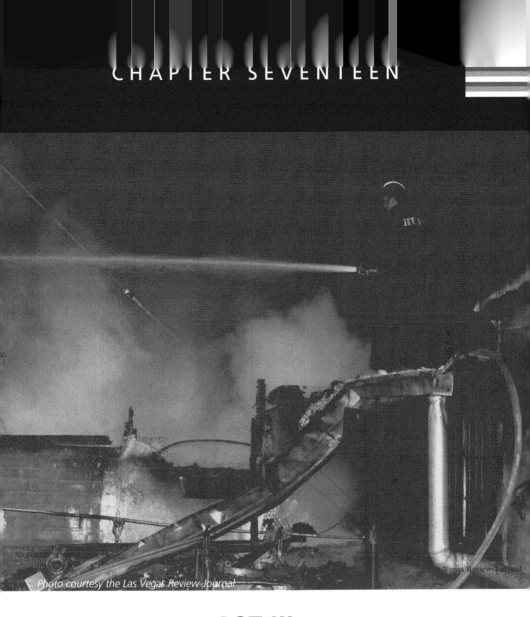

Photo courtesy the Las Vegas Review-Journal

# ACT III:
# GONE IN 90 MINUTES

J anuary 21, 1962 was any other Sunday at the El Rey Club. There were probably 150 people or more who had turned out to enjoy a night of fun and frolic. The crowd included five planeloads of people who flew in from California, according to Bob Martello, who was there that night managing operations for his uncle Willie alongside manager **Joe Speranza**. Regular patrons and good friends of Willie Martello, Ted Enoch, of South Gate, California's Enoch Chevrolet and Searchlight Judge **Jack Dillon** were there enjoying the comforts of the El Rey Club. Willie, the ever-present figurehead of the town and now *former* owner of the El Rey, was on-hand to entertain his guests and visit with friends. He was unsure of his future and took in another of his customary long nights. Willie looked visibly tired as he ate his steak dinner and posed for J. Florian Mitchell's camera.

As always, the bar and the gambling attracted the patrons and promised a night full of fun. After all, the El Rey had been known as THE place to drink or gamble in town for 15 years. Those not interested in either of those vices so familiar to Nevada may have been enticed by the lure of live entertainment. The night before, the star of TV's *The Bob Cummings Show* (aka *Love that Bob*), **Bob Cummings,** was in the crowd to check out a fancy new electronic keyboard called a Chamberlain. The idea behind his visit was because he hoped to invest in the production of the instrument. Past weeks showed customers enjoying the sensual allure of Sally Rand or the vaudeville comedy of **Mousey Garner**. No matter who was on the bill you were almost guaranteed to hear at least two bands, a "Las Vegas Show," and "Dancing" as so many advertisements for the club had promised. On this night, the headlining act was none other than the fabulous DeCastro Sisters and a seven-piece ensemble called the Tony Lovello Revue.

**Willie's last supper.**
*Nevada State Museum, Las Vegas [J. Florian Mitchell Collection]*

**Willie and an unnamed gentleman mere hours before the El Rey burned to the ground.** *Nevada State Museum, Las Vegas [J. Florian Mitchell Collection]*

Tony Lovello, largely recognized for generations as the greatest accordion player in all the world, described the act to me *"We had a six week contract there. Our review had seven members, two girl singers and five musicians. We put on three shows a night and the girls made five to seven costume changes per show."* The Tony Lovello Revue consisted of singers **JoAnn Conti** and **LaVonne Lovello** (Tony's wife), **Artie Stevens** (Joe Veronese remembered the name as **Art Toscano**) on string bass, **Joe Veronese** on drums, British tenor sax player **Barry Kaye**, and guitar player **Kenny Laursen,** who was noticeably unshaven for their first set.

The Tony Lovello Revue. Left to right: JoAnn Conti, Kenny Laursen, Barry Kaye, Tony Lovello, Artie Stevens (Art Toscano), Joe Veronese, LaVonne Lovello.
*Photos courtesy Kenny Laursen.*

*"Our show was the one of two groups playing the El Rey that week. We had played the first show and I had gone back to my room at the motel to shave,"* recalled Laursen. *"That afternoon I had driven 60 miles to Las Vegas to pick up dates for Barry Kaye and me. An accident had caused car travel on the highway to move very slowly and I arrived in Searchlight just in time for the show."* Nearly being late for a show was the least of his concerns.

*"We were off stage and they* [the DeCastros] *were on at the time,"*

recalled Veronese, *"and we were just sitting down to dinner."* While the DeCastro Sisters played their set and members of the Tony Lovello revue scattered to take their break, Bob Martello, working the casino pit, recalled a commotion emanating from the kitchen. At approximately 8:00 p.m. the chef came out, visibly upset and sweating, *"There's a fire in the kitchen,"* he told Bob. Unfazed and not wanting to cause alarm, Bob casually replied, *"There's ALWAYS a fire in the kitchen. Go put it out!"*

*"After the first show went off, I went to the kitchen to see if we could order a couple of hamburgers,"* said Lovello. *"I was surprised to see that there was a grease fire already going up the hood."*

The chef ran back out less than 30 minutes later to find Bob, *"There's a BIG fire in the kitchen!"*

*"I could tell it was a blaze,"* said Lovello of the fire. *"I ran out and told the girls to get to the dressing room as quickly as possible and throw everything out the dressing room window."* Fearing the fire could rapidly become worse, he knew it was time for everybody to start making an exit from the club. *"Needless to say, I told the band to not ask questions, get the band stand, and pack up now."*

*"As I put the lather on my face,"* said Laursen, *"the drummer, Joe Veronese, pounded at my door yelling that the club was on fire. I grabbed a shirt, wiping shaving cream as I ran."*

Laursen would continue to describe what appeared to be an otherwise normal night at any other club or casino. *"The other group was in the middle of their first show. People were drinking and gambling,"* he said. The fire spread rapidly in the kitchen, unbeknownst to the customers in the casino. *"Suddenly, a large bubble appeared in the paint of the ceiling above the middle of the casino,"* recalled Laursen. *"It was as if someone were inflating a balloon. It grew to about 5 feet across."* Soon, the paint bubble reached its maximum capacity and, *"as if it had been stuck by a pin, it returned to its proper place."* An eerie, smoky sigh emerged and echoed throughout the casino and accompanied the band who was still playing on stage. Veronese and Laursen ran to the dressing room.

Kenny Laursen continued to describe the frenzy to me. *"The building was concrete block construction with windows that had cranks to open and close. We opened two of them and started passing instruments, cases, and costumes out the window to another band member who stacked them up by the pool area. After we had removed everything, we*

Joe Veronese (L) and Kenny Laursen (R).
*Photo courtesy Kenny Laursen.*

Kenny Laursen in 1961.
*Photo courtesy Kenny Laursen.*

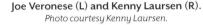

*went back into the casino and told our dates to leave the casino."* In spite of everything, the other band played on.

Kenny went up to the stage and subtly told one of the band members what was happening in the casino. *"About that time, someone from the pit came up to ask them to announce that the customers were to calmly exit to the parking lot."* Joe Veronese remembered a representative from the El Rey Club asking, *"Could you give us a hand clearing the place? We've got a little bit of a kitchen fire,"* which proved to be an understatement. *"We started to ask people to leave. We all headed in different directions toward different tables,"* said Veronese.

According to the *Las Vegas Sun*, Joe Speranza was the first to notice the fire and the first from the El Rey Club to begin leading the guests outside. Judge Dillon is credited with sounding the fire alarm.

*"Pit bosses were gathering up the money and asking the folks to leave the casino,"* recalled Lovello. Kenny Laursen confirmed, *"Security then came up to the stage and herded everyone out the front door."* Tony Lovello remembered, *"It was very orderly as they filed out."* As orderly as it was, not all of the customers were happy about their situation. *"I'll never forget the look on one guy's face,"* said Veronese. *"He had just handed the dealer a hundred and the guy dropped it when we told them he had to leave."* Veronese continued, laughing, *"The dealer handed him some chips and he took off!"*

*"Flames from the brick and wood building soared high over the small desert community,"* wrote the *Review-Journal* of the blaze. From as far away as the Railroad Pass Casino located just outside of Henderson,

Nevada, smoke and flames were seen by **Ethel** and **Buddy Martello** who were driving in from Las Vegas to start their night time shift. *"We saw the smoke and we just knew it was the El Rey,"* recalled Ethel. The couple increased their speed and hoped to arrive in time to put out the blaze. Kenny Laursen described the scene outside. *"The fire spread to more than half the roof area."* Joe Veronese recalled. *"Just about the time we got everybody outside, we looked back and the whole roof was in flames."*

*"Just across the street there was a gas station. We were standing out in front of it,"* said Veronese. The Tony Lovello drummer noticed there were no flames emanating from the back of the El Rey. *"I told Kenny the back part's not burning. I oughta go back, bust that window and get our stuff."* Against everyone's better judgment, Laursen and Veronese went to the back of the casino and noticed the back window was open. Joe Veronese crawled through the open window and began to shove equipment outside to Kenny. After successfully moving the equipment and clothing out of harm's way, the realization something had been left behind fell over them. A string bass and an amplifier were still inside the building. Veronese remembered Art, the bass player, asking if they could retrieve his string bass. According to Laursen, *"Joe climbed through the window into the pitch black dressing room and opened the door to the stage. That's when the lights went out,"* said Veronese. At that point, a massive swell of fresh air rushed into the burning building and let out a loud, thunderous sound. *"The concussion was tremendous,"* said Kenny. *"Kenny said, when I hit the wall across the room, my feet were on the ceiling,"* laughed Veronese.

After the booming blast of sound had subsided, Kenny called out to his band mate from outside the open window. *"I yelled for Joe and got no answer."* Kenny crawled through the window and hoped he would find Veronese but feared the worst. *"I found him barely conscious, lying on the floor. I dragged him to the window, lifted him upright, put his head and shoulders over the window sill, then lifted his legs up and shoved him through the opening,"* said Laursen. *"I could hear glass breaking and things crashing inside the casino by now and didn't waste any time following Joe out the window."* The two men walked across the street to safety *"just as the Searchlight Volunteer Fire Department pulled up in an ancient fire truck,"* according to Laursen.

*"It must have been at least 10 minutes before the one fire truck arrived,"* said Lovello. *"By that time, the whole building was engulfed in*

*flames shooting up about 50 feet high."* Almost everyone on the scene made attempts to aid in extinguishing the fire, including a bucket brigade of twenty prospecting miners from Chicago who were in town on an excursion to find gold. One man was seen standing on a ladder wielding nothing more than a garden hose.

**Prospectors from Chicago.** *Nevada State Museum, Las Vegas [J. Florian Mitchell Collection]*

While it sounds comical to think a garden hose would be sufficient to quell such a blaze, that hose provided a raging torrent compared to the equipment the fire department was using that night.

As in previous incidents throughout Searchlight's history, it was not the bravery of the Searchlight Volunteer Fire Department that was lacking. It was the condition of the antiquated and inadequate fire prevention equipment that was the story on this night. Judge Dillon said, *"The volunteer fire department, 'did a good job',"* but ultimately, *"the fire was too big to handle."*

The *Nevada State Journal* reported, *"Low water pressure hampered the efforts of the firemen."* Kenny Laursen, now safe with his friends, watched the action and said, *"They* [the fire department] *leaped to the street and dragged hoses from the truck to the front of the casino. The end of the hose was connected to the hydrant on the corner; a fireman with a wrench turned the valve and the hose began filling with water. Leaks were squirting water the entire length of the hose resulting in a weak two foot dribble."* Tony Lovello commented on the performance of the hydrant and hose. *"I was standing there watching the fire department trying to put out this hot fire with just a trickle of water."*

As people watched helplessly outside and waited for fire trucks from Boulder City, Las Vegas, and Needles, California to arrive, someone from the Searchlight Fire Department called out for more water pressure. Kenny Laursen remembered the event well. *"The hose was attached to the fire truck and another short hose from the truck to pump water* from the hydrant. On command, the engine revved up and a huge bulge worked its way to the end of the hose." Laursen later described that bulge to me

Las Vegas Sun headline, January 22, 1962.

as *"a scene from out of a Tom & Jerry cartoon,"* though Joe Veronese felt watching the Fire Department was more akin to watching the Keystone Kops. Laursen said the hose began to swell and grow, not unlike the bubble in the El Rey's ceiling paint he'd seen moments before. *"The pressure was so strong that it blew the nozzle off the end of the hose."* Joe Veronese remembered, *"The nozzle went right through the front window."* Adding, *"That brought a round of applause and laughter."* As the nozzle from the town's fire hose flew off into the distance, the El Rey Club became fully engulfed in flames. *"We just stood there and watched her burn. There was nothing we could do,"* said Veronese.

A lone figure of a man could be seen near the building, standing on a ladder, garden hose in hand. It was a feeble attempt to fight a raging fire with equipment at hand, but it was only marginally better than that of the town fire department. Kenny Laursen and Tony Lovello remember walking toward the ladder to discover the man in the smoky shadows was Willie Martello. According to Laursen, *"As the roof collapsed, Willie climbed down from the ladder with bitter resignation."* Willie's only remark...

*"Piss on it!"*

*"I will always remember Willie and his famous line at the time of the fire,"* said Lovello. Willie walked away from the ladder and noticed Tony Lovello and Kenny Laursen standing there. *"He asked if we were all right. I said, yes, and he told me to come see him tomorrow."* Soon thereafter, Willie walked away and headed toward the motel. Bob Martello stayed on the scene and guarded the motel as he sat up and kept looters away, shotgun in hand.

Eventually, fire engines from Las Vegas and Boulder City arrived. They contained and extinguished the fire, but the damage had already been done. While the El Rey Motel was unharmed, the El Rey Club, the casino, the café, Buddy's precious gun collection, the mural, the swimming pool, the memories, and all the hard work that 15 years' worth of love and dedication had built was gone. The fire razed the El Rey in just 90 minutes.

With the fire out and smoking coal left behind, the old fire truck made its way out of town and once again took its rest upon a Searchlight hillside.

A photo on the front page of the *Review-Journal* the next day summed it up in the first two words of the photo's caption: ***"ONLY EMBERS."*** The photo shows one of Searchlight's brave and valiant volunteer firemen standing on top of the remains, continuing to fight the blaze, ironically, with a full stream of water flowing perfectly through the hose. However, the remainder of the caption echoed what the people of Searchlight knew, not only that night but back in 1946 and 1949, ***"The stream looks strong at the moment, but low pressure has been indicated as a serious difficulty which hampered Searchlight volunteer firemen who tried to control the blaze."***

Tony Lovello and company returned to meet with Willie the next day. *"We walked into the still smoldering rubble,"* said Kenny. *"We found a burnt piece of name plate from our Fender Bassman amp and the peg from the bottom of the string bass. The slot machines had all melted into blobs of metal and silver."*

When they found Martello, *"He paid me for that week and wanted to pay off the entire contract,"* said Tony in an astonished tone. I asked Lovello about this as I was a bit shocked. As an entertainer myself, I'm very familiar with stories of club owners looking for excuses NOT to pay an act. Tony told me Willie's response was, *"I pay my people!"* Tony admitted to me he turned down Willie's offer to pay off the six week contract in full. *"I felt he had enough problems."* Willie was grateful for the gesture and promised that he would rebuild the club and invite the Tony Lovello Revue back to perform.

Miraculously, there were no injuries reported during the fire and evacuation of the building. The *Review-Journal* reported, *"Patrons had adequate warning and reached safety without difficulty."* Of course, nobody knew the terrifying tale of Kenny Laursen and Joe Veronese nor were they aware there was, in fact, one significant injury.

Buddy Martello, who arrived on scene with wife Ethel, started fighting the fire immediately. He hurriedly climbed a ladder and attempted to spray water onto the casino. During the confusion, he fell from the ladder and injured his leg but continued to try to fight the fire. Bob Martello remembered, *"We didn't see Buddy for a few days after that, and we were very worried about him. When he returned, we found out that Buddy had no idea his leg was actually broken."*

Along with the painful injury to Buddy's leg, I found out that another member of the Martello family carried a pain with him for nearly 50 years as a result of the fire. One man truly believed he was responsible for the disaster.

When I first began corresponding with Bob Martello via email, I had to tread carefully. The only knowledge any other Martello had of my interest in the El Rey was my childish interest in the prostitutes and the gambling. I frequently had to prove to him I wasn't just looking for "dirt." When Bob invited me to speak with him on the phone for the first time, I was convinced I'd have one shot to speak with him before everyone expected me to leave him and his family alone. By the time Bob and I were actually talking on the phone, I had a firm belief Bob knew I was truly interested in much more than whores and poker chips.

I had neither hopes nor expectations I'd hear tales about insurance fraud or other scenarios taken from the pages of a movie script about mobsters in Vegas. However, I did have questions. As with any casino fire, there were investigations into the cause and rumors of illicit plans for financial gain. When you consider Willie's recent announcement about the sale of the El Rey just one week before the fire, it is certainly fair for people to ask questions. In our first actual conversation, I simply asked Bob to tell me about the fire. I never expected him to be so open and honest with me right away.

*"Don't get your hopes up, kid. It wasn't that exciting,"* he said, laughing a little. Since I had only known him for a short time, I was rather taken aback by his next response. He sounded confident and vibrant all through the discussion, once he realized I wasn't a nosy jerk. Yet after that initial comment, his voice became noticeably quiet and reserved. After a pause and a deep breath, he spoke again. *"I was there, you know,"* Bob said. *"Willie had me out there often learning the ropes, running the business, taking care of his place. That night I was watching the place while Willie was relaxing with his friends."*

Though it was uncertain if it was a simple grease fire that got out of hand or faulty wiring in the lights that were strung throughout the kitchen that started the fire, he confirmed the fire began in the kitchen. He even laughed as I did when he recalled telling the chef, *"There's ALWAYS a fire in the kitchen!"*

*"When the chef came out to tell me it was a BIG fire, I went back there to see what the heck was going on,"* Bob said *"The fire had gotten out of control almost immediately. It was already into the flue. There was so much smoke."* He mentioned how dry and dusty the Mojave Desert could be and told me fires just smell different in the desert than they do anywhere else. According to Bob, the smell of the smoke in the kitchen was just awful, worse than any other smoke-filled room.

*"I got back there and saw that the fire extinguisher had already been used up. It was so difficult to breathe,"* Bob told me, *"I had to do SOMETHING."*

The fire quickly spread into the ceiling of the kitchen, and smoke was billowing everywhere. While it was probably already likely the fire was fully out of control, Bob had hoped he could contain the situation before it was too late. A flurry of coughing and mild panic was in the air along with that awful-smelling smoke. *"The back of the El Rey kitchen had these two metal doors with crash bar handles on them,"* Martello said *"I ran toward them and pushed them open as hard as I could. I thought I was helping, but it turned out to be the worst thing I could have done."*

When the doors were opened, a rush of fresh air entered and a loud whooshing sound as the outside air flooded the room and fanned the flames. *"I was trying to clear the smoke. Instead, I created a massive fireball,"* Bob reluctantly told me. *"It was over. The fire got into the ceiling, into the walls; it grew so fast."* Following that, evacuation of the guests and employees began.

*"I never had the heart to tell Willie about it. About what I had done,"* said Bob with shuddering breath. He took a long pause, cleared his throat, and told me, *"I've never told anyone this before."*

At the time, Bob had not heard about Joe Veronese reentering the building minutes later and had no idea a similar event had caused even more air to flow into the already burning building. He truly believed he was the reason the fire went out of control, when in reality, it was already too far gone by the time he opened those kitchen doors. Considering how dry the tinder was and how quickly a grease fire can spread, it was probably too late by the time the fire extinguisher had run out.

I took a moment before I said anything to Bob. As I began to speak, Bob regained a little bit of composure and said, *"That was Willie's place. He loved that club."* Another long passage of silence followed before I spoke.

*"Bob,"* I said, *"you do know that you were in a desert and the wood was extremely dry. You didn't start the fire and you didn't destroy the club. You were trying to keep from choking to death on smoke. ANYONE would have done the same thing. Anyone."*

*"I know,"* he said, *"but that was Willie's life. I should have been able to save it for him. I always thought I did something wrong. I could have done more to keep it from burning."*

Bob Martello circa 1960s.
*Photo courtesy Bob Martello.*

*"In the desert? With no working fire extinguisher or water?"* I asked him.

Bob emphatically said, *"YEAH!"* He then took a pause as if to listen to our last exchange in his head again and began to laugh. *"Yeah."*

I relayed to him some of the stories I'd heard about that night from Kenny and Tony, and he very quickly came to terms with the fact he'd been carrying guilt for no reason other than the fact he felt so badly for his uncle. *"He was just heartbroken. He wanted so much for that town."*

The entire town of Searchlight felt the sting of losing the El Rey. **Harley Harmon**, a member of the Clark County Licensing Board made a plea on behalf of Willie and the El Rey to allow Martello to move his operations into the Crystal Club across the street. Up to that point, it had been used mainly for storage. Remarkably, the Board agreed to waive close to $2000 in liquor and gaming fees for moving to a new location just to allow Willie to remain in business. The reason, in the words of Harmon, *"If you close the El Rey, you kill Searchlight."*

The *Nevada Star News* reported that an estimated $100,000 in checks and cash was lost that night. A piece in the *Reno Evening Gazette* quoted Martello as saying the fire represented a total loss of $800,000. He also stated it was fully insured. However, with the closing of the sale of Willie's property now in question, Martello's secretary commented to the *Review-Journal*, *"she did not know of the insurance status of the destroyed building."*

There were many questions in the aftermath of the devastating fire. The *Review-Journal* wrote, *"Martello, who fought the fire last night, was sleeping late today and could not be reached for comment."* What Willie did next was a topic on everybody's mind. Sharon Richardson recalled asking her uncle this very question sometime after the smoke had cleared. *"What am I gonna do? I'm going to live in Mexico and grow elephant garlic. That's what I'm going to do,"* insisted Willie.

Header artwork from Ray Chesson's **"Big Hearted Town on a Bald Headed Mountain."** *Originally appeared in the Nevadan, February 16, 1964.*

Richardson, in disbelief, asked, *"Garlic? You're going to raise elephant garlic? Come on, Uncle Willie, what are you really going to do?"*

*"I don't know. I can't really tell you what I'm GOING to do."* With that, a wicked grin took root on Willie's face, a look many in town and in his family knew all too well. *"But I can tell you what I already DID."* Sharon leaned in to hear of Willie's fire recovery plan. Willie began to speak, grinning the whole time, *"Last night, after the fire, I met this woman who'd just hit town. A hooker. She'd thought she could score big in Searchlight and found me. She scored big alright. I took her to the motel and spent the night with her. Paid her off with $100 chips from the El Rey!"*

The town's newest and possibly last prostitute never noticed the face of the man she'd spent the night with was on every one of those poker chips.

**A sampling of poker chips, all featuring Willie's picture.**
*From the author's personal collection.*

"Well, there are still plenty of things to do around here. There are still people left in Searchlight. They didn't all leave town when the El Rey Club burned.

I stopped in the Oasis to see who else I could talk to. Things were quiet in the Oasis. There was one customer, a man named Phil. Scoop was behind the bar.

'**When are they going to start rebuilding the El Rey?**'

Scoop looked at Phil. Sometimes, the natives are reticent. One has to dig for facts.

'**Next week?**' I prompted.

Scoop nodded. '**Next week.**'

'**It's going to be a big place, isn't it?**' I asked.

'**VERY BIG,**' Scoop said. '**They're going to pile up material on both sides of the road and keep going until it meets overhead. The highway will run right through the middle.**'"

Ray Chesson,
From The NEVADAN
"Searchlight Miners Shoo Camp Cooks From Stove"
Sunday, March 18, 1962

# BEST LAID PLANS

Some may have seen Martello's selling of his property in town (especially the El Rey Club) as an act of desperate survival by a man troubled with financial woes. While others probably saw the business transaction as a calculated decision by the town's most creative and crafty entrepreneurs. *"He was always thinking about the next big thing,"* said Sharon Richardson. *"The 'Willie Wheels' were always turning."* It seemed others who paid attention to news and listened to some of Martello's own self-promotion knew to ask the question, *"What's he got up his sleeve?"*

This book has pointed out ways Martello was innovative and revolutionary, but many could argue those ideas were simple extrapolations of ideas found at competing establishments and only seemed extraordinary when they were put into the context of small town Searchlight. What Willie had in mind firmly placed him among the true visionaries in Nevada gaming... if only his plans had materialized.

The sale of the Searchlight property was not necessarily the result of Willie's financial problems. For years, even before the complete remodeling of the El Rey in 1957, Willie had been planning his largest endeavor yet. He wasn't merely working to remodel the El Rey. He wanted to remodel the entire town of Searchlight.

This idea may have originally spawned from a meeting with a potential investor. Jerry Schafer spoke of a friend of his, **Bill Fiorito** (also Fio-Rito), who took rather a unique interest in Searchlight. Fiorito was related to workout guru **Vic Tanny** and, reportedly, had a stake in the famous Vic Tanny Health Clubs.

He had come out to the town with Schafer on one occasion and simply

From the *Las Vegas Review-Journal*, January 23, 1962.

**Sale of El Rey Completed Despite Ashes**

Sale to a Reno firm of the Searchlight El Rey Club—burned out casino and all — was completed late Monday several hours after the casino went up in smoke.

fell in love. He had the money to play around with and a new idea in his head, so he asked Jerry if Willie was willing to sell Searchlight. *"He wanted to buy the town,"* said Schafer in an interview. *"Willie pretty much owned the whole town, and Bill wanted to buy it from him."*

Schafer knew Searchlight was Willie's life and doubted he would sell it, but he told Fiorito, *"Everything is for sale. It can't hurt to ask."*

Fiorito approached Willie in the hope of making a major investment in Searchlight. *"Come up with a number,"* said Bill. Willie let Fiorito know he would consider his offer, but not before he asked about more of his plans for the town. Fiorito told Willie he wanted to turn Searchlight into a "Western Paradise," a town where the old west would never die. This idea appealed to Willie somewhat. Fiorito then went on to explain his vision further, *"No cars would be allowed in or out of Searchlight. The only way you could access the town would be by stagecoach."* The idea seemed a bit far-fetched and that's about where Willie's interests ended. He was always looking for a good money deal, and he did in fact consider selling all of his interests in Searchlight, making good on his promise to think the offer over thoroughly.

Martello called the potential investor three weeks later and told him he simply couldn't find a number popping up in his head. He told him the town wasn't for sale and stated, *"If I sold Searchlight, it wouldn't have anything to do with my life anymore,"* according to Schafer. Fiorito promised that if he sold the town, Willie could be the mayor, the chief of police, the justice of the peace—anything he wanted. Since he was already those things and owned the town, Willie declined. Fiorito eventually lost interest in Searchlight, but the idea he provided Willie began to take root.

As his friendship with Doc Bayley grew, so did his plans. The two men seemed oddly well-suited to one another as friends, as well as business partners. The two of them frequently discussed the potential of Searchlight. *"Doc recognized the value of a town where there was no competition, was not too far away from Las Vegas, and was controlled by one person,"* said Dick Taylor of his friend and employer. Willie saw the potential for big business in a professional marriage between himself and the Hacienda owner, and in the words of Dick Taylor, *"The same thought, no doubt, was in the mind of Doc Bayley."* There was a buzz going on about a re-design of Route 66 that would include passing through Southern Nevada and most definitely Searchlight. This prospect started the flow of creative juices in the minds of Willie and Doc. Between the mid-1950s and mid-1960s, the collaboration between Martello and Bayley produced some of the most progressive and bold ideas in Searchlight's history.

While most people read in the January 23, 1962 edition of the *Las Vegas Review-Journal* that the sale of the El Rey property had been completed, astute readers and those who KNEW there were bigger things on the horizon from Willie found something rather exciting. Martello spoke of plans for a $1.7 million hotel and casino in the works, right on the spot where the El Rey used to stand. Not much was said in the paragraph about the details, but people eager to see a revival of Searchlight could whet their whistles thinking about an **"all-western,"** 100-room hotel and casino designed by noted Los Angeles architect **Paul Revere Williams**. Among some of the historic buildings featuring Williams' design work were the La Concha Motel in Las Vegas and the newly re-designed Los Angeles airport (LAX).

*"I'm working very hard on this,"* said Willie in a later *Review-Journal* article, *"and I'm trying to work it out for the best interest of everyone –including the town of Searchlight."* Willie's plans were not small and grew as the days progressed. Some residents were being hired by Willie to raze the many dilapidated or unused houses and other buildings around town, but none were sure why. Willie and Doc needed Searchlight to be cleaner and more inviting. They also needed to clear the grounds for the grand design. When put into the context of 1960s Nevada, it appeared Willie wanted modern Las Vegas in Searchlight, or at the very least, modern Laughlin, Nevada.

Interviews with the Martello family, as well as newspaper articles in the wake and aftermath of the fire, helped illustrate the full scope of Willie and Doc's plans if not a futuristic vision.

*"We were trying to build a TOWN,"* said Bob Martello of his uncle's grand scheme. The new *"Frontier Town"* as Willie described it, would certainly be able to more efficiently take advantage of the airport runway. It would also offer some traditional amenities, just on an unusually large scale for such a small town: three casinos, three

**Unknown artist's rendering featuring a Captain's Walk and lighthouse.**
*From the author's personal collection.*

showrooms, a race book, a massive 450-room resort hotel, and rodeo grounds. More unconventional plans included staples of today's Las Vegas mega-resorts and showed a little bit of Willie's California lifestyle: bowling alleys, a health club, mineral bathing, assorted shopping, a convention hall, and a marina at Lake Mohave. As he delved into the unknown, Willie also had plans for a full-service motion picture facility on-site, no doubt to include his Hollywood friends, such as Rory Calhoun and Jerry Schafer.

He even saw there could be big money in attracting families to a dusty gambling town, a notion not embraced in Las Vegas until the 1980s. *"Willie always wanted to make Searchlight a place for families,"* said Sharon Richardson. *"He loved seeing families come into town on vacations. He also knew there was BIG potential in the family dollar."* The Martello Plan included a motel just for children and, according to Sharon Richardson and Bob Martello, an amusement park *"with rides and everything,"* said Richardson. Willie believed there was still gold to be mined in Searchlight, though this time around the gold could be found in the American family.

While not necessarily "Western" in either theme or appearance, a sketch I unearthed in my hunt for El Rey memorabilia even revealed a new look for Willie's Texaco station. The **"Desert Oasis,"** as it was described on the sketch, boasted the new look *"will advertise for miles around."* If Willie had his way, a revolving lighthouse tower would be erected on top of the station. The town of Searchlight would finally get a searchlight of its own complete with a "Captain's Walk" on the office roof, a beacon shining in the distance that would call out to weary travelers and invite them into town.

Martello and Bayley's plans also called for a golf course since golfing in the desert was already a big attraction for the vacationer. However, as Dick Taylor revealed to me in a never-before-told story, this golf course concept devised by Bayley would also be somewhat revolutionary. *"I know this to be completely factual, because I was involved with the land acquisitions in Searchlight township and the master planning because of my involvement with the Mt. Charleston development program,"* said Taylor.

Doc began purchasing parcels of land throughout Searchlight and set up headquarters in a mobile home on a hill at the southwest side of town. This would be no ordinary golf course. *"His plan was to construct an 18 hole golf course with home sites bordering all of the fairways and greens,"* according to Taylor. This design would grow and attract permanent residents into Searchlight by creating a private golf community; it would be a high-end suburban neighborhood with beautiful scenery and access to the casinos, theaters, and shopping. However, as with any private club, membership would have some requirements.

*"The rules of the club were simple,"* recalled Taylor. *"Each fairway, each green, would have a heritage requirement. All potential buyers would identify themselves and be shown only lots in consort with their heritage."* The concept stemmed from Bayley's belief that at least one part of human nature remained constant throughout the ages. In other words, birds of a feather flock together.

This **"like attracts like"** theory would prove true in major cities across the U.S. and flow through into the rural areas of the country. New arrivals at Ellis Island frequently found themselves choosing neighborhoods primarily filled with people of a similar background, such as New York's Little Italy neighborhood. Chicago had a large Irish contingency, as another example. You could find heavy populations of German immigrants throughout many parts of Wisconsin and Illinois and large concentrations of people with Nordic descent in places like Minnesota and northern Michigan. Bayley felt if this sort of ethnic congregation was happening naturally across the country then the creation of a community designed with ready-made neighborhoods would succeed. "[Bayley] *intended to capitalize on this inborn proclivity of people wanting to be near other people that had similar backgrounds,"* said Taylor.

Doc saw these simple rules as being desirable to the potential buyers. *"If your ancestors were German, you would be allowed to buy a lot only along the 4th hole and fairway. Scottish? Only near the third hole. Italian, the 2nd hole and fairway, and so on,"* recalled Taylor of Bayley's plan. *"He found wide acceptance among people he consulted, but he made no public announcement at that point and time."*

This kind of proposal today would surely incur the wrath of many. In theory, it invokes thoughts of racism and segregation. However, in the late 1950s, such an idea was quite groundbreaking. For people to naturally locate themselves into sectioned portions of the country based upon ethnic heritage was one thing, but to try and build an entire community with that sort of racial structure in mind and to attempt to bring people together in such a way could be considered rather progressive. Bayley knew it also held the potential for a firestorm of potential lawsuits and anger. According to Taylor, *"Bayley conjectured, a private club could have its own rules."*

Dick Taylor also stressed to me that the plan was very inclusive. The goal wasn't to keep any group out, but rather the creation of a place where any group could live as long as they could afford the lots within their demographic. An 18-hole golf course meant at least 18 different ethnic communities and all of the benefits that would come from such living. Opportunities to create restaurants and businesses in the town that would cater to their needs meant jobs, income, and growth for the town. If the concept was a hit, more people would come to live in their own neighborhoods. If more than 18 ethnicities, or if particular sections lured larger groups than on other fairways, the potential for growth became that much greater. There was always room for another 18 holes, after all.

Martello and Bayley had a grand design for Searchlight. The El Rey would one day be a part of a multi-million dollar western town, a themed tourist destination. Willie described it as *"a western Disneyland."* Decades before there were pyramids, volcanoes, and roller coasters in Las Vegas and long before Don Laughlin was creating his own gambling empire on the Nevada/Arizona border, there were blue prints drawn for this adventurous concept city.

Interestingly, Bonnie Canter vividly recalled a meeting with Willie Martello and Laughlin in order to discuss Don's plans for a town of his own. According to Canter, Willie's response was a resounding, *"**THAT WILL NEVER WORK!**"* Perhaps, Martello simply didn't want the competition. Maybe, he didn't want another man to go through the hell he had endured trying to do the same thing in Searchlight. I've spoken with Don Laughlin about this very meeting. Mr. Laughlin laughed very loudly and denied the story but did add, *"**Willie had a great town and great ideas.**"*

With all of Willie's connections, Bayley's acquisitions, and the sale to First Capital Development Corp., it seemed everything was proceeding according to plan.

What they didn't plan on was the fire.

# ON-AGAIN, OFF-AGAIN

There were five significant events that led to the ultimate demise of Willie's El Rey Club. The fire at the El Rey Club on January 21, 1962 marked the beginning of the end for Willie. Ethel and Buddy Martello set up shop across the street to open a bar, but it was not intended to be part of the El Rey. Over the years, Buddy found work at the Showboat Casino and the Desert Inn and eventually opened a successful bar in Las Vegas with Ethel. In the meantime, Willie worried about what would happen next. The sale of Willie's properties to First Capital ultimately did go through, but with no casino in operation, Willie had to act fast in order to keep the business running and the money flowing.

A *Review-Journal* headline on Wednesday, January 24, 1962 gave the people of Searchlight a glimmer of hope. *"Searchlight Gambling Not Dead"*. It detailed a story that stated the Clark County Licensing Board would approve a move of the El Rey gaming operations into Willie's closed Crystal Club across the street, pending approval from the state.

By Friday, February 23, 1962, just over one month after the El Rey Club burned, readers of the *Las Vegas Review-Journal* saw an ad that announced the triumphant Grand Opening of the NEW El Rey Resort. Among the scheduled entertainment for that weekend were **Tina Marsell and her "Beautiful Twisters,"** an all-girl revue of exotic dancers. TV and film star Bob Cummings would return as a special guest, though it was unlikely he would be there to see the charred remains of a Chamberlain keyboard.

It seemed as though Searchlight's premier promoter and the town's main attraction was poised to make a comeback. Unfortunately, that was only a fleeting vision. The resort that once served as a desert oasis was turning out to be only a mirage.

By April 25, 1962, readers of the *Review-Journal* read a front page article by **Colin McKinlay** that detailed the closing of the El Rey Club. If there were any doubts that Martello's resort was heading off into the sunset, one need only read the title, *"Casino's Death Casts Searchlight Shadow"* under the heading, *"El Rey Club Goes Under"*. The story continued on page two with a header that read, *"Searchlight Casino Folds."* The opening line of the column was equally as grim: *"The 'king' of this tiny community just shriveled up and died this week."* There clearly was no way to paint around this. Searchlight had to endure some bad news.

Despite the Clark County Licensing Board waiving their liquor and gaming fees and the approved move into the Crystal Club, the debts were catching up to Willie. While awaiting insurance payments to materialize, McKinlay wrote, *"Martello's possessions were attached by creditors, and about a week ago, he threw in the towel."* Willie reportedly headed to Seattle to meet with Estelle Longwell, the beautiful countess and dress shop owner who was his wife at the time. Just a few days after Willie left town, the El Rey shut its doors.

This was the second time in four months that Searchlight had to deal with possibly losing the El Rey Club. With it now a distinct possibility Willie had left Searchlight forever, one former employee of the El Rey summed up the gravity of the situation perfectly in McKinlay's article.

*"We might as well close up the town. There just isn't anything left."*

Within three days, Willie Martello emerged to defend himself and offer a ray of hope to the people of Searchlight. Willie called from Los Angeles and, in a phone interview, insisted he had not abandoned the town he loved and said emphatically, *"It's not so!"* Willie apologized for *"giving the impression he 'ran out' on the town,"* claimed the newspaper article printed on the 29th of April. He also quickly pointed out that some of his other operations, including the El Rey Motel, a bar, and his Texaco gas station, were still in operation.

The story, at least according to Willie, was he met with his investors and buyers to negotiate the building of his new and improved western resort town. *"The small casino that we had couldn't handle the business,"* Martello said. *"Consequently, we had to cut down our plane schedules to one airplane a day."*

He went on to say, *"Plans will be revealed shortly by Paul R. Williams, the noted Los Angeles architect."* He gave some more hints about the new resort that Searchlight would soon call home. He spoke of at least 100 new hotel rooms and promised the resort would be *"one of the smartest Western hotel-casinos in Southern Nevada."* Willie told the *Review-Journal* the only real factors that were holding up the plans involved fire insurance and *"minor technicalities."*

Those minor technicalities in all likelihood had to do with money such as payments Willie owed to his investors, W. Roger Barnard and Marshall W. Sawyer. Once the cause of the fire was determined to be just a kitchen fire that went tragically out of control, it was natural to assume there would be some big money coming from the insurance companies. With a disaster like a fire destroying the casino and with so few knowing of Willie's master plan for the new resort complex, the people who helped keep the old El Rey alive wanted their money back. Of course, there were some who knew of Willie's plans for the huge resort complex but didn't have much hope it would actually happen. The problem was there were far too many people claiming ownership of the property.

*"Willie was a funny guy. Willie owned 100 percent of the El Rey, but he sold 200 percent,"* said Stan Colton of his friend's hustling. *"There were so many claims on the money from the insurance company, when the money came through, the checks sat un-cashed for months and months. One of the investors refused to sign the check because he knew Willie would take the money."* According to the *Las Vegas Review-Journal* and a lawsuit filed by W. Roger Barnard, two investors actually refused to sign any checks: Marshall Sawyer AND Willie Martello.

By September of 1962, the El Rey had now been closed for nearly five months. Barnard, who held three deeds of trust on the El Rey property, filed a lawsuit against the seven insurance companies that offered coverage on the El Rey Club as well as Martello and Sawyer. Barnard alleged the insurance firm had paid Martello and Sawyer $71,000, but the amount of money they owed him was $101,594. Since Martello and Sawyer refused to assign the insurance money to him, Barnard filed a civil suit.

Martello stated in a *Review-Journal* article filed the following day that the $71,000 the insurance company paid would be applied to rebuilding the El Rey and that no money was due to Barnard. He also took advantage of the press coverage of the law suit (and the opportunity to dazzle the court) to extrapolate upon his plans for the new resort.

In my research and interviews with the Martello family, very little kindness was shared with me regarding Marshall Sawyer. Bob Martello, in my first interview with him, blared out, completely unprovoked by me, *"Marshall Sawyer was a BUM!"* Sharon Richardson relayed she and her mother disliked Sawyer. She also told me how he would frequently *"strut around the club as if he'd owned the place."* As it turned out, he actually did own the place. Or at least, enough of it to shut it down, possibly for good.

A year had passed since Barnard's lawsuit against Martello and Sawyer, and there were still no groundbreaking ceremonies being held in Searchlight. It was now Marshall Sawyer's turn to recoup some money from his investments, so on Wednesday, July 24, 1963, Willie found himself in court again, this time to prevent Sawyer from foreclosing on the two trust deeds he owned on the property. According to Sawyer, the deeds totaled nearly $200,000. The insurance money paid after the fire covered much of the loss but not the deeds Sawyer owned. It took two days in court before **District Judge John Mowbray** threw out Martello's action to prevent foreclosure.

Martello may have been running out of luck, but he was rarely without friends. Not too long after closing the El Rey Club, Willie was living and working in Las Vegas at the Hacienda, the casino owned by his good friend, Bayley. He and Doc had been working on ways to make the vision for a new El Rey Club come into fruition. In the meantime, Willie needed to make some money.

He moved into a suite at the Hacienda and acted as a greeter, for lack of a better term, for Doc. Bill Moore, a former Bayley employee, recalled seeing Willie in the hotel *"bouncing around as if nothing was wrong."* You always saw Willie with a big smile and a friendly demeanor as if he didn't have a care in the world. That was if anyone actually saw him. *"Willie slept late every day,"* Moore said. *"He was always out very late at night."* He loved the action and nightlife available in Las Vegas, so Martello later moved into a suite in Bayley's other property, The New Frontier. *"Willie liked the Frontier much better,"* according to Bill Moore. *"It was closer to the center of the Strip."*

Willie took advantage of Bayley's friendship and partnership as only a man who lived to Willie's level of excess could. He racked up large bills for food, alcohol, and just about anything he felt he could throw onto his tab as a way of showing his appreciation for Bayley's generosity. *"His bills were ENORMOUS! Doc would simply write off everything as a business expenditure,"* said Moore of his former boss. *"Willie did whatever he wanted at either of the hotels."*

**Doc Bayley, Liberace, and Willie Martello**
*Photo courtesy Bob Martello.*

According to some, Doc Bayley's wife, Judy, began to feel the same way about Martello as the Martellos did about the way Marshall Sawyer took advantage of Willie. She also reportedly grew rather resentful of Searchlight and the El Rey Club as rumors about Doc having an affair with a woman spread through the gaming community.

In addition to cavorting with Doc and greeting guests at the Hacienda, Willie continued to work on Doc about making an investment in Searchlight. There was, after all, still the prospect that Route 66 would be re-routed through Searchlight, which would have meant *"one hundred million dollars a year or more to Searchlight. Sixty million in casino, forty million in food and lodging. EASILY,"* according to Bob Martello. Even without the road, Searchlight's lack of competition and Willie's ability to somehow make things happen continued to appeal to Bayley.

In Vegas, Doc Bayley was getting in over his head though few knew it at the time. While he had made the Hacienda a success, in 1959, he overextended himself and bought the struggling New Frontier. He thought he could turn the business around much faster than expected and forged ahead with the purchase. The competition in the center of the Strip proved to be too much for Bayley and his team. All the positive momentum he had created with the Hacienda was now in jeopardy because of the casino that was closer to the action. The man everyone thought couldn't make a success of a hotel so far from the real activity on the Strip proved them wrong. Ironically, that same man could not make as great a success with a hotel in the heart of the activity. Just like Willie, Bayley never allowed a little financial trouble stand in the way of a good opportunity.

In August 1, 1963, one month after Sawyer foreclosed on Willie Martello, sports reporter, **Bill Burns**, reported in a Van Nuys, California newspaper column that Doc and Willie were *"feverishly pursuing a schedule which will this year open a motel and casino in Searchlight, NV."* Reportedly, the story was an exclusive to his column and offered, *"They will use the Hacienda's Constellation planes to fly patrons from Palm Springs, L.A., Phoenix, and other points to the new dice Mecca."*

Strangely enough, this same column listed both Willie and Doc together as owners of the Hacienda, but clearly, that was not the case. Other misconceptions in this article claimed that Bayley, Martello, and **Joe Hunter** (a close friend of **Jack "Doc" Kearns**, the recently deceased manager of boxing legend **Jack Dempsey**) were all working together to establish The Doc Kearns Memorial Boxing Hall of Fame in Searchlight and continue *"the advancement of Nevada as the tourism capital of the world."* While Kearns himself was a charter member of a Boxing Hall of Fame in 1954, an actual brick and mortar International Boxing Hall of Fame was not established until twenty-six years later in 1989. Kearns was inducted in 1990. The IBHOF was not named after Kearns nor was it built in Searchlight, but in Canastota, New York. I'll spare you any suggestion that indicated Willie was ahead of his time yet again.

This particular amenity, a Boxing Hall of Fame, seemed rather out of place, even after researching all the bizarre things for this book. Dick Taylor confirmed that Doc did want to create such a structure. When I asked Sharon Richardson about this, all she could report was all the Martello boys had a curious fascination with boxing and even had an actual boxing ring in their back yard as kids. Other than that, the motivation behind Bayley and Martello wanting to set up a memorial for Doc Kearns remains a mystery.

While little was known about this plan to make Searchlight the home for a Boxing Hall of Fame, it was becoming abundantly clear that Willie and Doc Bayley intended to revive the El Rey Club and not allow the casino or Searchlight to go down for the count.

Martello convinced Bayley to help rebuild the El Rey Club and expanded the operation at the Crystal-turned-El Rey-turned-ghost of Searchlight Past. They built on to the establishment and made it a bit larger, more like the size of its predecessor which sat across the street. The May 20, 1964 edition of the *Las Vegas Review-Journal* gave, yet again, a glimmer of hope for the residents of Searchlight with the headline **"El-Rey Club May Re-Open."**

Willie and Doc went into business. Willie ran the club but did not

# El-Rey Club May Re-Open

Wednesday, May 20, 1964

**From the *Las Vegas Review-Journal*, May 20, 1964.**

hold the gaming or liquor license. Bayley was listed as president and filed a request with the Gaming Control Board to re-open the El Rey with nine gaming tables and a bank of thirty slot machines. According to the *Review-Journal* column, Bayley invested $100,000 and owned 92% of the operation. A later report stated he and Willie shared a 46% split of the majority of the company. The remaining 8% was split equally between **Bonnie Gail Inman** (Bonnie Canter) and **Calvin Magleby**.

Magleby was a Las Vegas attorney and a licensed liquor store operator of Ace Liquor Store in Las Vegas. He held his license until the city found out about other, frowned upon, intoxicating entertainment offered at his store: strippers. He served as a corporate officer and legal counsel.

The 21-year-old Inman was a former California hospital receptionist and Doc Bayley's personal secretary. This spot in the El Rey Club hierarchy earned Inman a place in Nevada gaming history as the youngest woman to ever hold a gaming license and own a casino. She served as a corporate officer and lived in the trailer that was set up by Bayley in Searchlight, which no doubt added to his wife Judy's suspicions.

With the corporate officers in place, Bayley and Martello hoped for a grand re-opening by July 1st of that year. If all went according to plan, flights would resume on Bayley's Constellation aircraft, drinks would be poured, and gambling would once again take place at a casino called the El Rey.

It took a while before the Liquor and Gambling Licensing Board approved the new license, but on Monday, August 10, 1964, the new licensees, Bayley, Martello, Magleby, and Inman set out to open the El Rey Club. Just over two weeks later, on August 29, Martello was again in the coveted paragraphs of Forrest Duke's column as he announced the re-launch. Though his column did not state just who would attend the event, he did suggest that many Hollywood celebrities would be there to listen to the music and singing of **Mervin Brown**, Frank Sinatra's protégé.

Among the improvements at the new casino was the El Rey's first appearance of "high-tech" surveillance in the form of ceiling cameras. *"We had our own eye in the sky,"* according to Bonnie Canter. *"It was kind of a big deal back then in Searchlight. People*

# New El Rey Club Opens Tonight in Searchlight

**From the *Las Vegas Review-Journal*, August 29, 1964.**

*would come into the place just to look up at the mirrored ceiling!"*

By today's standards, the addition of surveillance cameras into a casino was something of a no-brainer. In the case of the El Rey Club, there was already a long-standing history of theft from so many of Willie's employees. However, it was a fairly common practice for casinos to avoid the use of such devices, particularly in the '50s and '60s. Perhaps, it was because he was broke or he feared the shipments of expensive surveillance equipment would be diverted or destroyed by the Vegas mob. It didn't matter what the reason was; Willie never felt the extra expense of cameras and half-silvered mirrors was necessary. Soon after their installation, the investment in a little extra security paid off.

*"I used to live in a trailer behind the new club,"* recalled Canter. *"One day I came in through the back and decided to take a look through the cameras."* She climbed up the stairs into the ceiling of the El Rey Club. *"Almost immediately I caught a pit boss stealing hundreds,"* she said. *"The dealer would push the cash through a slot but leave a tiny corner sticking out of the top. Soon afterward, the pit boss would come by the table on a routine check and use his handkerchief to hide his taking the bill. He'd cough or wipe his nose and then pocket the bill."* She was outraged, and the newest owner of the El Rey Club went downstairs to confront the thief. She quietly approached the pit boss from behind, watched him tuck a bill in his pocket, and then grabbed his hand. *"Put that bill back on the table and get the hell out of here,"* Canter remembered, *"Thank God for those cameras. Who knows how much cash was leaving the place before?"*

It seemed young Bonnie Inman was not the only one thinking about ways to recover monetary losses. According to Canter, Doc Bayley had devised a rather ingenious, if not humorous, way to collect outstanding gambling debts.

*"There was no legal way for us to collect, but banks could collect debts of all kinds."* The owners decided the El Rey Club needed its own bank

and its only location would be built inside the El Rey Club. *"The idea was, if a person didn't have the money to pay their marker, they could simply go right to the bank window and write out a check to themselves. The bank would cash the check, the customer would hand us the money to pay back the casino, and then either leave or keep gambling,"* Bonnie recalled. *"If they didn't have enough money in their account, the bank could legally go after them for writing a bad check and then we'd make even more money. Doc even suggested, if we didn't like the guy, we could have the bank issue a stop payment on the check!"* Canter laughed, *"We decided to call it the Searchlight Official Bank—The S.O.B.!"* The new bank never happened. *"I have no idea why we never did it,"* said Canter. *"It would have been a first for any casino so far as we knew. Either way, we all got a good laugh just thinking about the S.O.B."*

Though it never quite recaptured the high numbers of people and the glamour, what glamour there was in Searchlight at least, the new El Rey Club attracted attention and brought in sizeable amounts of cash. *"At that time, things were booming,"* recalled Bill Moore. *"Searchlight brought a lot of money back to Vegas."* Large sums of cash coming out of such a small and unlikely location would not go unnoticed. They needed to take precautions. *"I used to travel back and forth with Doc's secretary to bring the money back, and we would take different routes so that we wouldn't be followed,"* said Moore.

While they made plenty of money in Searchlight, many believe most of it remained in Searchlight. Some believed, rather than simple bank deposits, the money that left the El Rey Club was primarily used to keep Bayley out of debt, although it is difficult to believe such a small club could make Vegas-sized income. It was clear none of the cash was applied to the bigger, grander plans for the western theme town and resort. It was too soon in this new arrangement to say if those plans were still on the horizon or if the constant removal of cash from the El Rey's coiffeurs was draining the life out of the casino. Dick Taylor, Bayley's right-hand man, is quite certain no such skimming or reallocations of funds ever occurred.

*"I would have known about it had it been done,"* said Taylor. *"The Hacienda, after the first five years of being on the edge of big time trouble, was doing just fine in the early 1960s. But not the Frontier!"* Taylor went on to explain money was brought to the Frontier but not from Searchlight. *"I personally took big time money down to the Frontier cage,"* said Taylor.

*"We didn't need money from Searchlight. Owners don't start skimming at a brand new club! They* [Willie and Doc] *had too much money invested."*

Flights came in through Searchlight and business continued. The new El Rey continued to bring in top quality entertainment such as the very popular Nancy Kaye and once again offered Vegas-style fun in a respectable establishment. However, before long, the El Rey Club would hit another bump in the road, the next of the final death blows Willie would encounter on this long and winding road.

One day after Christmas, on December 26, 1964, Warren "Doc" Bayley passed away. A heart attack took away one of the Las Vegas area's more colorful daredevil casino promoters and owners as well as Willie Martello's last true ally.

With the death of Doc, majority possession of the El Rey property went to Doc's widow, Judy. *"Judy Bayley didn't want to have anything to do with Searchlight. Doc was playing around here in those days with his girlfriend,"* said Stan Colton. *"She knew about it and didn't want anything to do with the place."*

It was now time for Judy to put an end to a lot of the shenanigans that had been upsetting her all these years, which stopped Willie's gravy train. Colton recalled Judy was not a fan of Willie's, at all. *"She took all of Willie's stock* [in the El Rey Club] *because he owed Doc so much money,"* said Colton. According to Colton, Judy Bayley explained to Willie, *"You lived in the hotels all those years. You didn't pay any rent. You owe me money!"* With that, the Widow Bayley took control of all Willie's stock, and he and Bonnie Inman (by then, Bonnie Canter) later sued for controlling interest in the company.

Willie tried to remain unfazed by this setback. In the interim, business needed to continue. Nobody was going to make any money if there were no customers in the El Rey. If he could prove the El Rey could not only survive, but exceed expectations and thrive once again, he might gain Judy's trust and finagle a way to own the El Rey Club once again. Until all legal matters related to Doc Bayley's death and proper ownership of the El Rey could be sorted out, he still had use of Doc's DC-3's and Constellation airplanes and intended to make hay while he could.

Unfortunately, Willie soon faced another major setback.

*Photo courtesy Nevada State Museum, Las Vegas [J. Florian Mitchell Collection]*

# GROUNDED

Among Willie's proudest achievements during his years in town was when he convinced the county to turn the military's dusty emergency runway into a viable airport. This airstrip meant countless dollars and visitors to Searchlight and offered him and the people of Searchlight hope for a better future. His hope was the runway would play a major part in the development of Searchlight into a major tourist destination. Though it cost him plenty to keep the planes flying, he knew such a modern amenity could clear the pathway to Searchlight becoming a heavy hitter in Nevada's gaming industry. This accomplishment would set him apart as one of the state's biggest and best-known moguls.

Shortly before his death, Bayley had some problems of his own related to those same airplanes. The man with the hotel and casino so far away from all the action in town was somehow leading the entire city in occupancy rates for his hotel. This was due predominantly because of some crafty marketing by Dick Taylor, and Bayley's airplanes.

The traffic flying into McCarran airport was brisk, but it was not the major airlines of the day that brought so many tourists and gamblers into Las Vegas. It was Bayley's private flights. Reportedly, Bayley's fleet of planes brought in more tourists than all of the major airlines COMBINED. This caused the Civil Aeronautics Board to shut him down in July of 1962, stating the sheer volume of flights and business they generated constituted a de facto airline. Since Bayley didn't have a license to run his own airline, the flights into Vegas had to stop. Where did those flights go? To Searchlight.

**One of the many large groups en route to the El Rey Club. May 29, 1961.**
*Nevada State Museum, Las Vegas [J. Florian Mitchell Collection]*

The timing for Willie couldn't have been better. He had a runway and needed planes. Doc was losing his ability to provide airline transportation to Vegas and needed to make money. For a while, it seemed to be a perfect match. Unfortunately, by April of 1965, not quite four months after Doc's death, Willie's runway faced closure.

The news about an airport in Searchlight sounded quite impressive to people who read the ads that

From the *Las Vegas Review-Journal*, April 21, 1965.

SEARCHLIGHT RUNWAY

# Willie Can't Get Off the Ground

announced the free flights to Searchlight, and to those whom Willie directed his promotional efforts. To those who saw the planes it appeared almost epic. However, once you approached Searchlight, the reality was unavoidable.

Jim Sarra and his gambler father took a junket to Searchlight in the spring of 1965. Sarra vividly remembered the airport runway being less than glamorous. *"I flew in from San Diego in 1965. That Constellation was a tad too heavy for that runway! The runway was little more than sand and asphalt."*

Indeed, Sarra's opinion was all too correct. The runway Willie fought so hard to bring to life and spent so much money on over the years was too thin and unstable to handle the heavy aircraft he was bringing in so regularly.

**Erle Taylor,** the newly appointed Director of Aviation in Clark County, had caught wind of the flights coming in and out of Searchlight. When he heard the name "Doc Bayley" and realized it was his DC-3s and Constellations landing on that runway, he immediately took action. He knew it couldn't handle such massive aircraft.

The county commissioners banned all aircraft heavier than 10,000 pounds from landing at the Searchlight airport after the recommendation of Erle Taylor and test results from the county engineering department's **George Monahan**. Twin engine DC-3s weighed in at about 18,300 pounds empty and just over 25,000 pounds when fully loaded. Hearing that any DC-3s were successfully landing in Searchlight was amazing enough. However, a Lockheed Constellation like the one Bayley allowed Willie could weigh an astonishing 137,500

CHAMPAGNE FLIGHT — Guests of the El Rey Club in Searchlight landed by DC3 at the Boulder City Airport last weekend from Los Angeles and were transported to Searchlight by bus. That town's airport has been declared unsafe for the larger planes to use.
(Knighton photo)

From the *Henderson Home News*, June 24, 1965.

pounds when fully loaded.

On Tuesday, April 20, 1965, Willie pleaded with the county commissioners to change their decision. He was certain the runway was safe based upon its history of successful flights and a soil report conducted by the United Testing Laboratory. Monahan's tests were all the commissioners needed to declare the runway unsafe for larger aircraft.

**Willie on the runway, May 3, 1961.** *Nevada State Museum, Las Vegas [J. Florian Mitchell Collection]*

There were only about three inches of asphalt that covered the runway, which was well below Federal Aviation Agency standards, and their own density tests of the soil proved inadequate.

In a desperate attempt to save the El Rey's hopes for financial stability, Willie tried to explain he had all the proper insurance coverage for the airport. This pleased neither the commissioners nor Deputy District Attorney **John Porter.**

*"At this time,"* Porter admonished, *"my main concern is lives. If that airport is not up to standards, it could cost a lot of lives."* Porter went on to demonstratively state, *"Until such a time that the safety of it is worked out, the insurance coverage is not the important thing."* The decision to limit the weight of the planes using Willie's runway stood.

The airstrip eventually reopened, but it remained open only to planes with a gross weight of less than 10,000 pounds. There just were not enough of those small planes to bring in the quantity of people necessary for the El Rey Club to succeed. The sad truth was, even if there were, in all likelihood Willie couldn't afford to pay for them, anyway.

# THE LONG AND WINDING ROAD

1965 continued to be a bad year for the new El Rey. In July, the El Rey Club lost money in a different way. It was robbed by masked marauders.

In a July 29, 1965 *Review-Journal* story that seemed filled with two tons of irony and pain for Willie, it reported three and possibly four men in masks entered the El Rey Club at 3:00 a.m. when *"there were apparently no customers in the club."* If this had been Willie's El Rey of a few years earlier, the place would have been packed. The criminals wielded long-barreled revolvers similar to those from Buddy's lost collection and stole $1,000 from the El Rey before they made their hasty getaway. One of the thieves prevented employees from calling for help when he tore apart the telephone and wire inside the club, a phone line that might not have existed without Willie's efforts. As roadblocks were being set up by the Clark County Highway Patrol and California's San Bernardino County Highway Patrol at all points that included Railroad Pass, Nipton, Needles, Kingman, and Davis Dam, a small airplane was called to aid the search and took off from the Searchlight airport. The plane weighed less than 10,000 pounds.

On August 11, 1965, the *Review-Journal* reported a new liquor license was being granted to Judy Bayley on behalf of her late husband for her stake in the Hacienda and the El Rey Club. However, the ability to sell a few drinks wasn't a sign that things might improve for Willie and his club.

Curiously, an article in the April 13, 1966 edition of the *Review- Journal* listed neither Martello nor Bayley as owners of the club even though it was widely known Bayley was in fact the primary owner of the property.

Regardless of whom was named the owner on paper, the story reflected many of the growing

**MASKED BANDITS GET $1,000**

# El Rey Club Robbed

From the *Las Vegas Review-Journal*, July 29, 1965.

tensions and declining quality seen at the once great El Rey Club.

Fifty-six year-old **Floyd Keller**, the reported owner of the club, was arrested and taken to the Clark County Jail after a fight with dishwasher **Douglas Stewart** nearly turned deadly. Keller was charged with assault with intent to do great bodily harm after he grabbed a meat cleaver and wielded it in a threatening manner. Stewart grabbed a kitchen knife in self-defense, and the two men faced off in the El Rey kitchen. Cooler heads prevailed and both men slowly put down their weapons. However, once Stewart put down his knife, Keller allegedly cracked Stewart across the head with a knife sharpener. What started this near fatal altercation? Keller was displeased with Stewart's dishwashing abilities. The El Rey was clearly no longer the place to find a friendly atmosphere.

Judy Bayley was interested in selling the property she owned in Searchlight and set out to do so by September of 1966. Willie was not ready to let go. The partnership that had been formed in 1964 (with Judy Bayley assuming Doc's part) had now split into two factions: Judy Bayley and Calvin Magleby (now her attorney) on one side and Willie Martello with Bonnie Inman (now Bonnie Canter) on the other.

Martello and Canter, acting on behalf of themselves as officers of Searchlight Development, Inc., filed a $1,375,000 lawsuit against Bayley and Magleby. The suit claimed Doc Bayley had coerced his secretary into signing a deed of trust on the property *"with the assignment of rents to Casino Operations Inc. as beneficiary and Pioneer Title Insurance Co. as trustee."* This meant, if Bayley, Magleby, and Pioneer sold the properties, they would be in breach of said trust.

There were three principal things Willie wanted to accomplish with the lawsuit.

Martello and Canter sought damages of $500,000 against Bayley, $500,000 against Casino Operations, Inc., $75,000 in attorney fees, and an additional $250,000 against Judy Bayley for *"alleged malice."* In addition to damages, Martello wanted the court to declare him, Canter, and Willie's accountant, Louis Cooper, officers and directors of Searchlight Development, Inc. and remove Bayley and Magleby as officers and directors in the company. The plaintiffs also wanted to have the deed of trust declared a fraudulent instrument, stating Bayley was not a stockholder of Searchlight Development, Inc.

"Willie leaves Searchlight," an image with a prophetic name taken on March 23, 1961.
*Nevada State Museum, Las Vegas [J. Florian Mitchell Collection]*

This tactic stalled the sale of the property for a while, but ultimately, things did not go Willie's way. *"He won his case against Judy,"* according to Canter, *"but it was too late. The damage had been done."* Shortly thereafter, Canter pulled out of the El Rey Club business.

According to Bill Moore, the property was eventually sold to mafia yes-man **Allen Glick** and his partner, **Gene Fresch,** of the infamous Argent Group. By this time, Willie's El Rey Club was dead, but insult was always added to injury, so the final nail in the El Rey coffin would soon be struck.

Bob Martello described this period as *"not the best of times."* The possible re-routing of the historic Route 66 was among the many factors that pushed Willie to grow and develop his little casino. If that road wound its way into Nevada and through Searchlight, the town would clear over $100,000,000 a year without even trying. As Bob put it, *"A great incentive for Nevada...but not for California."*

That re-routing never happened. Nevada never had a piece of Route 66 to call its own. According to Bob Martello, the governor of California, **Pat Brown**, *"a former crooked D.A. put into power by gamblers,"* Bob alleged, had an interest in a million dollar bridge project. That bridge was to run through nearby Needles, California. As any governor of a state would do, whether corrupt or otherwise, Brown backed Needles, California and not Searchlight, Nevada. Whether Governor Brown used his power and influence honestly or dishonestly, the bridge in Needles happened and the re-routing of Route 66 through the dusty mining town of Searchlight, Nevada never did. The project that helped inspire dreams for Willie was nearly twenty years old and would ultimately never even move past the "what if" stage.

Willie, as lost a soul as he was when his family first told him to head to Searchlight and make a go of things, went back to California.

# LONG LIVE THE KING!

One thing that is rather unfortunate when one sets out to write a book about someone else is the book generally turns out to be more about the author than the subject. I am hopeful you will not accuse me of this offense as I have tried to stay out of this book as much as possible. When necessary, I've referred to myself in references to interviews with various members of Willie's family or in things I have discovered along the way. However, this story is not about my journey to write the book. My original goal was to write about Willie Martello and what happened in this little known casino called the El Rey Club, and to that end, I feel I have achieved that goal. For a brief moment, I have to tarry from the path a bit and relay something along the way that does pertain to me.

I was at the Las Vegas Library on Flamingo Avenue on September 27, 2010. Aside from other reading and all the interviews I have conducted, much of the research I've compiled has come from tracking down as many newspaper stories from various publications as possible. Many of these are only available on microfilm these days.

Previous to September 27, 2010, I had amassed a rather large listing of dates and page numbers where the El Rey Club, Willie, or other key players were mentioned. I knew what days they appeared and had an idea what the article would be about thanks to some thorough archiving by the folks at the Nevada State Museum.

Long before I had ever gotten to that stage of the research, before I knew I was actually going to write a book, and before I'd acquired my first piece of El Rey memorabilia on eBay, I knew Willie Martello had passed away in 1968. I'll repeat this. I *knew* in 2005 that Willie Martello was long gone. As early as 2006, I had a copy of a column by Ray Chesson that stated Willie had passed on January 9, 1968. This was incorrect information; the correct date was actually the 3rd. I blamed this inaccuracy on Chesson not always needing the facts to make a good story. When I went to the library that day, I realized just how deeply into this project I had really become.

After I tried to locate some clearer, easier to read clips from previous years, I picked up where I had chronologically left off during my last trip to the Nevada State Museum, where I usually conducted a lot of this type of research. I found out a few things about some rather unpleasant behavior at the new El Rey that involved an arrest, and a few other equally upsetting pieces that revealed how this truly was not the original El Rey anymore. Then, I found a headline from an article in the January 4, 1968 edition of the *Las Vegas Review-Journal* that stopped me in my tracks.

### *"Pioneer Searchlight Casino Owner, Martello, Dies at 53"*

I stopped in shocked disbelief over what I had read, as my hands actually shook in front of the microfilm machine. It was as if I were reading a headline about one of my own family members. I'd forgotten that this was a headline from 1968 and felt a wave of emotion overcome me as if this were someone I knew, someone I'd known my whole life. Incredibly, tears welled up in my eyes.

I already knew Willie was dead. If he had been alive, this book would have been much easier to write and research. If he were still alive, somebody else would surely have already written the story of Willie Martello long before I showed up. Instead, I was sitting in a library I'd never visited before while I used a machine rarely needed these days, and cried over somebody I had never met, and in all likelihood, wasn't related to anyway.

The simple fact was, after all the research, photos, calls and emails to friends and family, poker chips, dice, eBay auctions, and all the excitement I had enjoyed, and still enjoy as a result of this nonsense that started in a downtown Las Vegas museum, I simply wasn't ready for Willie to be gone. Even writing this paragraph now, I find it silly that I, a reasonable and often cynical adult man, would have some sort of emotional outburst after reading a 42-year-old headline. Admittedly, I just wasn't ready. I was having too much fun.

I wondered if that was how people other than Willie's immediate family felt back then. When Willie was alive, there was always a sense of fun in the air, a genuine feeling that something outrageous could happen at any time. Sometimes, that could be a little more than you may be able to handle. Other times, that may have been somewhat charming and harmless in nature. At all times, people felt, if Willie was around, there was potential for a great time.

Willie had *become* family to me as had everyone with whom I spoke while I researched this book. Even the folks I'd only spoken to briefly now had become a major part of my life. I have rarely had time for sentimentality. I didn't just drop everything on a silly whim for a HOBBY, even though I have thrown myself into my hobbies rather definitively. I couldn't feel loss because someone I never knew was STILL DEAD. Well, up until that moment, I couldn't.

William Joseph Martello died of a heart attack on January 3, 1968 at Hawthorne Community Hospital in Hawthorne, California. In the time that led up to his death, Willie's health was something of concern for everyone. He certainly LOVED to live the wildest of lives and never took particularly good care of himself. Anyone who lived in Searchlight, Nevada during that time lived a hard life regardless of personal habits. Add in Willie's outrageous habits and one simply aged harder and faster than almost anyone else. While you view some of the photos in this book, pay particular attention to those from 1960-1962. Willie was only in his late 40s during that time, but the level of exhaustion and age on his face certainly suggested otherwise. It was no coincidence that Willie's first heart attacks occurred during those years.

Willie suffered four heart attacks between 1961 and 1968, all with varying degrees of intensity. The first came in April of 1961, reportedly, while he was running around on his wife and seducing one of the young Hollywood starlets he had invited to the club, an act that caused more than one family member to kid Willie over time. That heart attack, a relatively minor one by all accounts, was the first of *THREE* Willie suffered in a single week according to a column by Forrest Duke. **"Work-Horse Willie wouldn't let the first two attacks stop him – just laughed them off,"** wrote Duke. The third and most severe attack during that week happened in the home of Jerry Schafer.

*"I just can't bear to think about that day,"* said Schafer in an interview we had. *"I am still shocked about it to this day. I can't even remember what happened. It was just too much."*

Suzan Riddell and her mother, Joan Gilbert, heard of the first heart attack Willie suffered thanks to friends and Horseshoe Club employees **Georgia** and **Hal "Speedy" McCormack**, who always kept them abreast of Willie's life. She told me about the relationship the two maintained over the years. *"The last time I saw him was at the Hacienda Hotel in 1962. My mother had heard he had a heart attack, and so we went to see him as she'd carried a torch for him forever,"* Suzan said. *"Mom took the name Martello as her own, once again. She told me she did it because he was the love of her life."*

What was most unfortunate about his last heart attack (in 1968) was that Willie's chest pains were initially misdiagnosed at the hospital as a bad case of the flu. He was given medications to treat influenza and sent home. Willie's symptoms failed to improve and his pain increased. By the time his current wife, Estelle, had called an ambulance, Willie's skin was gray in appearance, and he was clearly in pain. Since it was believed he only had the flu and presumably did not need immediate attention, the ambulance drivers opted not to take him to the hospital closest to his house but one considerably farther away. Even with Willie's past history of poor heart health, somehow, they categorized this as a fairly treatable ailment and, was kept at the hospital for observation. Willie later died from this bad case of "influenza."

In what can only be classified as that special kind of fate and irony that proves there is a sense of humor in the universe, Willie's last heart attack started while he was in bed with a woman. Even those who teared up the most over Willie's death, smiled a little bit at that fact.

The good news, if there is any from this unfortunate set of events, is the heart attack did not occur while he was trying to seduce a young Hollywood actress or while cheating on his wife. Rather, this happened while he was making love to his wife, Estelle Longwell, whom many in Martello's family claimed was Willie's true love. Estelle was a dress shop owner and a countess, though nobody in the family can remember the details of her royal connections. They just knew she and Willie were a great match.

Estelle and Willie always had a rather heated, on-again, off-again romance. Usually, it was "off-again" because Estelle grew tired of Willie's frequent infidelities. He may not have been the most faithful of men, particularly with Estelle, but he did love her tremendously. He even brought along a briefcase to most of his meetings with potential business partners that included two things: information about his El Rey Club in Searchlight and photo after photo of his beautiful wife, Estelle. The two things Willie loved above all else in the world were with him almost everywhere he went.

Mickey and Lou Cooper remained good friends with Estelle until the end of her life. Mickey recalled the last days of "Royal Couple" Willie and Estelle fondly. *"I was so happy to see the two of them finally, truly together,"* said Mickey. *"I remember telling Estelle that I thought it was such a shame that Willie died so soon after they finally made their lives together work."* According to Mrs. Cooper, Estelle was not one bit regretful or saddened by this. *"She told me, 'I wouldn't have it any other way! I was with Willie when he needed me the most and that's what mattered.' She just loved that man so!"* Lou added, *"Everybody loved Willie. It was just too hard not to love him."*

Jerry Schafer remembered when he met Willie for the first time in Hollywood and listened as he described both Searchlight and Estelle. According to Schafer, it was hard to tell which he thought was more beautiful. *"Willie was a heck of a salesman for Searchlight because he loved it so much. He had photos of the casino, Cottonwood Cove, his runway, the swimming pool, his family, and he simply couldn't wait to show everyone in the room photos of Estelle,"* Jerry said. *"His face would just beam looking at them."* When Schafer described how Willie waxed on about his plans for the future and his beloved Estelle, it became clear the countess was really King Willie's queen, Searchlight was his kingdom, and

Left to right: Estelle, Rory Calhoun, Luigi Scirocco, Willie, and Calhoun's wife, Lita Baron. *Photo courtesy Ethel Martello*

the El Rey Club his castle.

Schafer received a phone call from Estelle as she broke the sad news to him at his L.A. home. *"It was terrible. I really liked that man,"* said Jerry. *"He was always nice with me. He was appreciative of everything."* Jerry had spoken with Willie shortly before his death, *"I knew he had been sick,"* recalled Schafer. *"I called him on the phone and he told me he was O.K.."*

During his last years, Willie tried in vain to stop the sale of his many other Searchlight properties. He hated to lose all he had worked so hard to build. He spent time off and on in the Vegas area, but primarily, went to California to spend time with Estelle and run some of the other family businesses, mostly night clubs and restaurants.

A casino with the El Rey name continued in Searchlight in one form or another until 1973. Some contended that Willie himself didn't die in January of 1968 but in January of 1962 after his original club burned to the ground.

Willie had never really regained any of the success or the modest grandeur with the new club he had when his original club was thriving. In the words of Stan Colton, *"His little place was gone."*

Chef Luigi said of his long-time friend, *"He was a fellow who wanted to go first class, and he went that way if he had to hock himself to the hilt."* Willie wanted a western-themed Nirvana in the middle of the desert, a place where families could breathe in some fresh air and snap photos of Joshua trees, where the kids could enjoy their own carnival rides and the adults could act like high rollers. Unfortunately, that never happened.

At the end of it all, Willie didn't do too badly. Ray Chesson wrote about the glory days of the El Rey Club and the town of Searchlight after Willie's death and put things into some perspective. *"He may have hurt a few people, but he helped a lot."* At one point, nearly all the town's residents enjoyed some level of gainful employment as a result of Willie's efforts. Searchlight had not turned into the ghost town everyone expected once Willie arrived in 1946. Phone calls were being made on permanent lines, airplanes full of tourists had a place to land, folks were now aware of the beauty available at Christmas Tree Pass, Cottonwood Cove, and Lake Mohave. Some children got to play a little baseball with their friends and enjoy the cool waters of a luxurious swimming pool. What happened between the years of 1946 and 1962 in Searchlight paved the way for the town to thrive and survive to this day.

Willie Martello was laid to rest on Tuesday, January 9, 1968 at Rose Hills

Cemetery in Los Angeles. It shouldn't be surprising to know he was buried in a glistening white suit. Attended by many friends and family, the service was held at St. Rose of Lime Catholic Church in Maywood, California, where all of the Martello children grew up and where Willie was once an altar boy, if you can imagine that. Legendary casino owner and land developer **Del Webb** and Clark County Assessor **James A. Bilbray** were on hand to serve as pall bearers. At the funeral, one sentiment was heard and repeated by so many friends and family members: It was a shame Willie died at such a young age. When Luigi Scirocco heard this, he smiled and pointed out the simplest of facts, *"Don't feel sorry for Willie. He did more living in fifty-three years than you or I could do in two hundred."*

**Willie at the Stardust's Continental Cafe.**
*Photo courtesy Suzan Riddell.*

# "YOU KNOW ABOUT THE GIRLS, RIGHT?"

As I have mentioned previously in this volume, I started on my journey to learn more about Willie after hearing his El Rey Club was a brothel. What little information that was available, online or in print, only discussed the prostitutes and referred to Martello as little more than a common pimp. You hardly ever read about the generous man buying presents for the town's children on Christmas, the fun-loving guy who conducted mock trials over a lost bowling ball, the creative man who used carrier pigeons when there was no telephone, and the fearless promoter who commissioned a mural to honor Searchlight's history and did so much for the fly-speck on the Nevada map called Searchlight.

As we reach the end of this book, it is only fitting that I place here the chapter about the El Rey Club and its history with the world's oldest profession. If you have made it this far, you have come to learn as I have the simple fact there was so much more to Willie Martello and his unique little casino. It is my hope this will bring closure to Willie's family, healing to Willie's legacy, and context to a part of Nevada's history we all acknowledge but only secretly embrace. Let these be the last words about Willie the pimp. He was no saint, but, at least now, I hope fewer people will view him only as the sinner history has made him out to be.

I've always admired the state of Nevada. It is a state with a population of only about three million people and yet you can always find at least that many people simply visiting the state due to the fantastic marketing of tourism and amenities offered in the state. It abounds in excessive habits and adult pleasures while still offering some amazing scenery, wholesome attractions, and generally the best in entertainment for all ages. I've mostly loved the fact that there were numerous places throughout the state where fully grown adults could act like complete children.

The gambling is something that allows Nevadans to enjoy lives free from state income tax and taxes on consumable goods. The arguments against gambling have always been the same everywhere since the dawn of time, namely the crime, bad influence, adverse effect it will have on the community, and the list goes on. Somehow, every city I've visited that wised up and allowed riverboat gaming or, maybe, a few more Indian casinos, benefited greatly from their presence. It appeared Nevada always knew gambling was NOT the root of all evil.

There's plenty of alcohol to go around, which, if you are one to imbibe responsibly, is a truly great thing. The combination of the gambling and the booze provide each resident plenty of hilarious stories of drunken tourists that make jackasses of themselves. Ask any Nevada resident *"What's the craziest thing you've seen out here?"* and I promise you the stories you hear will have less to do with spotting alien aircraft in the sky and more to do with random tourists vomiting on somebody's pet snake on the Las Vegas Strip.

I'll apologize in advance for adding some personal opinion to this next paragraph, but another thing I always admired about Nevada, was until recently, you could still smoke damn near anywhere in the state, something this non-cigarette-smoker used to love. I know it seems ridiculous, but currently, you cannot smoke in Nevada except in a casino. Okay, I'm completely over-simplifying the law. You can smoke in approved places and in your home, but not in public buildings or places that serve food. This law mirrors those found in the increasing number of states across the country foolish enough to embrace smoking bans. I do not smoke cigarettes, but I do enjoy a fine cigar and believe any ADULT that wants to enjoy tobacco, a legal product that funded and helped grow the nation, should be able to smoke in places where adults gather to enjoy adult vices. At the very least, if there is only ONE place in all of the world where an adult should be able to enjoy a cigarette without any fear of persecution or scrutiny, it should be Nevada and, more specifically, Las Vegas. It makes no sense that anyone with enough cash can rent a hooker for the night and not enjoy a cigarette afterward. I guess the mint the girl leaves on the pillow for you qualifies as food. This brings me to another reason why I think Nevada just does things a little bit differently and, maybe, even better than the other states.

Prostitution and the state of Nevada have gone hand-in-hand for as long as anyone can remember. Being the only state in the Union with any form of legalized prostitution sets the state apart from the others. By using something most consider morally, spiritually, and in the remaining 49 states, LEGALLY dishonest, Nevada appears to hold on to an honesty all other states deny; people very much enjoy sex and many are willing to pay for it.

This doesn't mean the practice doesn't have its fair share of detractors. Just like anywhere else in the world, you'll find people eager to spout about the evils of consenting adults enjoying one another in a sexual, consensual, and (at least, for one) profitable manner. However, Nevada in general does have more people who just "get it," both the concept and the actual "it" of it all.

The Old West contains plenty of stories of men who found satisfaction within the arms of comfortable strangers. In fact, when one puts it into the context of "the Old West," prostitution takes on a certain romantic quality. It stimulates fascination and curiosity from a wide and varied array of people.

During the brief time I spent as a tour guide when I brought families to the Hoover Dam or the Grand Canyon, I spent much of my time answering questions about prostitution in the state as opposed to providing facts about the wonders of both the natural and modern world. In my travels across the country as an entertainer, I've not only encountered many ladies willing to sell themselves for a little bit of cash *("HOW SHAMEFUL!")*, but also many places dedicated to presenting the history of brothels and the women who represented so much more *("Aww, how quaint!")*. While on a road trip in Tombstone, Arizona, I took tours of old saloons, hotels, and of course, brothels. I recall a trip I took to Kansas to see the Dalton Gang hideout in between shows and learned about some houses of ill repute along the way. All of these stories were told with a nod and a wink, which implied just a hint of the guiltiest of pleasures.

In Butte, Montana, you can visit the **Dumas Brothel Museum**, which was a legal, working brothel from 1890 until 1982. Cripple Creek, Colorado features the **Old Homestead House Museum** and all the sordid tales of the "soiled doves" who worked inside. A short drive from Las Vegas,

Nevada takes you to the **Brothel Art Museum**. The Brothel Art Museum resides in Crystal, about 25 miles north of Pahrump, Nevada, the home of several legal brothels in operation today.

## Searchlight Is Banned By Army; Vegas Is Studied

From the *Las Vegas Review-Journal*, April 23, 1943.

It should not be surprising that the aforementioned homes of brothels were also the homes of the mining industry. In fact, you will frequently find one of three things near a brothel:

1) men 2) mining 3) a military base. Searchlight had all three.

At present, prostitution is not legal in Clark County, Nevada where both Searchlight and Las Vegas are located. However, the bigger cities in Nevada such as Reno and Las Vegas did have their own fully-functioning Red Light Districts up until the early 1950s.

In 1942, President Roosevelt had issued an order restricting the presence of brothels near military bases. This order was lifted in 1948, but both Reno and Las Vegas had shut down their Red Light Districts by 1951. Reno successfully shut down a local brothel, listing it as a public nuisance in 1949. This action was upheld by the Nevada Supreme Court. However, even though these towns were much smaller than they are today, they were still considered to be large towns in Nevada. Searchlight, while celebrating a brief life as a boomtown, was still very much isolated and remote and, therefore, not necessarily as scrutinized by the law. With the remaining presence of prospectors and miners in the area and servicemen at Camp Ibis a stone's throw away, it was clear that Searchlight didn't feel obligated to rules governing prostitution. In short, the girls were in Searchlight and they were there before Willie Martello ever set foot in the town.

*"I believe the fact there were always 'girls' in town,"* according to Joyce Walker. *"Willie had very little to do with Searchlight's checkered past,"* she went on to say. *"During the building of the Boulder Dam, there was a very active 'house' near where the* [city] *park is today. I remember it was run by the grandfather of some school kids. No little girls were stolen or raped."*

On April 23, 1943, three years before Willie Martello arrived in Searchlight, the *Las Vegas Review-Journal* reported the town of Searchlight was listed as **"out of bounds"** for the soldiers of Camp Ibis. Apparent increases in cases of gonorrhea and other social diseases were occurring among the fourth armored force.  They suspected both Las Vegas and Searchlight as potential sources.  Las Vegas, with its investigation in progress for two weeks, feared an unfavorable result that would place it, too, on the list of "out of bounds" cities.  According to **Sheriff Glen Jones**, "[Searchlight] *may be tabooed, also."*

Being listed as "out of bounds" by the military was taboo enough publicly.  However, to the servicemen, Searchlight suddenly became not just a name for a town, but quite literally a shining beacon in the distance.  The light led you home to the exact location of "you know what."

*"Once they told us Searchlight was off limits,"* said one [unnamed] soldier in an interview, *"we knew exactly where to go! We might not had ever even known about Searchlight were it not for the ban."*

Nevertheless, Searchlight was officially tainted by stories of the painted women of an unclean nature.  Soldiers were not allowed within the city limits except to pass through town on the main highway.  The liquor licenses of the City Café and the Miners' Café were revoked, and at the request of the Army, the two establishments were subsequently shut down.  Military police  patrolled the establishments and enforced the ban.  By May 1st, Sheriff Jones declared, *"All those formerly connected with the two places have 'moved on."*  While the sentiment of the statement may have been true, it is far more likely the ladies simply moved on to a different establishment than moved out of the town.  There were always ways to make money in Searchlight.

Searchlight fought the military ban in May of 1943.  The town board simply refused the terms imposed by the Army officials and accepted the fate of being a city tabooed because of prostitution and remained off limits to the military.  The liquor board  revoked a couple of licenses and the town board  closed a couple of establishments.  However, one military request crossed a line  Searchlight was not  prepared to cross.

According to a *Review-Journal* report *"...liquor might be sold between the hours of 3 and 11PM only if the ban were removed from the military personnel's entering the town."*  All of this was contingent upon the removal of all gaming devices, including slot machines, from all establishments in Searchlight.  It seemed, at least in the mind of the commanding general, no gambling meant no prostitutes (more of that *"gambling brings in bad influences"* thinking, I imagine).  Liquor, apparently, was not responsible for any such shenanigans and, if regulated by time constraints, was acceptable.

A *Las Vegas Review-Journal* article stated there were at least three establishments that offered slot machines in Searchlight at the time, and the revenues from licensing fees they paid to the city were far greater than the need to get servicemen into the town, whether it was for sex, alcohol, or just a pass through town. The town board was basically saying the gambling dollar was the king. Moreover, it had always been generally understood servicemen would eventually find what they were seeking. The gambling remained in Searchlight establishments and the military ban stood.

While *Fuller's Index of Nevada's Gambling Establishments* provides an extremely informative listing of casinos and the games they offered, one thing it failed to report were the "other" adult games available at these establishments. Prostitution was reported or rumored to exist in almost every business in Searchlight that offered a beer or a table game. Senator Harry Reid wrote in his book, *The Good Fight*, that there were at least 13 brothels in the town including the Crystal Club and the Searchlight Casino.

Establishments that had their own hotels were able to utilize the rooms accordingly, while businesses without their own facilities such as the Searchlight Casino simply sent the eager men to any one of the Searchlight "cribs," a small number of mini houses located along Searchlight's main drag. Photographs from the time period show at least five cribs behind the Searchlight Casino on Highway 95. However, with the opportunistic nature of prostitution, there were more than likely other such locations throughout the town. These cribs were small and unassuming in appearance, designed to look more like a cluster of affordable homes in a burgeoning suburb if such a thing existed then. If you drove past, there would be little outside to suggest anything of an untoward nature in place there. While there is something rather brazen about having miniature houses of ill repute along the town's main thoroughfare, these cribs were designed not to attract attention.

One thing is clear, interviews with Martello's family and an interview with Joyce Dickens Walker show prostitution was not on the menu in the early days of the El Rey Club. *"Adding the girls was NEVER Willie's idea,"* according to Bob Martello.

When Willie joined his brothers Buddy and Albert in 1946, he began to envision bigger things for the humble El Rey Club. He knew the El Rey

Club could be successful, and that the Martello brothers could use their knowledge of the night club game and make it a place where people would want to spend time and money. He saw a lot of potential and money coming into the town of Searchlight though not necessarily into the El Rey. At least, there was not enough money coming into the El Rey by his estimation. Money was good, but not THAT good...yet.

Willie eventually became the P.T. Barnum of Searchlight and boasted he had the biggest, brightest, and most exciting place to relax and have a good time. However, with the situation as it was, Willie would have been more like the guy cleaning up after the elephants if he couldn't bring more money into the club.

He had big plans for the El Rey Club. The plans were big enough to match the personality and ego of the man who thought of them. He wanted to add a café that served top-notch food, expand his gaming venture, bring in live entertainment, and build a motel. All of these ideas cost money he simply didn't have.

*"Once the Club was up and running,"* Richardson said, *"he needed revenue."*

Enter: *Daisy Mae and Her Ladies*.

Sometime in 1947, Willie was approached by *Daisy Mae*, a madam who was interested in running prostitutes out of the El Rey. Willie's club was one of the few gambling establishments in town that was not already offering such services, and Daisy took it upon herself to try to expand her business. While the Martello family took pride in running a clean business, the addition of the working girls made perfect business sense. Since nearly every other gaming house in town doubled as a whore house, potential dollars for the El Rey Club were lost, dollars that Willie could use to make the aforementioned improvements.

The Martellos made the decision to allow Daisy Mae to bring in her ladies, a decision that didn't set well with everyone, including Willie himself. Joyce Dickens Walker recollects, *"One day Willie dismissed me saying he was hiring girls. I was very mad at Willie for this, but he sweet-talked me and I forgave him and went to work at the grocery store next door."* Personal feelings about the addition of the ladies aside, it was a difficult decision to make but an easy one to justify. *"It was a means to an end,"* says Sharon Richardson. *"He did whatever it took just to keep going until the dream was realized."*

Bob Martello quickly pointed out the addition of the girls and the casino operations were two separate things. *"She ran the girls. He ran the club. That was that. Willie was no pimp!"* Running the girls through the El Rey improved the financial situation of the club very quickly. Willie and Buddy already had a good reputation in town for having a comfortable place to drink and gamble. The addition of Daisy Mae and her ladies only made the El Rey seem more desirable.

Searchlight had the Camp Ibis army base nearby and did not seem to be affected by 1943's "off limits" status. There were still miners and prospectors in town interested in spending time with willing ladies. There were also enough people traveling either to Las Vegas or California, all needing or wanting to stop in Searchlight. Willie's goal was to get as many of those people as possible to not only stop but also STAY in Searchlight. The money brought in as a result of the ladies now made that a genuine possibility.

Willie was able to add blackjack and roulette to the club, and slot machines would soon follow. A café would soon open and brightly painted signs that announced *"This is it! El Rey Club Bar & Casino"* were now found on all sides of the building. A rather modest neon sign with a curved arrow that pointed down to the entrance of the club would lead people into what Willie called *"The Gayest Spot on U.S. Hwy 95."* While there was no official motel offered, the neon sign out front did advertise cabins were available both for the road-weary traveler and those in search of comfort of a more salacious kind. Presumably, these were the "cribs" found between the Searchlight Casino and the El Rey, as photographic evidence from the time suggested. A full service, 17 room motel would not be fully operational until the mid-1950s.

While the drinking, gambling, and café brought in customers, the ladies were really the big moneymakers. Almost any place in town at the time contended gaming brought in big dollars, but prostitution brought in consistent cash. Willie Martello himself once joked to long-time friend Jerry Schafer, *"If it weren't for the miners and the servicemen, I'd go broke! God bless the hard working men in and out of uniform in the U.S.A.!"*

The extra revenue and Willie's overwhelming need to promote and be recognized as the big man in town brought about the most notable improvement to both the town of Searchlight and the El Rey Club around 1950 when he built the town's first and only swimming pool within the city limits.

Although it was nestled about 57 miles from Las Vegas, the temperature of Searchlight was generally cooler but far from cool. They were still in the desert, and the desert got hot. With all the ladies on hand, some of whom were actually working as dealers in the club, there was a need for a place to cool off and relax. Willie called **Harold Blasiola**, Sharon Richardson's father, and contracted with him to build a spacious swimming pool for Daisy Mae and her ladies.

The swimming pool was specifically for the ladies and employees. I've heard stories that stated guests of the El Rey were allowed to use the pool as well, but in the early days, this may have been limited to those also interested in procuring the skills of the ladies. In later years, the pool was treated as an amenity of the resort and offered to guests.

Willie never missed an opportunity to generate a lot of buzz for his establishment, and being the man who brought the first swimming pool to Searchlight, cashed in on the opportunity and offered use of the pool to the children of Searchlight every Thursday afternoon. Jeff Reid, Jr. remembered the pool as being

**Left to Right: Ralph Stewart, Joyce Dickens, & Jeff Reid, Jr. at the El Rey Pool.**
*Photo courtesy Joyce Dickens Walker.*

**Willie and friend lounging by the El Rey Club pool.**
*Photo courtesy Sharon Richardson.*

219

specifically for the kids. *"Willie built the pool mostly for us,"* he recalled. *"When it was finished, he had the girls there and they got to use it too. But I remember being there on weekends all the time."*

Among those who were happy to enjoy the cool waters of the town's unique attraction was future Senate Majority Leader, Harry Reid. Reid stated in *The Good Fight* never more than a dozen kids were allowed in the pool at a time and all were invited to live *"the life of Riley"* for a few hours.

Had the Reid boys or anyone else in Searchlight known of the golden secret lying beneath the refreshing waters of the pool, the excitement would surely have turned into a chaotic frenzy.

The building of the pool was exciting enough for the town and the club. This kind of thing simply hadn't happened before, and people soon became very eager to see the new El Rey amenity. However, none of the townspeople of Searchlight knew the truth that was revealed to me; something was buried in that pool.

In an interview I had with Bob Martello, he recalled a story never before told and one I've always been hesitant to share.

As the workers were pouring concrete for the pool, Willie stopped its progress and had a wicked grin on his face. According to Bob, *"Willie took off his gold ring, worth about $25,000, and tossed it into the wet concrete!"* Immediately afterward, Willie instructed them to resume the work. *"He thought it would be funny knowing people were swimming on top of all that money, completely unaware. That's just how he was. He didn't care about money, at least, not his money. That was Willie!* [laughing] *The ring...it's probably still there!"*

Hearing a story like this one not only fit into the many outrageous tales I've heard about Willie Martello, but it also scared the hell out of me. Seriously. In today's world, a $25,000 gold ring could be worth a heck of a lot more, and lord knows, in a small town like Searchlight, there are plenty of people more than willing to start digging and hacking into concrete for the chance to find some "whore's gold." After I laughed at the tale, I told Bob I couldn't print that story for fear it would cause a panic. Bob's only reply was, *"Print what you want, but that's what happened.* [laughing] *Willie loved a good joke."*

Thankfully, after I took several trips to Searchlight myself, I realized all traces of the El Rey pool were gone. To my knowledge, aside from a few inflatable or privately owned pools in back yards, there is no swimming pool in Searchlight and certainly no swimming pool with a gold lining. Put away your metal detectors and pickaxes.

Business was booming for the El Rey Club. Revenue was up in all departments, and within a few years of arriving in town, Willie also owned and operated The Crystal Club which sat across the street, down from the Searchlight Casino. It seemed that Searchlight, a town that really only had a few hundred permanent residents, was starting to thrive once again.

By early 1951, the heat was on again in Searchlight and prostitution was the main target. District Attorney Roger Foley was acting upon a public nuisance petition that was signed by ten Searchlight residents. Willie was already feeling a bit of a pinch after his gaming license was revoked on February 27th for "irregular gambling operations" as mentioned in a previous chapter. While Martello was eventually able to get his license back and continue gaming operations, the last thing he needed was a decrease in revenue because of the loss of the girls.

On May 10, 1951, Las Vegas attorney **Harry Claiborne** applied for a reinstatement of Willie's gaming license. At that same time, District Attorney Roger Foley was getting ready to shut down four reported houses of ill repute in Searchlight. **William R. Dingwall's** Searchlight Casino, **John Norheim's** Oasis Club, and both of Willie's establishments, the Crystal Club and the El Rey Club, were named publicly, and all three men were facing the prospect of losing both liquor and gaming licenses. On May 25, 1951, Foley essentially shut down the houses and gave Dingwall, Norheim, and Martello until Tuesday the 29th of May to completely clear out all the girls. **Archie Teague** of the *Las Vegas Review-Journal* wrote, *"The last of the good-time girls in this town were packing their bags today and starting to look for greener pastures on the tenderloin circuit. District Attorney Roger Foley has given the four night clubs here until Tuesday to get rid of their prostitutes. But most of the love-for-money ladies weren't waiting around."*

The three men were brought before Roger Foley by Sheriff John Silveira to answer for their crimes: running illegal houses of prostitution within 300 yards of a school and on a public highway. They were each given a choice: pay a fine and remove the girls or lose your liquor and gaming licenses. Realizing there was more long-term money possible from drinking and gambling in Searchlight, Willie Martello and the other men named agreed to pay a fine of $50 ($25 on each of two counts) per person. There was also an understanding that Foley would go for the maximum penalties if there were ever any future *proven* violations. One of the men told Archie Teague, *"We struggled along without 'em before, so I guess we can do it again. But it ain't gonna be the same."*

The fine was noticeably small at the recommendation of Foley who felt the men's promise to remove the girls would be sufficient punishment. Foley, also on the board that granted or revoked liquor licenses in Clark County, felt safe all parties would comply. In reality, a small fine may have been cruel and unusual punishment for the town of Searchlight who feared financial ruin without the ability to

Searchlight's Halls of Fun Are Quiet Now

From the *Las Vegas Review-Journal*, May 25, 1951.

provide men with this valuable service. The *Review-Journal* even went on to describe Searchlight as *"the soon-to-be ghost town."*

The investigation and subsequent closure of the houses in Searchlight started with a petition signed by only ten local residents and resulted in a situation that threatened the financial stability of the entire town. A counter-petition signed by 76 residents who wanted all business operations to remain untouched was a little over one tenth of the town's population. Something seemed fishy to the people of Searchlight and the *Review-Journal's* Archie Teague.

Teague wrote a three-part series of stories detailing the petitions, investigation, and closure of the houses. At first, it appeared the complaints that came from the ten residents mirrored those heard from any town that didn't want gambling or other more adult activities happening in their town.

The working girls of Searchlight were certain the brouhaha started when one very unhappy local woman felt she was being cast aside by her husband in favor of the ladies plying their wares in town. *"The gentleman was supposedly spending more time in the roadside rendezvous than his ex-wife cared for. He later married a blackjack dealer from one of the local clubs and that was more than the lady could take,"* wrote Teague, quoting an unnamed prostitute. According to his article of May 25, 1951, it was the belief of many of the girls that this anonymous jilted ex-wife, *"a busy body,"* as they labeled her, started to float the petition around town.

The girls vehemently denied anyone in their profession was ruining any marriages, claiming it simply wasn't their policy. Two such ladies, who surprisingly gave their first names to Teague, defended their professional ethics and practices, insisting they were simply not allowed to market to the locals. One lady whom Teague described as a young blonde named Lynne said, *"We respect the family life here."* Her colleague, listed as Carol, insisted, *"It's strictly HANDS OFF the married men."*

As with any town across the country that has had gambling or prostitution, legal or otherwise, people complained of an increase in violence and riffraff in their town, though there is little evidence to confirm this type of information. One long-time resident, unwilling to put his name in print, told Teague, *"Beatings outside the clubs were a regular occurrence."*

Whether or not the old chestnuts of destroyed marriages, loss of family values, or increased bar fights were to blame, it was the signatures of exactly ten people that drew the attention of D.A. Foley who later recommended a Grand Jury investigation into prostitution in Southern Nevada. Ten people AGAINST versus seventy-six people FOR prostitution halted the flow of thousands of dollars into Searchlight, Nevada? Archie Teague believed otherwise. According to Teague, there may have been a busy body at work, but it was not likely it was some angry Searchlight wife. Not entirely.

Listing only *"informed sources"* as his references, on June 1, 1951, Archie Teague completed his three-part series on page two of the *Review-Journal*. He posited that the entire issue of a petition naming the Searchlight sin shacks as public nuisances was the work of an anonymous man who had his own sights set upon being the ONLY whoremonger in town.

Although Teague was not able to find anyone willing to go on record about the mysterious pimp or prove the allegations, he felt he had enough evidence to publish the story. One man, a dark stranger, wanted to own the prostitution trade in Searchlight.

*"He picked a time when a few natives here have had beefs against the club operators and their girlies and talked an especially irate woman into passing the 'nuisance abatement' petition,"* wrote Teague.

The *Review-Journal* reporter painted a picture of a powerful and imposing man who may have intimidated the ten locals and acted as a puppet master, calling the shots from behind the scenes. He pointed out the mysterious man in question was not among the ten who signed the petition. Though it was not specifically stated in the article, it seemed as though the man was not only absent from the petition but among those absent from the town as well. What happened to the angry woman who started the petition in the first place? According to Teague, she *"left Searchlight as soon as the great debate got going and hasn't been heard from since."* Teague continued, *"Most of the signers left town for a while."*

Whether Teague's account is accurate or not, one thing was clear, Searchlight did not want to remove the working girls and the revenue stream they generated. At the time of Foley's investigation, the Searchlight town board was looking into incorporating the town.

Had Searchlight been incorporated it would still be subject to the law that allowed fines to be imposed if you ran a house of ill repute within 300 yards of a school or on a public highway. However, as an incorporated town the decision of exactly what constituted a public nuisance would be decided by the town and not by the district attorney of Clark County. In essence, an incorporated town could decide for itself what was or wasn't a nuisance to the people.

Still, the unincorporated town of Searchlight had their ladies removed and the club owners, including Martello, agreed to run their businesses from that moment on without the aid and added revenue of the world's oldest profession. Perhaps, it was the threat of losing their liquor and gaming licenses, but if Teague's account was accurate, it is not beyond belief to suspect a genuine fear of the mysterious stranger mentioned in the newspaper article. Surely, a man capable of coercing some of Searchlight's hard-edged and resilient residents to sign a bogus petition, threaten the livelihoods of those living good lives within the town, and then flee the scene can certainly possess a degree of intimidation strong enough to convince a man of Martello's confidence and resolve to play by the rules. It also stands to reason if District Attorney Foley, a man also on the liquor board, was willing to pay such close attention to tiny little Searchlight, perhaps that constant presence would stave off the advances of this anonymous thug.

Searchlight was quickly growing. The amount of money being generated by gambling, drinking, prostitution, and the efforts of Willie Martello to use the allure of the town's surrounding areas such as Lake Mohave and Christmas Tree Pass, were not going unnoticed. Could it be that Searchlight's good fortune and increasing coiffeurs attracted the attention of a bigger, seedier element from neighboring Las Vegas? Was Searchlight becoming a threat to the flow of traffic and cash 57 miles to the northwest? Was this so-called prostitution kingpin the first hint that organized crime was interested in setting up shop in Searchlight? Unfortunately, we'll never know. No official investigation was ever launched into the story of a slithering sin lord working his way into town. Archie Teague wrote no more about the financial woes of a Searchlight without whores, and his own theories of a mysterious stranger in town remained confined to that single column.

At this point, the mere notion of a sultan of sin or organized crime organization is simply speculation. Archie Teague's three-part series, particularly the third installment that alluded to a dark figure in the background, could have been like so many tales from the Wild West and factual only up to a point.

I'm no investigative reporter, and I love a good story, but even I have to wonder about the veracity of a report or wonder if a friend of Teague's planted it when I see such a glaring absence of people willing to go on record. With that in mind, I realize I may encounter the same level of doubt from readers of this book. I, too, have found it very easy for people to offer a tale but difficult for them to willingly be associated with the tale. In this instance, I choose to remain curiously skeptical about the presence of an elusive and imposing whoremaster and any criminal conspiracy. If there was a man causing that much of a stir in the small town of Searchlight, his identity remains a mystery.

The same is true concerning the true identity of Daisy Mae, the madam who brought her ladies to Willie Martello. Interviews with members of the Martello family affirm that Daisy Mae was actually **Daisy V. Clapsaddle**. If that is the case, it certainly adds to the mystique and intrigue surrounding the whole tale, but without legal proof or any confirmation from any members of Clapsaddle's family, I cannot confirm the madam's identity.

Daisy V. Clapsaddle was the wife of the respected sheriff, John "Big John" Silveira. Clapsaddle and Silveira were reported to have quite an outrageous relationship. *"John and Daisy were FABULOUS together,"* exclaimed **Diane Kendall**, Searchlight resident and daughter of Jr. Cree. Their marriage seemed to be more of the "on-again, off-again" variety, with a serious slant toward the "on-again" side, with John and Clapsaddle marrying and divorcing on more than on one occasion. When I asked about Clapsaddle, one Searchlight resident said to me while laughing, *"She married John a lot!"* However, this same person is rather insistent Clapsaddle couldn't have been the El Rey madam.

If Daisy Clapsaddle were the infamous Daisy Mae, it would not be altogether that shocking when put into the context of life in 1940s through 1960s in Searchlight. It was, after all, a story about a man who left his wife for a dealer prostitute of Searchlight that started the entire Foley investigation. In my research, I've been told repeated stories of notable Searchlight businessmen who settled down and married local working girls, quite literally making "honest women" out of them.

At the time of this writing, efforts to locate and interview descendants or relatives of Daisy Clapsaddle or John Silveira have been unsuccessful, and therefore, any sort of confirmation that Clapsaddle was indeed Daisy May cannot be made. While the comedian in me cannot stop laughing at the wonderful irony of a madam with the last name Clapsaddle, I cannot say with certainty that the two Daisys were one and the same. Besides, what man would willingly order a prostitute from any madam with "CLAP" in her name?

Along with these puzzles surrounding Searchlight's history with the ladies of the evening comes a lack of ability to pinpoint an exact time period when prostitution began and ended in the town – specifically, the El Rey Club. Perhaps, it is simply because Searchlight bore such a reputation for being a place to find working girls. Based upon comments from several Las Vegas area long-timers, it was the belief of everyone but the Martello family that the girls never really stopped being a part of the scene. Bob Martello had insisted to me, *"When they were gone, they were gone for good."*

While writing an article about the El Rey for **Mark Englebretson's** Nevada Casino Ashtrays website, I wrote, *"For a period of not more than five years, guests of the El Rey could procure the services of Daisy Mae and Her Ladies."* Bob Martello confirmed this time frame for me. As time passed and more people found my own website and research, more stories came out and led me to amend the story.

Jerry Schafer, a long-time friend of Willie Martello and one-time Las Vegas law man himself, was one of the first people who returned a phone call and eagerly told me tales about Willie Martello. Thankfully, he never looked behind his shoulder and whispered, *"You know about the girls, right?"* However, he did have a few stories to tell about the girls, nonetheless.

Schafer, who did not become acquainted with Martello until about 1960 and filmed *Wide Open Spaces* at the El Rey in 1961, recalled seeing lines of servicemen outside many of the 17 motel rooms at the El Rey Resort, *"Willie had a guy he called his 'whoremaster' who would stand outside of the motel rooms. He would stand out there holding a stop watch and wore one of those change-making machines around his belt. The kind bus drivers used to wear."* Why the stopwatch, you ask? According to Schafer, the servicemen were able to avail themselves of the lovely ladies of Searchlight for the bargain price of one dollar per minute, and every second mattered.

*"Can you imagine?"* Schafer laughed, *"This poor guy's job was to watch the clock and make change for the guys getting laid inside! I saw plenty of guys who paid for 5 or 10 minutes only to come out after a minute or two and want a refund for the difference. One guy left the room wanting fifty cents back. He had only paid a dollar!"*

Jerry recollected these stories with fondness and without any judgment for Willie or the El Rey. He never had to worry about making any arrests or imposing any fines. Willie was a good friend and business was business in a town like Searchlight. While not the exact phrase I've heard so often during this research, one of my first emails from him asked, *"Did you know that the El Rey was a house of ill repute?"* This was long before I got such a tale from Schafer.

Dick Taylor recalled it differently.

*"Contrary to popular opinion, the El Rey was NOT a house of ill repute,"* said Taylor, respected Nevada historian and former owner of the Moulin Rouge Hotel and Casino in Las Vegas. However, his assertion comes with a bit more clarity of terms. *"I don't deny that there were girls there at some point. It was a common thing in Searchlight. There were brothels in Searchlight, but those were run-down shacks. Filthy places. The El Rey was a nice place, not what you'd call a whorehouse. When I was there, it was a legitimate business."*

Dick Taylor knew Willie Martello through his own business relationship with Warren "Doc" Bayley, who became friends with Willie Martello in the mid-1950s and entered a business partnership with Martello by the 1960s. All of this happened after the now infamous prostitution scandal of 1951. *"The El Rey was a respectable place. Willie ran a wonderful, clean club out there."*

Since so much of Taylor's dealings with Martello happened in the late '50s and early '60s, it certainly suggested Willie kept to his word when he promised D.A. Foley he wouldn't have any girls in the El Rey. All of this muddies the waters a bit. We have two men who were there and knew Willie offering two different accounts. Both were men of honesty and integrity who were there during the same time period. Fascinating!

Of course, the loudest voice in Searchlight proclaimed the loudest that the El Rey was on the up-and-up. On March 5, 1952, not quite one full year after Roger Foley had Sheriff John Silveira bring in Norheim, Dingwall, and Willie Martello to pay a fine or lose their livelihoods forever, the opening sentence of a column on page three of the *Las Vegas Review-Journal* read, *"There is an unhappy man in Searchlight these days and his name is Willie Martello."*

Willie was upset with the negative publicity and was eager to recreate a more favorable view of his beloved El Rey, so, promoter that he was, went to the press to state his case. In a story more filled with quotes than questions, Willie went on to tout the virtues of his establishments.

*"If I was running what you folks in Las Vegas are pleased to call a bordello, I wouldn't have a squawk coming. But I am trying to run a decent place, where people coming to Southern Nevada can relax and enjoy themselves without having a bunch of hoodlums come in and insult them."*

Martello continued, *"The goops who hear all about the supposed lovemaking that goes on down here, come in to the bar, get a beer or two and get high, and then start insulting my customers in the bar. It's just not right."*

This *Review-Journal* article, credited to no specific author, was as much an advertisement for the El Rey Club as it was a plea for forgiveness. Willie, rather unfairly became the face of prostitution in the now twice-tabooed town. Being the town's biggest promoter and most powerful man clearly had a big drawback once the Foley investigation made headline news.

I recall my first encounter with any of Willie's family members. It started with a comment left at my blog. The post I wrote showed an admittedly juvenile fascination with the prostitution aspect of the El Rey and took a line about Willie from Harry Reid's book, *Searchlight: The Camp that Didn't Fail.* I didn't know much about Willie or the El Rey at that point and referred to Willie as Reid did: *"The King of Prostitution in Searchlight."* The comment left by Ed Darling, one of Willie's nephews, showed me that a scar that lasted nearly 60 years started with a very deep cut. *"Didn't think my uncle was so notorious. I will forward this web page to his wife. I don't think it would be appropriate to send it to his daughter. Willie was not a bad man. I hate the name you have hung on him."*

Suddenly, this became all too real. I realized while most everyone I've spoken with understood and actually enjoyed hearing tales of prostitution and gambling in the heyday of Southern Nevada, real people were likely scorned plenty for it, and I was perpetuating the rumors.

By the time I connected with Bob Martello, there was a lot of tension during our first few encounters, both online and on the phone. In what I'd call a hesitant, protective, and defensive tone, Bob said to me on the phone, *"Look, if you're going to write something, try to write something nice. My family has suffered enough because of this. Willie was no pimp. There are more than enough bad things written about Willie. He was such a wonderful man."* I told Bob I'd write the truth, both good and bad, if he'd be willing to share the truth with me. I think we finally clicked when I said, *"Bob, hookers in Nevada aren't anything new to me, but facts about Willie and the El Rey are. I know this could be a sore subject, but I was scared shitless to call you. It took a lot of nerve for me to call you KNOWING that you probably already thought I was an asshole. If you have the nerve to tell me what's not in Harry Reid's book, I'll tell as many people as I can."* With that, after a pause, Bob laughed and said, *"Pinky?"* (Harry Reid's nickname) *THAT GUY'S got nerve! You can call me any time."*

I had won him over, but clearly the stigma attached to the prostitution scandal was still very much a part of the Martello family. The kind of exchange that required me to prove my intentions as honorable took place nearly every time I met someone else in Willie's family.

The fact remains I have met people who can confirm both the presence and the absence of prostitutes in Searchlight and at the El Rey post 1951. I have just as many first-hand accounts insisting it was a brothel as there are people denying it happened after the scandal. Frankly, I choose to believe both are true to some extent.

This was still a very remote part of Southern Nevada, and Willie was always in need of more money. *"Every dime he ever made went back into the town or the club,"* said Sharon Richardson. Willie's plans never diminished and neither did his reputation for the grandiose. It is reasonable to believe publicly there were no prostitutes at the El Rey after 1951. Privately, you can safely assume, whether or not he liked it, Willie Martello was the man to ask if you wanted to procure such a thing. There is enough evidence to support both prospects.

In addition to Jerry Schafer's eyewitness accounts from 1961, there are other clues.

In the March 1952 *Review-Journal* column, Willie asserted, *"My places are the cleanest in the country. I defy any of the law enforcement agencies to find any of these wandering love-makers in my spots."* One only needs to be reminded that Sheriff Silveira was married to Daisy Clapsaddle to speculate once again.

Willie admitted to spending the night with a Searchlight prostitute in January of 1962 after his casino burned to the ground. This, at least, proves the presence of working girls in or traveling to Searchlight for fun and profit after 1951.

One of my contacts who wishes to remain nameless has supplied me with several fantastic artifacts from Searchlight and the El Rey, and provided me with several items reportedly from the home of a Mary Patterson, also known as **"Kissy Mary."** Kissy Mary was alleged to be a prostitute in Searchlight and possibly an employee at the El Rey at one point. When I asked if she was definitely at the El Rey or even a prostitute at all, I received the reply, *"I don't know if she was a girl at the El Rey, but if she wasn't a prostitute then she sure was by the time I last spoke to her! That's what she told me."* Again, not conclusive proof of anything other than the existence of prostitution in Searchlight after the scandal and further evidence that a working girl could always make money in Searchlight.

Perhaps, the best evidence suggesting a connection to Martello and the girls can be found within his own literature promoting the El Rey. In my collection of El Rey memorabilia, I have one original brochure. This is a great piece of 1950s era advertising, and it did well to sell the amenities of the El Rey Resort. The photos and fonts place the origin of the brochure from the early to mid-1950s. The subtext of one photo caption suggests something more. Underneath a wonderful picture of happy gamblers surrounding an El Rey roulette table, the subtext reads, *"We 'got lucky' at their exciting gaming tables."*

Much like the identity of Daisy Mae or that of the nefarious pimp wanting to invade Searchlight, we'll never know exactly how long the girls were available in Searchlight or the El Rey. As with so many aspects of the El Rey story, *"nobody knows nothin'"*. At the very least, nobody wants to be responsible for pinning blame or shame on anyone.

**A suggestive excerpt from an El Rey brochure.** *From the author's personal collection.*

If you do a search online or at your local library of the names John Norheim or William Dingwall, you are unlikely to find the labels **"pimp"** or **"whoremonger"** as you would with one Google search of Willie Martello. I believe this is an example of what I call "P.T. Barnum Syndrome".

Much in the way Barnum is immediately associated with the circus, Babe Ruth remains the face of baseball, or Muhammad Ali represents the persona of "The Champion of the World" to boxing fans, Willie Martello is forever linked to Searchlight's darkest and most intriguing topic. To all the world Willie Martello was Searchlight, Nevada, and rightly so. His constant promotion of the town and his desire to create a legitimate tourist destination to rival Las Vegas made him the most recognizable and powerful figure in town. When his name became associated with a scandal involving the world's oldest profession, who in Nevada or elsewhere was really going to recall the names Dingwall or Norheim?

The fact of the matter is, prostitution was and still is a large part of Nevada's history and in no way exclusive to the El Rey. I believe Bob Martello said it best, *"It's not like Willie invented prostitution in Nevada!"*

I'll close this chapter with the last quote from the March 5, 1951 article from the *Review-Journal* and let you decide for yourself.

*"Please, will you tell the folks in Las Vegas that Willie Martello is running a first class establishment, and if they're looking for these ladies of the evening, they ought to go somewhere else and leave us alone? So far as I know, there are none of those women in Searchlight, now."*

# WHAT'S IN A NAME?
# AKA, UNCLE WILLIE AND THE SCARLET LETTER

I t is with a certain amount of joy (and some breathless exhaustion) that I can lay claim to getting more people to ask a question about Willie other than, *"You know about the girls, right?"* In the time it has taken to research this book, all of the letters and phone calls to total strangers in the hope I would receive some new information, all of the casino collectibles shows I've attended to look for more knick-knacks for my home, and all of the family members I have encountered have brought up at least one other question with equal frequency.

*"How are you related to Willie?"*

This is something I have wondered from day one. The thought of finding a whole new branch to the Martello family, and one who owned a casino no less, was thrilling to me. My mother, my brothers, my sister, my cousin, my aunt – everybody in my family that has taken time to listen to this nonsense from me – has wondered if we have a new uncle or cousin to talk about and extended family members to add to the Christmas card list in December.

It always seemed perfectly plausible. According to Ancestry.com, in 2000, there were only 826 Martello families in the United States which made it a much better prospect than if my last name were Smith or Jones. From photos I found early on, there were certainly some resemblances

**Tony & Buddy Martello in front of the first El Rey Club in South Gate, CA, in 1939.**
*Photo courtesy Bob Martello*

that could either be a result of being Italian or from being related. When my mother first got word of this mysterious casino owner in Nevada, she told me about someone in her family being a croupier at the Sands in the 1960s. Granted, my mother was not Italian, but I had to gnaw on something until this hunger was sated.

Within a few minutes of the beginning of our first conversation, Bob Martello was wondering if we were somehow related. We started looking for similarities other than the common last name.

Among the things that intrigued us both was his branch of Martellos and my own came through Ellis Island within a few years of each other. Better still was the fact many Martellos from both families settled for a spell in Ohio, especially the greater Cleveland area. In fact, my **Aunt Louise,** who was married to my **Uncle Nick Martello,** and several cousins, including cousins **Nick** and **Johnny Martello,** still reside there, as do quite a few Martellos from Willie's branch of the tree.

Bob Martello has a son, **Matt Martello.** My younger brother's name is **Matt.** I bet you thought I was going to say **John Martello** was my younger brother. No, John Martello is actually my older brother (using his middle name, **Marty,** makes things a lot easier at reunions).

I, **Andy Martello** from Chicago, while doing a little ego-surfing online one day, found another **Andy Martello** who lives in St. Louis. This Andy Martello is the son of a **Nick Martello** from Ohio, but NOT my cousin Nick or my uncle Nick (both from Ohio), but one that actually is related to Willie Martello. The kicker for me was I contacted this Andy Martello years BEFORE I'd ever heard about Willie Martello. I just found it to be good blog-fodder to post about another Andy Martello.

By the way, I do have an uncle named Bill, but he's on my mother's side and not Italian, at all. In fact, he's not even a Martello and certainly not a

Willie. I'm getting confused.

There are many Nicks, Johns, and Tonys in our families. However, just like the facial resemblances, this could simply be because Italian families tend to name a lot of kids, Nick, John, and Tony. What can I say? Some stereotypes are true. Deal with it. Still... gnaw, gnaw, gnaw!

Physical similarities, common names, and geographic locations weren't the only ways we could find we had new family. Choices in professions started popping up that made us think there certainly was something to this theory of relativity. There are a fair amount of teachers, salespeople, entertainers, antique dealers, and most significantly, tavern owners in both Martello families.

**Uncle Nick (L) and my father Don (R) in front of their dad's saloon.**
*From the author's personal collection.*

By this point in the book, you should be more than aware of the history in the bar and night club business on Willie's side of the family. As it turned out, my grandfather, **Giambatista "John" Martello,** owned a saloon in the Little Italy neighborhood of Cleveland for many years. This fact prompted Bob to send me a couple of photos of his father (Tony) and Uncle Buddy standing in front of the El Rey Club that started it all, the one in South Gate, California.

Staring at that photo, I looked at the two brothers happily posing in front of the family business, smiling, and holding some ice cold beers. I got a chill as I pulled out an old photo of my Uncle Nick and my father, **Donald Martello** (Don??? We must have filled our quota for Nicks and Johns by the time he was born). The photo showed the two brothers on the steps of their father's saloon, laughing and toasting one another with ice cold beer. It was a veritable family reunion!

Bob and I promised each other we would do a little homework and solve this mystery. He was certain we were somehow related. By the time he and I were emailing more frequently and speaking on the phone somewhat regularly, we had both forgotten about actually getting an answer. So far as we were concerned, we were already family and that was that. We spoke often, sent each other little messages around holidays, and we shared stories with one another about things our crazy relatives had done. There were times Bob would give me pep talks about my career without provocation and times when I'd ask him for advice.

Soon, I was in contact with Suzan and Sharon, **Angie Tune** and **Louette Harmon**, more family members with info on Willie. Ed Darling, Ethel, and I have shared a few conversations—the family was getting bigger every day. In fact, I think I've spoken with Sharon Richardson as much, if not more, in the last few years than I have any one of my siblings. Of course, to be fair, my sister **Lisa** keeps moving and forgetting to update her contact information.

We are all exchanging photos with one another, sharing stories that should likely be kept private, and I even sent gifts to a few of these folks around the holidays. Bob received his very own copy of *Tonight for Sure!* and Sharon opened a box one day to find both a matchbook and ashtray from Willie's club, Marsal's in South Gate, California.

We call each other when family members are sick or dying. We cry and laugh based upon the results and the stories that follow.

Isn't that what families do?

As a result of all this poking and prodding into the past, many of Willie's family are speaking a lot more frequently, trying to share more memories before they're gone. Whether we're actually related or not is no longer relevant. We simply are a family of some kind and Willie is the guy who brought us all together. Sharon even told me in an interview, *"Family was always so important to Willie."*

Still...gnaw, gnaw, gnaw. I had to know. Not so much because I think it is that important to find out this quest has a greater purpose like finding lost relatives. I need to know because everyone from historians to casual acquaintances of Willie and presumably any media personalities I may encounter trying to promote this book will not stop asking the same question.

*"How are you related to Willie?"*

The comedian in me has the perfect answer...

*"By accident."*

The writer in me has a more clever answer...

*"By chance."*

The genealogist in me...has no answer, at all. Why? Because I'm just not that interested anymore. I'm not an investigative journalist kind of a guy. I'm certainly not patient enough to look into the minutiae of a family tree. However, the genealogist in the family DID have an answer.

Remember Nick Martello? Not my uncle Nick or my cousin Nick (both from Ohio). The Nick from Ohio with an Andy Martello for a son that is not me? He has done a lot of painstaking research over the years to fill in the family tree. While my hobby has been to research Willie Martello, his hobby has been to research all Martellos. He contacted me out of the blue one day to continue his research.

It just so happened, just as I'd contacted his Andy Martello years before, Nick had been in contact with my aunt, Louise Martello, in Ohio years before. After plenty of laughs, questions, and prerequisite hand-waving while talking, Nick had the answer.

Nope.

It turned out his Martellos came from a markedly different section of Italy than mine and lived there at somewhat different times. Normally, that wouldn't be enough to make a big difference, but learning that Willie's Martellos from the old country used to have an "**a**" at the end of their name and later changed the "**a**" to an "**o**" sometime after coming to America certainly was enough. My Martellos were always Martell**O**s, dating back to the Italian city of Vico del Gargano, near Foggia.

Martell**A** vs. Martell**O**. The difference of one simple letter may not seem like much, but by genealogical standards, it is ENORMOUS.

So, there it is. I've been betrayed by my own first initial. A big "A" emblazoned on Willie's beautiful white suit, if I may steal and adapt a literary reference.

In fact, this entire journey was really a result of pure coincidence. It was a one-in-a-million chance my wife would find a photo on a wall in Las Vegas which bore my last name. That sliver of probability and random happenstance would start a multi-year project which has culminated in this book. That one perfect storm unearthed a whole lot of history and quite possibly brought about a world that may now look at Willie Martello in a completely different light. Whether this is your first time hearing about Willie or the El Rey Club, or the 100th, that little bit of luck, a gift to me from the seventh son of a seventh son, has made an immeasurable positive impact on my life. I hope Willie and his family are proud.

What are the odds?

(just) A Martello

# EPILOGUE

To this day I continue to be fascinated with the El Rey Club and the many antics and actions of Willie Martello. When I am not working my "real job" as an entertainer in Las Vegas or across the country, I frequently find myself organizing notes, looking through photos, visiting the Nevada State Museum, haunting antique stores, or surfing eBay hoping to find just one more piece of arcana that is not in my collection.

One of the things that IS in my collection is the photo that started it all. I don't mean a copy of the photo. THE actual framed photo is now hanging on my wall. I purchased this within the first year of moving to Las Vegas. The Lost Vegas store closed its shop at the Neonopolis location, but thrived as one of the dealers at the Main Street Antiques for a long time. That is where I found THE actual photo complete with the sticker bearing Willie's name across the top. The kicker? I walked right past the photo at the store. If I had not been there with, you guessed it, my wife April, I'd never have even noticed it was now something I could actually own. It's a good thing we're still friends even after a divorce. Who knows what else I'd miss? For those interested, Main Street Antiques had to shut its doors to make way for the new Las Vegas Government Center, but Lost Vegas has a new location on Las Vegas Blvd. very close to the *Pawn Stars* pawn shop.

Interestingly, after moving out to Las Vegas, my wife and I never visited the Neon Museum and Boneyard until December 18, 2010. The Neon Museum, while still offering tours, had been undergoing major renovations and simply wasn't something we were able to do since moving here in mid-2007. Shortly after I completed the book and geared up for editing and proofreading, I heard the Boneyard was offering an open house, and we decided to check it out. Among the great "new" things we found there were the Moulin Rouge and Stardust signs, the sign from the Chapel by the Courthouse (where April and I married several years earlier), and the La Concha Motel lobby had been moved from the Strip and preserved as the main entrance to the Neon Museum. It was very nice to see something designed by the architect of what would have been Searchlight's future preserved in the place that helped start my El Rey journey. There is also something else of note about our visit to the Boneyard. Our first visit back to this genuine jewel of Las Vegas fell on the same day April finished reading the first draft of this book. It seems I've come full circle with all of this El Rey fun. Perhaps, I was destined to tell this story.

Even though it has been gone for so many years, and I have so many things already, my heart won't allow the place to truly be gone; I am, therefore, forever hopeful of finding just one more item for safekeeping. My website is still up and running, and I am always ready to speak with someone else who has a story to share or memorabilia to sell. I have other book projects in the works including some follow-ups to this one. Such is the curse of accidentally becoming a historian, I suppose.

When I first began researching the El Rey Club, online primarily, I found little information. While I cannot remember which website provided me with this tiny shred of information, I do recall learning the El Rey Club reportedly burned to the ground twice in its lifetime. Twice. When I made email acquaintances with a few folks who sold me El Rey memorabilia, they had heard roughly the same thing, but again, couldn't quite recall the source of the information. Eventually, I wrote and repeated this information on my blog. As a result, I am now the point of reference when people talk about the El Rey Club and its two historic fires. It is still online to this day. Go ahead and see for yourself. I'll wait.

Since then, I've found my research located on eBay listings and in online price guides for casino collectibles. I've received random emails from people curious to know more about the blazes and the casino. Much of the research which I shared on my web log was used in the recent New York Times Best-Seller *The Girl in Alfred Hitchcock's Shower* by Robert Graysmith. I can't vouch for the accuracy of this statement, but I am considered the "expert" on the subject of the El Rey Club. Long before I even thought about writing this book this expert got it WRONG!

As the book has clearly stated, more thorough research showed the El Rey Club only suffered one horrible fire in 1962. I believe the confusion can be attributed to the fact a fire did occur in Searchlight in 1946; this was the same year the El Rey opened its doors. That fire scorched one wall of the El Rey Club, but it clearly did not raze the building. Since so much of Searchlight's history between the 1940s and 1970s is something of a mystery compared to its history at the turn of the century and the boomtown days, it is easy to conclude people just assumed the El Rey was one of the businesses that perished in 1946.

I write this here neither to tout my stellar research nor to be self-deprecating. I write this to cite an example of just how easily speculation can turn into history. The last version of ANY El Rey Club closed its doors in 1973, which really isn't that long ago, yet, prior to this publication, many people believed the El Rey burned twice. Willie Martello installed the first telephones in Searchlight, single-handedly built a full-service airport, and had the second license plate ever issued in Nevada. Above all else, they also "knew" Willie Martello was little more than a common pimp or a whoremonger. These facts were all the result of the *perception* regarding what happened in Searchlight. As with so many tall tales and taller lies, they all started with some elements that were true and have changed over time.

I hope this volume achieves success as the new authoritative source of what happened in Searchlight and answers exactly who Willie Martello was. While there have been times when even I resorted to relaying the rumors and stories told most often, I've done my absolute best to find people and newspaper accounts to corroborate the stories. Even keeping all of this in mind, the expert can still be wrong.

I've joked throughout the book that without a doubt in my mind there will be people who will spring from the woodwork to tell me now just how wrong I am. After somehow missing my ads in the newspapers, the fliers shoved under car windshield wipers and under front doors, the brochures, the seminars, the website, and every other plea for stories, information, and memoirs, somebody will most assuredly come forward to tell me, *"That's just not what happened!"* If that is the case, the result will be just one more example of how perception can alter the truth.

I am happy to allow you to decide for yourself just how well my perception, my interpretation of the data, and my research fits into a historical context. I also welcome the sequel books that all of the *"You got it wrong"* crowd will inspire.

Until that backlash or praise comes forth, I will try to tell you to the best of my ability what has happened to some of the key players mentioned most often in this book and how Searchlight has been affected by the presence of one Willie Martello. First, a little about Searchlight today.

Searchlight has grown since the days when Willie was in town. At one point, there were as few as 50 people living there, but today about 1,000 permanent residents make their homes in Searchlight. The town still boasts some of the freshest air in the world, and I am not about to dispute that claim. While I never want to see a fire in any part of the Mohave Desert, I can say with confidence that the firemen in town are just as brave but much better equipped to handle a fire. However, for the longest time, when you entered the town from Las Vegas on Highway 95, you found on your left hand side two most amusing things: an actual searchlight with a "Bat Signal" emblem on it, and...a dilapidated fire truck.

If any small town like Searchlight can survive boom town days and beyond, it would appear the presence of one or two families as principal land owners and businessmen will keep the town alive. This was true of the small farming community where I grew up in Illinois, and it has always been true of Searchlight. Whether it was the Colton family of the earliest days, the Martello family in the 1940s through the 1960s, or the Doing family today, if the town has thrived and survived, you can bet it will lead back to one or two families.

After the Argent group owned the El Rey (the Crystal Club-turned-El Rey Club), the last building to house any form of Willie's dream was purchased by the Doing family who later donated it to the city. The building remains standing today and is now the home of the Searchlight

Senior Center. Searchlight/Nevada gaming history enthusiasts may want to stop at the K-Million Mine art gallery and antique store. Next to the complex you will be in the building that once housed Sandy's Casino. The original bar is now being used as a display case and cash wrap.

The El Rey Motel is still intact and in business. If you wish to relive the moment, you can rent out room seven of the motel where Kenny Laursen stayed the night of the fire. Make sure to arrive unshaven when arriving in town, and if you do find you've left a musical instrument in a burning building, leave it there!

There is an empty lot with an old planter across the street next to the El Rey Motel. That vacant lot is where the El Rey Club once stood. Mysteriously, nothing has been done with the property since the fire. Even more unusual is the current owner of the property is listed as William J. Martello of Searchlight Development, Inc. However, that is a falsehood considering the property recently went up for sale and Willie is certainly NOT the one selling it.

Sometime after the fire in 1962, the ultimate ownership of the lot went to Lou Cooper, but not for the purpose of rebuilding the casino. *"I was doing all this* [accounting] *work, but he wasn't paying me any money,"* said Cooper. *"He had lots of property in town, and eventually, he offered some of the parcels as security and payment."* This proved to become a bit of a comical arrangement when the time came for Martello and Doc Bayley to make improvements to the motel or the new casino. *"When Willie told someone to 'Build it there', he didn't care if he owned the property or not,"* said Cooper's wife, Mickey. *"As it happened, I owned something like half of a room of the motel and the restrooms of the service station,"* laughed Lou as he reflected upon a time when Willie wanted to start some new construction. *"When Willie needed those small pieces of property, he offered me the bigger vacant lot in exchange and that seemed like more than a fair trade to me."* As the years passed, and Doc and Judy Bayley, Willie, and eventually the El Rey Club died, the Coopers simply held onto the property with no real idea what they'd ever do with it, if anything at all. *"We held onto it and would pay the taxes on it every so many years,"* recalled Mickey. *"It wasn't really worth a lot, so we wouldn't rush to pay the taxes on time every year. Only when it started getting sizable. One day,"* according to Lou, *"a few years back we finally sold it to the nice man who has it now."* When I mentioned to the Coopers the current owner is asking approximately $300,000 for the land, Lou laughed out loud. *"Well, he sure didn't PAY that for it!"*

That motel and most of the town is owned by Verlie Doing who also owns the Searchlight Nugget Casino. In February of 2013, Verlie announced she was selling her 62 parcels of Searchlight land totaling 41 acres. This sale included the casino and the El Rey Motel—you could have purchased nearly the whole town lock, stock, and barrel.

The Doing family arrived in Searchlight in 1967, roughly about the time Searchlight's last town owner was making his exit, and lasted a good 20 years longer as the town's primary landlords. Perhaps, the secret to their success was they didn't strive to make Searchlight another Laughlin or mini Las Vegas. There were improvements to the town, and many successful businesses came and went after 1967; however, there was never a master plan to make Searchlight bigger and better in a rapid and spectacular way. Maybe, it was Willie's ambition that led to his demise while it paved the way for folks like the Doings to become successful.

My dream is to one day own that land where the vacant lot still sits— the ultimate addition to my collection of El Rey memorabilia. Should this dream come true, I'd rebuild the El Rey as close to the original plans as possible. Not as a casino nor a brothel but as a larger museum for El Rey and Searchlight history. I might even include a little café and an area for private events. The most important thing to me would be the installation of a community swimming pool for the town to use. I think it would be poetic and satisfying to know another Martello brought back such a beloved city amenity and placed it in the spot where the town's first swimming pool once stood. Of course, with a $300,000 price tag on the land, I'd need to sell a lot more books. Until then, I enjoy knowing Willie still "exists" today as the owner of the vacant lot and that broken-down planter.

The planter, installed by Harold Blasiola, stands as the last vestige of the original El Rey. However, thanks to the generosity of a long-time Searchlight resident, in January of 2012, one piece of El Rey history rose from the ashes.

Nearly 50 years after a fire razed the El Rey Club, **Mike Madden** sent me a few grainy cell phone photos of what looked like advertising from the El Rey. After a phone conversation revealed he also had some newspaper clippings and an original promotional photo from Sally Rand's appearance

The El Rey Club billboard with at least 50 years of wear and tear.

at the casino in his collection , I decided yet another trip to Searchlight was in order. I was not prepared for what Mike had in store for me.

As promised, Mike owned a rare Sally Rand photo in addition to some fantastic bits of information, all of which he graciously shared with me at no cost. Since he was a bit of a Searchlight historian in his own right, he was more than happy to help me preserve a valuable piece of the town's history. After that exchange, he asked if I wanted to take a little walk into the desert.

We left the Searchlight Nugget Casino and headed a bit farther south to the Terrible's Casino, which houses a truck stop and Searchlight's only McDonald's. Fans of Oprah Winfrey will remember seeing this McDonald's as a stopping point on her cross-country trip with best friend Gayle. After parking the car, we headed on foot toward the section of barren desert just south of the casino. We were only about 100 feet from the side of Highway 95 when he proudly proclaimed,

*"Here it is!"*

At first glance, it was just a large hunk of metal surrounded by rotten, dried redwood. Closer examination revealed it was actually a roadside billboard for the El Rey Club that measured five feet high and twelve feet long. The hand-painted lettering on the sign was barely legible after at least 50 years of baking in the desert, but it was clearly a billboard for the El Rey.

The restored El Rey Club billboard today.

As far as anyone could recall, this billboard stood on the highway and greeted you as you came from Laughlin long after the El Rey Club was history. It was torn down sometime in the 1980s to make way for the rather large, modern-day billboard that was installed around the time Terrible's was being built. Miraculously, it was discarded in the desert and never picked up for disposal. More incredibly, no school kids looking to make a skateboard ramp, no hoodlums looking to fire a shot gun at something worthless, no wild burro looking to chew or stomp on something because it was there even touched the thing after its removal from the ground. I was blown away.

In all likelihood, this once sturdy sign comprised of redwood planks and sheet metal was hand-painted by Bob Martello who was responsible for many of the El Rey's advertising in and out of the casino. Mike was eager to hear my reaction to this incredible find. I was eager to find out what he wanted for it regarding price. Mike was, among other things, a miner. Miners in the West definitely live by a "finders, keepers" code. However, nobody mines for something that doesn't have value and, therefore, everything they find has a price. After what amounted to several years of education in casino collectibles, I was prepared to hear a big number for something like this billboard. I asked him what he wanted for it, expecting a finder's fee, if not a price for the item, himself. Mike smiled, looked me squarely in the eyes and replied, *"I could really go for a cold bottle of beer."*

That is exactly the kind of incredible generosity that has followed me throughout this journey. Whether it has been the gift of people's memories, the sharing of artifacts, or in some cases, people buying El Rey items for me simply because they knew I couldn't afford them, gestures like these have led me to believe in my heart that telling this story was something I was meant to do.

Fans of the popular History Channel program, *American Restoration,* saw that very billboard brought back to life in April of 2012. Within the program, there

The nearly 6ft tall Willie Martello monument, placed by the Clampers in Searchlight on June 2, 2012.

was quite a lot of history discussed about the casino and Willie. While the program mentioned the brothel, it placed more emphasis upon how Willie essentially saved Searchlight from extinction. For the first time in over half a century, Willie Martello was not portrayed as a lowly pimp or a whoremonger, and in grand Willie fashion, it was on national TV. Realistically fearing this book may never see the light of day, I took great pride in knowing I had some part in getting his name cleared on such a grand scale.

On June 2, 2012, Willie was given his due once again in the form of a plaque that honored his casino and his lasting contributions to Searchlight, Nevada. This plaque was placed by the Queho Posse Chapter #1919 of E Clampus Vitus®. Also known as The Clampers, this wonderfully eclectic group is dedicated to preserving some of the rich, unusual, and lesser known parts of American history throughout the West. Mark Hall-Patton, best known as the rock star historian from Pawn Stars, is the administrator for the Clark County Museum and the Searchlight Museum as well as a proud Clamper. At the Searchlight birthday celebration in 2007, Jane Overy read many of the facts I'd uncovered about the El Rey Club and Willie Martello, particularly one that mentioned there was no street, school, or any sort of plaque in town that honored Willie. The Clampers stepped

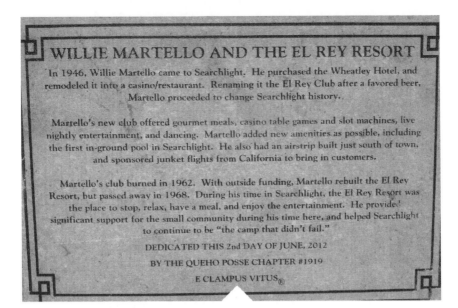

WILLIE MARTELLO AND THE EL REY RESORT

In 1946, Willie Martello came to Searchlight. He purchased the Wheatley Hotel, and remodeled it into a casino/restaurant. Renaming it the El Rey Club after a favored beer, Martello proceeded to change Searchlight history.

Martello's new club offered gourmet meals, casino table games and slot machines, live nightly entertainment, and dancing. Martello added new amenities as possible, including the first in-ground pool in Searchlight. He also had an airstrip built just south of town, and sponsored junket flights from California to bring in customers.

Martello's club burned in 1962. With outside funding, Martello rebuilt the El Rey Resort, but passed away in 1968. During his time in Searchlight, the El Rey Resort was the place to stop, relax, have a meal, and enjoy the entertainment. He provided significant support for the small community during his time here, and helped Searchlight to continue to be "the camp that didn't fail."

DEDICATED THIS 2nd DAY OF JUNE, 2012
BY THE QUEHO POSSE CHAPTER #1919
E CLAMPUS VITUS®

The engraving on the historical marker honoring Willie Martello.

up and set upon the path of rectifying that error. Mark has been a good friend and supporter, and he appeared in the aforementioned episode of *American Restoration*, lending his rather weighty credibility to this project.

A restored billboard, several gaming artifacts, and a shiny plaque are not the only parts of Willie's legacy that survive to this day. The Searchlight airport is still in use. In recent years, it has even gone through some vast improvements. A development company has purchased the runway and much of the surrounding land to create modern, upscale homes that will serve as a "fly-in community" for people with their own private planes. Though development has slowed considerably since the housing and economic crises hit Southern Nevada, it promises a bright new future for Searchlight and Willie's runway. Perhaps, they'll use more than three inches of asphalt on it this time around.

In modern days, Las Vegas and Hawaii have grown to share a rather amazing symbiotic relationship. Some of the biggest numbers of tourists heading to Las Vegas come from Hawaii. Among the largest demographics of people who relocate to Las Vegas are from Hawaii. The California Hotel and Casino in downtown Las Vegas caters almost exclusively to the customer wanting that Polynesian flair. For several summers, the Imperial Palace (now the Quad) offered a Hawaiian Luau and attracted many customers, both locals and tourists. To some Las Vegas is considered "The Ninth Hawaiian Island." While I do not possess any knowledge of Willie Martello being the first casino owner to host a Hawaiian luau, one cannot discount the success of his promotion and how similar ideas exist in Las Vegas today.

Residents are still making phone calls on the permanent lines Willie helped get installed in the town. Car phones became a part of American life and were followed by the cell phones nobody of any age can seem to live without. One need only look at Laughlin, Nevada or think about the era of family entertainment in Las Vegas to see some of Willie's ideas were not that farfetched.

At the time of this writing, here is what I can say about some of the people I've had the great fortune to interview and come to know as friends.

**Jerry Schafer**, still Las Vegas' most prolific and most unsung live variety show producer, is still as active in entertainment today as he was 50 years ago. Though you will rarely find his name listed on the Internet Movie Database, Jerry continues to write, produce, and direct movies and television shows around the world including the international hit, *The Contender: Asia*. At any given point during my research for this book, Jerry could be half-way around the world in places as far away and exotic as Bangkok or as local as Las Vegas. He always has a script ready to go into production and a cigar in hand. He's given me permission to write his official biography, but I told him, *"Let's see how this one goes, first,"* which prompted a big laugh from a big man in Las Vegas history.

**Dick Taylor** left Las Vegas and his high-end position with Doc Bayley's Hacienda in 1963, because he wanted to take his family away from the trappings of a Las Vegas lifestyle. *"I didn't want to raise my children as a Daddy in the 'mob' kinda business,"* is how he described it. He moved to Palm Springs, California to become a securities broker. In an ironic twist of fate, a New York brokerage house hired Taylor as their resident manager in...Las Vegas, where he returned a couple years later. Since then, his countless accomplishments have included owning the fabulous Moulin Rouge Hotel and Casino and the development of the land in Mt. Charleston to make it the wonderful resort property it is today. A very prolific author, he published several books on Nevada history.

Sadly, Dick passed away on March 10, 2011, after a battle with metastatic melanoma. In my opinion, he was the last of the true giants from the

Golden Age of Las Vegas, and yet, few neither knew his name nor of his influence on Vegas. In the three short years I knew Dick Taylor, he became quite a good friend and a tremendous influence on my life.

We were introduced by historian **Lisa Giola-Acres** after Dick mentioned to her he wanted to write a book about Willie Martello and publish his story about Doc Bayley's plans for the ethnic golf course in Searchlight. Lisa did a little research of her own and found my blog online. When I first spoke with Dick, I feared all my hard work would be for nothing, knowing a respected and well-published author was hankering to write about Willie. Instead, Dick met with me and reviewed my research himself. He came to the conclusion this was my story to tell and marveled at some of the things I'd uncovered; he even suggested I should write the definitive book about Doc Bayley one day. Being such a fan of preserving history, Dick graciously shared his story about the golf course. It was an amazing story since he was the last living person to even know about it. I'd heard about the big plans for Searchlight from Bob Martello, but the details about the golf course and Doc Bayley's involvement bridged a very big gap in the story for me. It would have been lost forever if it hadn't been for the generosity and pure enjoyment Dick Taylor shared for this project. I'd found a man who shared my enthusiasm for this ridiculous subject and one with a lot of clout and credibility to boot.

Among my fondest memories of Dick Taylor was the day he asked if I wanted to head out to Searchlight to hand out fliers and *"try to shake the rafters loose."* We went out there hoping we would find just one more person, one more morsel of information to add to the tale. We both knocked on doors and placed information in the businesses of storefronts. What was great to see was this 79-year-old man actually running up and down the streets of Searchlight to meet people and spread the word about this project.

Dick Taylor was a true friend and ally along the way. He provided many great leads and added clarification or confirmation to stories that would only have been rumors otherwise. Without his help, I know with certainty many people would simply not have taken my call or read a word of this manuscript. He introduced me to very important people in Las Vegas as if I were someone they needed to know, and he printed up brochures that announced the project and sent them to anyone with a mailbox and an interest in Nevada history, hoping some momentum would flow my way.

He told me not to expect much from my efforts and told me, *"Preserving history is more of a labor of love than anything else."* I cannot agree more with that statement. What he didn't realize and what I wasn't counting on was the fact that our brief friendship, much like my friendship with people like Jerry Schafer or Sharon Richardson, was more than payment enough. A man simply could not ask for a better friend, resource, and mentor than Richard Blackburn Taylor. He is missed by many, and I think about him almost every day.

**Kenny Laursen in 1961.**
*Photo courtesy Kenny Laursen.*

**Kenny Laursen** quit the music business but has always stayed close to the entertainment world, owning a successful video production company, Aladdin Productions, in Las Vegas. In an interesting twist of fate, **Joe Veronese**, the man Kenny saved from the burning embers of the El Rey Club, saved Laursen's life in a boating accident several years later. Fire and water, Alpha and Omega...Kenny and Joe. They remain good friends to this day. I hear Kenny recently picked up his guitar and got the bug to play again. He has even been in contact with some of the members of the Tony Lovello Revue, though I wouldn't expect a reunion tour any time soon. Why? Tony Lovello is too darned busy.

**Tony Lovello**, the world's greatest accordion player, also left the music business after a long and successful career. He became a hotelier in Kentucky and enjoyed an equally long and successful life as an owner of fine hotels. Today, he's ostensibly out of the hotel business and touring the world with his accordion, once again, much to the delight of his many adoring fans. Kenny Laursen told me Tony took some fantastic 8mm footage of the El Rey fire and tried unsuccessfully to sell it to the local media back in 1962. Again, in a perfect world, he'll find that footage in an old trunk somewhere and give me another call. Tony...Search those old boxes!

**Joyce Dickens Walker** passed away in 2012, but not before she made several phone calls, sent several emails, and provided me with many photos and stories that were invaluable to this book. Joyce was a character

A seemingly despondent Sharon Blasiola (Richardson) sitting at an El Rey blackjack table, circa late 1950s/early 1960s. *Photo courtesy Sharon Richardson.*

in every sense of the word and a true Las Vegan. I was honored to get to know her, and I know her rather large, beautiful family is eternally proud of her, if not inspired, by her outrageous free spirit.

**Sharon Richardson** is living in California, and though retired from her several happy years slinging drinks to gamblers in Las Vegas, she keeps very busy with a family-run antique store. Always the loudest of Willie's family members wanting SOMEONE in the world to recognize what her uncle did in Searchlight: Sharon frequently surprises me with another story, an envelope with a new photo, or an email just to say hi. More than you'll ever know, I'm thankful for her input and hopeful she is proud of the book you're now reading.

**Bob Martello** passed away in January of 2010. He led quite an amazing life himself, full of accomplishments too numerous to mention here. Perhaps, a book about his life is in order. More than any note about what he did in his life professionally, the fact he was truly a great father to his three children and a wonderful provider for his family says the world about the man who was among the very first to offer any sort of information about Willie and the El Rey.

Bob was always very interested in my entertainment career — as interested as I was in his El Rey connection. We got along very well and spoke on the phone often. He always said, *"If I know anyone out there in Vegas and can help you out, I'll do what I can."* He was also quick to say, *"Just keep telling people out there your last name. Eventually, some doors will open."* I always told him just the fact he took time to respond to my ridiculous questions was more than enough.  Once we connected, and he knew I was sincere in my intentions,   I came to the conclusion he was truly happy someone was taking such an interest in Willie.  I secretly thought he looked forward to my random interruptions to his day.

I received my last email from Bob in November of 2007 while I was working a casino comedy club in Laughlin, Nevada, one of my first events after I moved to Las Vegas.  This email came on the heels of learning about some of the sadder times in Nevada: The El Rey closing, Willie's death, his own father's passing.  I worried I'd dug too deeply and upset him too much.  Later that same day, I received another email from Bob, which fittingly was forwarded from Ed Darling, THE first of Willie's family to say a darned thing to me about this El Rey fascination of mine.  The email was one of those animated e-greeting cards.  Bob simply asked, *"Could you use a laugh?"*  One click and a cartoon groundhog sprung up on the screen to sing a silly little tune which, while more for kids than anyone else, had a wonderful little sentiment that told me it was just as okay to ask him the tough questions as it was to ask the easy ones.

Per high-pitched, singing groundhog...

*"Today you came to mind and it made me smile wide.*
*I appreciate the things you do.  You are so very kind.*
*I want to tell you just how much I appreciate you, friend.*
*You are the very bestest one that there has ever been.*
*This card I thought was very cute.  It says the things I'd like to say.*
*I hope it makes you smile like me.  I hope it makes your day.*
*Have a great day."*

Yeah, I know it is a little corny, but I still click the link every so often and think about Bob.

We spoke a few more times after that, but as so many of our conversations had done before, it quickly turned into a chat like friends or family would have rather than one an interviewer and subject would have.  I've no problems with that as he gave me so much in such a short amount of time.  During one of our last phone calls, Bob complained he was very tired and felt a bit off.  Soon afterward, I noticed my emails and phone calls were not being returned,  so I knew something was up.  I didn't pry as it was not my place, and I felt I had intruded upon his life more than enough.  When I got the phone call in 2010, I was so very sad I never got to meet him in person and simply shake his hand.  I hope that, if he were alive to read this book, he'd smile and know I didn't come up with something that was *"250 pages of dirt."*

**Buddy and Ethel Martello** remained in Las Vegas where they owned and operated the very successful **Elbow Room** on Flamingo Avenue. The Elbow Room opened its doors in August of 1968 and, just as he had done in 1946, Buddy's brother, Al, was a partner in the venture. Buddy and Ethel were happily married for 50 years before Buddy passed away in 1994. Ethel now lives in Texas where she remains tough as nails, soft spoken, more active than almost anyone I know, and cares for her sister. She's internet savvy but admits she lets her sister have much of the computer time as it is almost her only entertainment. However, she's never turned away a call or an email from me. Like many people from that era in the Vegas area, she holds true to the fact that *"nobody knows nothin'"* but seems to remember an awful lot once you get her started. What she does remember is crystal clear in detail and vivid with color and life. I'm hopeful I'll get the chance to meet her and present her with a copy of this book in person, if I am not fortunate enough to meet her sooner. Maybe then, after we've met and she's read what I have written, she'll have a better understanding of just why the heck anyone would even care about what happened in Searchlight.

---

**Ethel and Buddy Martello at the Continental Café inside the El Rey Club, circa late 1950s.** *Photo courtesy Sharon Richardson.*

# SPECIAL THANKS

A few years back I won a small award. The *Business Ledger*, a business publication in the western suburbs of Chicago, honored me and my entertainment company by bestowing upon me their Annual Award for Business Excellence. I have their snazzy trophy in my office to this day.

Since I had never won an award before, it followed I never had to make an acceptance speech. While my speech ended up being very funny and memorable, I forgot to thank my wife at the time who was there to watch me accept this award. I've never stopped feeling awful about forgetting to thank the one person who had been the most supportive of me over the years.

While I am certain that April Martello, now April Sperk, has been duly acknowledged within the pages of this book, I will make doubly sure not to make the same mistake again.

If you are among the people to whom I owe a debt of gratitude and I have inadvertently omitted your name, please accept my apologies and hope this volume sells well enough to warrant future editions so I can remedy my error.

*Special heartfelt thanks belong to the following people.*

## My Family
April Sperk,
Don & Wyn Martello, Marty Martello, Lisa Hayward, Matt Martello,
Nick Martello, Louise Martello, Nick & John Martello,
Mary Morrison Martello,
Susan Sperk, Samantha Mckie, Ray & Dolores Blaetler

## My Extended Family

Sharon Richardson, Bob Martello, Suzan Riddell, Ethel Martello, Robin Clark, Ed Darling, Matthew Martello, Christy Martello, Louette Harmon, Angie Tune, Nick & Betsy Martello, April Sperk

## Interview Subjects

Jerry Schafer, Dick Taylor, Lou & "Mickey" Cooper, "The Boys in the Band" - Tony Lovello, Kenny Laursen, & Joe Veronese, Joyce Dickens Walker, Jeff Reid Jr., Diane McBain, Bill Moore, Bonnie Canter, Donna & Gail Andress, Anthony Luigi Scirocco, Don Laughlin, Jim Sarra, Diane Kendall, April Sperk

## Friends and Helpful People

Kellie Bowers, Kristin Newton McCallum, Lisa Giola-Acres, Melia Skinner, Mike Madden, Patrick Bertelson, Rick & Kelly Dale (and the Staff at Rick's Restorations), Rebecca Bowers, Mark Walberg, Todd Newton, Laura Enright, Victor (my neighbor) for use of his truck, Phil Jensen, Carey Burke, Rebecca Doing, Kathryn Costello, Doc Mac, Wendy Van Vacter, Ed & Lynne Clemmens, Steve Fischer, Susy Martian, Stephanie Gardellis, Susan Hurst, Thomas Reed , April Sperk

## Museums and Organizations

Jane & Carl Overy of the Searchlight Museum, Crystal Van Dee & Dennis McBride of the Nevada State Museum & Historical Society, Mark Hall-Patton of the Clark County Museum, Mark Englebretson of the Nevada Casino Ashtray Project, The Las Vegas Media Group, The Clark County Library, The *Las Vegas Review-Journal*, The April Sperk is Awesome Foundation

**Very special thanks go to April Sperk, for her continued patience, love, and dedication. She also has a great sense of humor.**

Copyediting by Brenda Coxe, Brenda Coxe's Writing Services
http://www.joyofwriting.wordpress.com, bscoxe@comcast.net

Revised edition proofread by Leslie E. Hoffman

Graphic Design & Layout by Gregory Barrington

# Gofundme.com Supporters

When the decision was made to self-publish this book, I realized the cost of licensing so many photos could very likely bring the project to a screeching halt. Even though the licensing fee from the Nevada State Museum was not unusually high, the sheer number of photos I wanted to use made this a potential deal-breaker.

Knowing that so much of the interest in this project came from my blog posts on the Internet, I decided to utilize the World Wide Web once again to raise the money to license the photos and pay for professional services. The crowd-funding website, GoFundMe.com, and the generous donations from many people made it possible to bring you the book you hold in your hands today. Everyone who donated, regardless of the amount, was guaranteed a thank you in the book, and it is my honor to make good on that promise.

**The following people have my eternal gratitude and friendship for their generosity, friendship, and support. I simply could not have finished this project without the following wonderful individuals.**

| | | |
|---|---|---|
| Sharon Dynek | Nate Pincus | Samantha McKie |
| Joe Vecciarelli | Sheldon Smith (twice) | Edward Clemens |
| Michael Lawson | Mark Engelbretson | Michael Hopper |
| Eric Predoehl | Julie Thompson | Susan Snyder |
| Jo Hammel | Mike Hammer (twice) | Mark Walberg |
| Will Glenn | Robert Pardue | Nick Martello |
| Jose Martinez | Steve Miller | Robert Sivek |
| Kellie Bowers | Doug "Cigarman" Smith | Jules Sparks |
| De'Reen Vyleta | Alan Schuyler | Frank Messina |
| Luanne Triolo Newman | Nicholas Martello | Jim Steffner |
| Sondra Harris | Mark Geary | Kurt & Colette Lindemann |
| Jessi Owens | Todd Newton | Non-E Moos |
| Charles Bastian | Phillip Jensen | Dave Lester |
| Patrick Bertelson | James Jensen | Gemma Martello |
| Sue Sperk | Charlie Urnick | Deric Harrington |
| Hania Mikdadi (twice) | Marty Martello | Alan Martin |
| Andy Hughes | Stephanie Rambosek | Karl Waterbury |

Bud Buckley

Kevin Lepine

Barbara Potter

Gillian & Greg Gardellis

Gary Kuehl

Michelle Ingram

Kelly Hawley

Nick Cassiano

Scott Stewart

Alan Altur

Chuck Knisley

Chris Flondro

Bethany Thomas

Audrey Schulze

Kristen McCallum

Brian Schultz

Denise Eppel

David DeRose

Alex Schneidinger

Julie Ewry

Krista Boyens

Mike All

Kimberly Croteau

Randy Hayward

Pete Parker Coppni

Jeff Siena

Julie Trygar

Thad Shirley

Bill Judge

Sharon Egger

Richard & Crystal Wittlief

Brenda Bowen

Wendy Lippert

Jim Sarra

Brian Hinz Sr.

Tommy Vinci

Emilie St-Pierre

Eric Brashear

Rebecca Bowers

Eric Jurisch

James M. Sklena

Laura Enright

Mike "Captain Q" Quinlivan

Annette Hassalone

The Honorifics

Oscar & Bernie

Chris Temple

Captain J. Tuttle

Christy Martello

Gerry Feldman

Henry Cartledge

Jen Frieden

# BIBLIOGRAPHY

The vast majority of information and quotes were taken from interviews conducted by the author. The following bibliography lists additional sources of reference.

## *Books*

- Searchlight: The Camp That Didn't Fail, By Harry Reid, ©University of Nevada Press, January 1998
- The Good Fight, By Senator Harry Reid, Copyright © 2008 G.P. Putnam's Sons, a member of Penguin Group (USA) Inc..
- Index of Nevada Gaming Establishments , By Harvey J. Fuller
- Kiss Tomorrow Goodbye: The Barbara Payton Story, By John O'Dowd, © 2007 BearManor Media
- I Am Not Ashamed, By Barbara Payton, ©1963, 2008 Holloway House
- The Martello Name in History, From Ancestry.com, © 2007 The Generations Network, Inc.

## *Newspapers and Magazines*

### Las Vegas Review-Journal
Las Vegas Review-Journal Copyright © Stephens Media LLC

- October 3, 1941, Announcements
- April 23, 1943, "Searchlight is Banned by Army; Vegas is Studied," Author unknown
- May 1, 1943, "Searchlight Vetoes Army Proposal for Lifting Taboo," Author unknown
- April 11, 1946, Advertisement
- August 26, 1946, "Searchlight Gutted by Bad Blaze," Author Unknown
- August 29, 1946, Searchlight Fire Photo, Photographer unknown
- December 3, 1946, legal notices
- April 8, 1947, "Searchlight Asks Better Fire Wagon," Author unknown

- February 10, 1949, "Nevada Hotel, Famed Searchlight Landmark, Razed by Night Fire," Author unknown

- September 1, 1949, Advertisement

- Feb 1, 1950, "Carrier Pigeons End Dilemma of Searchlighters," Author unknown

- Feb 28, 1950, "El Ray Club Game Permit is Revoked - Tax Commission Meets Again Today," A.P. Story

- May 25, 1951, "Searchlight's Halls of Fun Are Quiet Now," by Archie Teague

- May 30, 1951, "Scratch Searchlight; Roxies May be Next," by Archie Teague

- June 1, 1951, "Hint Not All On Level In Searchlight Fuss," by Archie Teague

- March 5, 1952, "Searchlighter Complains of Unfavorable Publicity," Author unknown

- February 24, 1953, "Martello Produce Celebrates Second Anniversary Here," Author unknown

- August 6, 1953 "Slot Machine's 'Percentage' Takes a Big Jump," Author unknown

- August 9, 1953, "Man Arraigned for Operating Slots Illegally," Author unknown

- December 11, 1953, "Deny Gaming License to West Side Men," Author unknown

- August 9, 1953, "Man Arraigned for Operating Slots Illegally"

- July 1, 1954, "Brothels Grand Jury Target - DA Tells of Open Bawdies," Author unknown

- December 24, 1954 "Land Ownership Row Halts Resort Building," Author unknown

- March 2, 1955, "Royal Nevada and Riviera Get Approval," Author unknown

- October 17, 1957, Advertisement

- December 31, 1958, Advertisement

- April 24, 1959, Advertisement

- May 25, 1960, "El Rey Bar in $25,000 Legal Suit," Author unknown

- July 26, 1960, column by Forrest Duke

- November 22, 1960, "Lodge Owner Dies in Calif. Auto Crackup," Author unknown

- December 29, 1960, Advertisement

- April 10, 1961, Column by Forrest Duke

- May 19, 1961, Advertisement

- June 29, 1961, Column by Forrest Duke

- January 15, 1962, "Martello Reveals Resort Sale," Author unknown

- January 22, 1962, "Only embers" Photo, Photographer unknown

- January 22, 1962, "Fire Guts Searchlight's El-Rey Club," Author unknown

- January 23, 1962, "Sale of El Rey Completed Despite Ashes," Author unknown

- January 24, 1962, "Searchlight Gambling Not Dead," Author unknown

- February 23, 1962, Advertisement

- April 25, 1962, "El Rey Club Goes Under, Casino Death Casts Searchlight Shadow," by Colin McKinlay

- April 29, 1962, "Martello Tells New Hotel Plan," Author unknown

- July 20, 1962, column by Forrest Duke

- September 7, 1962, "El Rey Boss Hit by Suit," Author unknown

- September 8, 1962, "El Rey Boss Answers Suit," Author unknown

- July 25, 1963, "El Rey Club Owner Loses Court Round," Author unknown

- December 31, 1963, Obituary, Achilles Martello

- May 20, 1964, "El Rey Club May Re-Open, Bayley Seeks License," Author unknown

- August 11, 1964, "El Rey Club Set to Open," Author unknown

- August 29, 1964, "New El Rey Club Opens Tonight in Searchlight," Column by Forrest Duke

- October 16, 1964, "DI's Davis & Reese Say 'Show Must Go On'," Column by Forrest Duke

- April 21, 1965, "Searchlight Runway, Willie Can't Get Off the Ground," by Don Beale

- July 29, 1965, "Masked Bandits Get $1000, El Rey Club Robbed," Author unknown

- August 11, 1965, "Liquor Licenses Get Okay," Author unknown

- April 13, 1966, "Club Owner Faces Charge," Author unknown

- January 4, 1968, "Pioneer Searchlight Casino Owner, Martello, Dies at 53," Author unknown

- January 7, 1968, "Martello Services Set for Tuesday," Author unknown

- August 21, 1968, "Riviera, 10 Others, Get County Licenses," Author unknown

### NEVADAN, a supplement to the Las Vegas Review-Journal
The NEVADAN, Copyright © Stephens Media LLC

- March 18, 1962, "Searchlight Miners Shoo Camp Cooks From Stove," by Ray Chesson

- February 16, 1964, "Big Hearted Town on a Bald Headed Mountain," By Ray Chesson

- February 11, 1968, "Willie Martello: King of the Mountain," By Ray Chesson

### Las Vegas Sun
© Las Vegas Sun, Greenspun Media Group, Henderson, NV

- May 1, 1961, "'Airline' Service To Searchlight Inaugurated," Author and photographer unknown

- January 22, 1962, "Fire Destroys Casino, $1 Million Blaze Hits Searchlight," By Jim Combs, with a photo by Frank Maggio

- January 25, 2008, "Deadly casino fires helped rewrite safety standards," Author unknown

- Web archive, http://www.lasvegassun.com/news/2008/jan/25/las-vegas-fire-history/

- May 6, 2009, "Four-alarm blaze at Moulin Rouge leads to site demolition," by Mary Manning

- Web archive, http://www.lasvegassun.com/news/2009/may/06/moulin-rouge-fire-reported/

### The News (Van Nuys, CA)
- August 1, 1963, SporT-Views column, "Hall of Fame," by Bill Burns

### Reno Evening Gazette
- May 10, 1951, "Tax Commission Studies Binion License Plea," Author unknown

- May 30, 1951 "Housed Closed in Searchlight," Author unknown

- July 18, 1952, Tiny Town of Searchlight Finally Gets Connected with Outer World by Phone," Author unknown
- September 1, 1953, "Martello Loses Gaming Permit," Author unknown
- January 24, 1962, "Clark Casino Claimed Sold Despite Fire," Author unknown

### Henderson Home News
© Henderson Home News, Greenspun Media Group, Henderson, NV
*Archives available through their website, www.digitalcollections.mypubliclibrary.com*

- July 3, 1958, Advertisement
- January 15, 1959, Write-up and advertisement
- May 4, 1961, Advertisement
- August 4, 1960, Notice
- October 30, 1962, Legal Notices
- November 6, 1962, Legal Notices
- November 13, 1962, Legal Notices
- November 20, 1962, Legal Notices
- July 9, 1963, Legal Notices
- June 24, 1965, Photo, Caption: CHAMPAGNE FLIGHT, Photo by Knighton
- December 20, 1966, Legal Notices

### Searchlight Journal
- August 29, 1946, "Sunday Fire Levels Three Buildings, Townsmen Battle Blaze with Antiquated Equipment," Author unknown
- August 29, 1946, Editorial, H. E. Mildren
- October 3, 1946, Advertisements
- October 17, 1946, Advertisements
- October 24, 1946, Advertisements
- March 20, 1947, "Prospecting Guitarist Becomes Deputy," Author unknown
- March 20, 1947, Advertisement

### Nevada State Journal
- February 28, 1950, "El Ray Club Game Permit Revoked, Tax Commission Meets Again Today," by UNITED PRESS, Author unknown
- September 9, 1953, "Tax Commission Devoting Time to Assessments, Searchlight Man Gets Order," Author unknown
- January 23, 1962, "Searchlight Club Razed By Flames," UPI, Author unknown

### Star-News (CA)
- January 22, 1962, "$1 Million Fire in Searchlight," UPI, Author unknown

### Press Telegram (Long Beach, CA)
- December 26, 1962, Advertisements

### Paper Unknown (Clipping only, provided by Bob Martello)
- September 5, 1966, "Court Order Puts Skids On Searchlight Property Sales," Author unknown

## Real West
*Real West Magazine, ©1968, Charlton Publications, Inc.*
- January 1969, Volume XII, Number 67, "Searchlight Was a Live Wire," by Doris Ceveri

## Adam
*Adam Magazine, ©1961, by Knight Publishing Corp.*
- Volume 5, No. 8, "Wide Open Spaces," Article, Pictorial by Jack Schafer

## Fury
*Fury Magazine, ©1962, by J. B. Publishing Corporation*
- July 1963, Volume 26, No. 2, "Tonight for Sure!" Author unknown

## Harlequin
- Harlequin Magazine, ©1963, ROYAL PUBLICATIONS, INC.
- November 1963, Volume 1, Number 3, "Harlequin Goes to a Nudie Movie," Author unknown

## Modern Man
- Modern Man, The Adult Picture Magazine, ©1961, Publishers' Development Corporation
- October 1961, Vol. XI, No. 4-124, "A Rootin' Tootin' Rawhide Reel," by Max Harris

## Desert
*© 1965, Desert Magazine, Palm Desert, CA*
- June 1965, "The Light is Green in Searchlight," by Royce Rollins

# Video

- Sharing of Memories, Recorded at the 110th Birthday Celebration, October 4, 2008, Produced by The Searchlight Museum Guild and Aladdin Productions

- "Putt Mossman Motorcycle Acrobatics 1960," YouTube http://youtu.be/7rUF8PXUYm0

# Websites

- The Internet Movie Database (IMDB) listing for "Tonight for Sure", http://www.imdb.com/title/tt0153167/, Copyright © 1990-2013 IMDb.com, Inc. , an Amazon Company

- The Internet Movie Database (IMDB) listing for Paul "Mousie" Garner, http://www.imdb.com/name/nm0307063/, Copyright © 1990-2013 IMDb.com, Inc. , an Amazon Company

- Hollywood.com listing for "Tonight for Sure", http://www.hollywood.com/movie/Tonight_For_Sure/184234, ©1999-2013 Hollywood.com, LLC

- ambidextrousfilm.com, http://ambidextrouspics.com/html/tonight_for_sure.html

- The Huffington Post, http://www.huffingtonpost.com/sen-harry-reid/the-good-fight_b_99228.html, Copyright © 2010 HuffingtonPost.com, Inc

- Global Oneness, http://www.experiencefestival.com/prostitution_in_nevada_-_history, © 2010 Global Oneness

- Clark County Fire Department website, http://fire.co.clark.
  nv.us/%28S%28ilytero4mskoh4qqxnh53kwu%29%29/MGM.aspx, ©2005 CCFD

- Online Nevada Encyclopedia, http://www.onlinenevada.org/red_rooster

- USC Thornton School of Music, http://www.usc.edu/schools/music/about/board/
  lemel.html

- AllMusic.com, http://www.allmusic.com/artist/gary-lemel-mn0000661847

- I'm Learning 2 Share, http://learning2share.blogspot.com/2007/08/78s-from-hell-polly-
  possum-and-joe.html,

- Christine Jorgensen Official Website,  http://www.christinejorgensen.org, © 2006
  ChristineJorgensen.org

- Biography.com, Christine Jorgensen Listing, http://www.biography.com/people/
  christine-jorgensen-262758, © 1996–2013 A+E Television Networks, LLC. All Rights
  Reserved.

- U.S. Air Force, http://www.af.mil/information/heritage/person.
  asp?dec=&pid=123006462

- EarlyAviators.com, http://earlyaviators.com/emacread.htm

- Nevada Aerospace Hall of Fame, http://nvahof.org/?page_id=640, Copyright © 2011
  Nevada Aerospace Hall of Fame

- VPNavy.org, http://www.vpnavy.org/vp17mem_28jun98.html, © 1996-2013, VPNavy.org

- Ghspaulding.com, http://www.ghspaulding.com/vp-17%20bulletin%20board.htm

- Historic Dumas Brothel website, http://www.thedumasbrothel.com/. © 2011,
  HOWLING WOLF PRODUCTIONS

- Only in Butte website, http://www.butteamerica.com/dumas.htm, © 2010 by George
  Everett.

- Visit Cripple Creek website, the official website for the city of Cripple Creek, CO,
  http://visitcripplecreek.com/businesses/old-homestead-house-museum, © 2008-2012
  Cripple Creek, Colorado

- RoadsideAmerica.com, Cripple Creek, Colorado: Famous Wild West Brothel, http://
  www.roadsideamerica.com/tip/1539, © Copyright 1996-2013 Doug Kirby, Ken Smith,
  Mike Wilkins.

- The Museum of Flight, http://www.museumofflight.org/aircraft/douglas-dc-3, http://
  www.museumofflight.org/aircraft/lockheed1049g-super-constellation,
  © The Museum of Flight

# About The Author

Andy Martello is a comedian, actor, variety entertainer, and freelance writer. Originally from Chicago, he now makes his home in Las Vegas, Nevada. A writer since birth, his work has appeared in the pages of the *North Las Vegas Voice* newspaper and *Strip Las Vegas* magazine.

Aside from his very popular (and rarely updated) blogs, his humor and opinion columns can be found at TheCheers.org, AbsoluteWrite.com, MaliciousBitch.com, and GapersBlock.com.

This is Andy's first (and probably his last) book.

www.andymartello.com
www.kingofcasinosbook.com
www.elreyclubbook.com
www.facebook.com/kingofcasinosbook
www.facebook.com/andymartelloentertainent
www.twitter.com/THEandymartello

16672439R00172

Made in the USA
San Bernardino, CA
12 November 2014